**W9-ADO-092**

The PMP Cram Sheet

This Cram Sheet provides the distilled, key facts about the PMP exam. Review these important points as the last thing you do before entering the test center. Pay close attention to those you feel you need to review. A good exam strategy is to transfer all the facts you can recall from this Cram Sheet to a piece of paper once you sit to take the exam.

IMPORTANT PMI THEMES

1. The project manager is ultimately responsible and accountable for the project.

2. Projects should be aligned and prioritized with the organization's strategic direction.

3. The earlier in the project lifecycle, the more risk for the project and the more influence management has on it.

4. Historical records and lessons learned are very valuable.

5. Stakeholder management is an ongoing, continuous process throughout the project lifecycle.

6. The success or failure of a project is determined during project planning.

7. The Work Breakdown Structure (WBS) is a "must-have" for any project manager and serves as the basis for most project planning.

8. The person (people) who will do the work should estimate the work.

9. The most important task and skill of the project manager is effective project communication.

10. The project team should be involved in all project-planning activities.

11. The project plan is an all-encompassing document and must contain cost and schedule baselines in order to determine project performance during execution.

12. Project changes will occur. Changes should be expected, planned for, and well managed when they occur.

13. Earned value is the best project-controlling technique.

14. The project team should solve its own problems and resolve its own issues whenever possible.

15. Quality is planned into a project, not inspected in.

16. Risk management is an ongoing, continuous process performed by the entire project team.

17. Preventing a risk event is always preferred to mitigating a risk event.

18. Closing processes (administrative closure) should occur at the end of each project phase, not just at the end of the project.

19. "Lessons learned" describe the knowledge the team and stakeholders gained by actually performing the project and are an invaluable source of project management information.

PROJECT FRAMEWORK

1. A *project* is a temporary endeavor undertaken to create a unique product or service.

2. A *program* is a group of related projects managed in a coordinated way.

3. *Project management* is the application of knowledge, skills, tools, and techniques to project activities to meet project requirements.

4. A *deliverable* is a tangible, verifiable work product.

5. The PMBOK project management process groups are Initiating, Planning, Executing, Controlling, and Closing.

6. Project management processes can repeat within the project lifecycle, and they generally repeat with each project phase.

7. The three organization types are functional, matrix (weak, balanced, or strong), and projectized.

8. As an effective project manager, you are expected to be a good manager and a good leader.

9. The "triple constraint" paradigm is used to show the effects that competing demands can have on a project.

PROJECT CLOSING

1. Administrative closeout includes the updating and finalization of records.

2. The goal of a procurement audit is to review the successes and failures of the procurement process in order to transfer the knowledge gained to other procurements.

3. The requirements for formal contract closeout are defined in the contract terms and conditions.

4. The person responsible for contract administration should provide formal acceptance to the seller in writing.

5. The criteria necessary to ensure project closure are formal customer acceptance and meeting the requirements of the delivering organization.

6. Lessons learned should be documented throughout the project lifecycle.

7. Administrative closure should be performed at the end of each phase in a project.

PROFESSIONAL RESPONSIBILITY

1. Conduct yourself professionally in your work with clients. This includes the following:

    - Doing the "right" thing
    - Being respectful and cooperative and treating everyone fairly
    - Following the correct procedures
    - Being assertive and taking responsibility of any issue or problem
    - Being cognizant and avoiding any conflict-of-interest issues

2. Ways to increase the professionalism of project management include the following:

    - Maintaining high standards of personal integrity
    - Continually striving to improve and become more knowledgeable
    - Continually looking for ways to improve the project management practice and the project management knowledgebase.

32. Quality management addresses both product (goods and services) quality and project management quality.

33. The project manager has ultimate responsibility for the project *product* quality.

34. Quality is planned in, not inspected in.

35. The PMI definition of *quality* is "conformance to requirements" and "fitness of use."

36. The identification of risks is an iterative, continual process throughout the project.

37. Risk management will change the project plan during planning, executing, and controlling.

38. After procurement planning, the other steps of procurement management (including solicitation planning) are only performed if a "buy" decision is made.

39. All requirements should be specifically stated in the contract and should be met.

40. Project communication dealing with procurement management should always be formal and written.

41. Incentives should be used to align the seller's objectives with the buyer's.

42. The risk management plan, risk response plan, procurement management plan, quality management plan, communications plan, and staffing plan are all considered part of the project plan.

43. The three main types of contracts are cost reimbursable, fixed fee, and time and materials.

PROJECT CONTROLLING

1. Project changes should be expected, planned for, and well managed.

2. Out-of-scope extras (gold-plating) add no value to the project and should be avoided.

3. Scope verification ensures that the work product is formally accepted. Quality assurance ensures the correctness of the work product.

4. *Lessons learned* are important resources for planning and future projects. Maintaining the lessons learned during project control is important.

5. All change-control systems should include guidance on the following factors;
   • How to influence the factors that cause change
   • How to detect when a change has occurred
   • How to obtain agreement on a change activity
   • How to manage the change

6. Earned value is the preferred project controlling and performance reporting technique.

7. Cost variance (CV) = earned value − actual costs

8. Cost Performance Index (CPI) = earned value / actual costs

9. Schedule variance (SV) = earned value − planned value

10. Schedule Performance Index (SPI) = earned value / planned value

11. Estimate at completion (EAC) = budget at completion (BAC) / CPI

12. Estimate to complete (ETC) = EAC / actual costs

13. Variances are always "earned value" minus something. Performance indexes are always "earned value" divided by something.

14. Performance indexes of less than 1 are unfavorable.

15. Quality control focuses on measurement. Quality assurance focuses on all the planned and systematic quality activities within the project.

16. The key quality control tools and techniques are control charts, pareto analysis (80/20 rule), Ishikawa diagrams (cause and effect, fishbone), trend analysis, and statistical sampling.

17. Preventing a risk event is always preferred to mitigating a risk event.

18. A key goal of effective risk management is to have a response plan ready (that is, a mitigation strategy) to be implemented if the risk event occurs.

19. Risk management may require replanning, developing alternate strategies, and re-baselining the project, depending on the severity of the risk.

PROJECT EXECUTING

1. The project manager is ultimately responsible for the quality of the project.

2. The project team should solve its own problems and resolve its own issues whenever possible.

3. Team development occurs throughout the entire project lifecycle.

4. The five types of power are legitimate, coercive, reward, expert, and referent (the most common type for project managers).

5. The five conflict-resolution techniques are confronting (preferred method), compromising, withdrawal, smoothing, and forcing.

6. The performance evaluation process of an individual should include everyone who has had significant interaction with that individual.

7. Maslow's Hierarchy of Needs, in order, is physical, safety and security, social, self-esteem, and self-actualization.

8. Herzberg's Hygiene Theory suggests that pay is not as motivating as work satisfaction, learning new skills, and promotions, and it suggests that relationships only prevent job dissatisfaction; they do not motivate.

PROJECT INITIATION

1. Initiation is the first step in the scope management process.

2. Initiation formally authorizes a project to begin or to continue to the next phase.

3. Initiation formally links a project to the work and to the strategic objectives of the organization.

4. Someone external to the project team and higher up in the organization must issue the project charter.

5. The project charter gives the project manager authority to "get the job done."

6. The project charter establishes the targets for the project.

7. A signed contract can serve as a project charter.

8. The two types of project selection methods are benefit measurement methods and constrained optimization methods.

9. Management by Objectives (MBO) supports project initiation by linking projects to corporate objectives.

10. MBO supports project management through its use of goal-setting and periodic reviews.

11. Many project management activities during initiation are further elaborated during planning.

PROJECT PLANNING

1. The project planning process entails 21 of the 39 PMBOK processes.

2. The project plan is much more than a project schedule. It is an all-encompassing document used as the basis for project controlling and executing.

3. A project charter is not a project plan.

4. The WBS is not the project schedule.

5. The WBS serves as the foundation for most project-planning activities.

6. The WBS should include all the work of the project and should be developed with the project team.

7. The granularity of the WBS depends on what detail is needed for effective management and control.

8. Scope definition generates the WBS. Activity definition generates the activity list.

9. A project schedule must meet three key criteria to be complete: It must have buy-in, be achievable, and be realistic and formal.

10. Developing a project schedule is a four-step process: (1) define work activities; (2) identify activity/task relationships; (3) estimate effort and duration of each activity; (4) apply calendar and resources to build a schedule.

11. Network diagrams highlight relationships among project activities.

12. The three types of project network diagrams are Activity-on-Node (most popular) , Activity-on-Arrow (uses dummy activities), and GERT (uses loops and conditional branches).

13. Estimating should be performed (or approved) by the person doing the work.

14. Key project success factors (cost, time, scope, resources) should be managed to baselines and only changed when an approved project change has been executed.

15. All assumptions used in estimating should be documented.

16. Historical information is vital to improving estimates.

17. The key facts about the "critical path" in a project schedule are as follows:

    • It's the longest sequence of activities.
    • There is zero slack (float).
    • It's the focus of any schedule-compression activity.

18. The three scheduling techniques are CPM (uses one estimate), PERT (uses three estimates), and GERT (can show various project outcomes).

19. The Monte Carlo technique is the most popular simulation scheduling technique and is also used for risk analysis.

20. The three methods for presenting the project schedule are milestone charts, Gantt charts, and network diagrams.

21. The two most popular methods for compressing the schedule are *crashing* (adding resources to critical path tasks) and *fast tracking* (performing critical path tasks in parallel).

22. Cost estimates for an activity are affected by activity duration, resource rates, and risk level.

23. The three levels of estimating accuracy are order of magnitude (-25% to +75%), budget (-10% to +25%), and definitive (-5% to +10%).

24. The risk management plan is not a risk response plan.

25. All project management activity should be "thought about" and planned.

26. Effective project management is proactive.

27. The "core" planning processes are those that must be done in a specific sequence.

28. The "facilitating" planning processes are always performed, are not optional, and directly impact many of the core planning processes.

29. The formality and detail of each supplemental plan will vary depending on project need.

30. Ninety percent of a project manager's time is spent communicating. Communication is the most important project management skill.

31. Remember the three C's in project communications: Be clear, concise, and courteous.

PMP

David Francis

Greg Horine

CERTIFICATION

PMP Exam Cram 2

Copyright © 2004 by Que Publishing

International Standard Book Number: 0-789-73037-5

Library of Congress Catalog Card Number: 2003109199

Printed in the United States of America

First Printing: October 2003

06   05   04   03   4   3   2

Trademarks

Warning and Disclaimer

Bulk Sales

Que Publishing offers excellent discounts on this book when ordered in quantity for bulk purchases or special sales. For more information, please contact

U.S. Corporate and Government Sales

1-800-382-3419

corpsales@pearsontechgroup.com

For sales outside of the U.S., please contact

International Sales

1-317-428-3341

international@pearsontechgroup.com

Publisher
Paul Boger

Executive Editor
Jeff Riley

Acquisitions Editor
Steve Rowe

Development Editor
Steve Rowe

Managing Editor
Charlotte Clapp

Project Editor
Elizabeth Finney

Copy Editor
Bart Reed

Indexer
Erika Millen

Proofreader
Tracy Donhardt

Technical Editors
Sara Strock
Jerry Thompson

Team Coordinator
Pamalee Nelson

Multimedia Developer
Dan Scherf

Interior Designer
Gary Adair

Cover Designer
Anne Jones

Page Layout
Bronkella Publishing

CERTIFICATION

Que Certification • 800 East 96th Street • Indianapolis, Indiana 46240

A Note from Series Editor Ed Tittel

You know better than to trust your certification preparation to just anybody. That's why you, and more than two million others, have purchased an Exam Cram book. As Series Editor for the new and improved Exam Cram 2 series, I have worked with the staff at Que Certification to ensure you won't be disappointed. That's why we've taken the world's best-selling certification product—a finalist for "Best Study Guide" in a CertCities reader poll in 2002—and made it even better.

As a "Favorite Study Guide Author" finalist in a 2002 poll of CertCities readers, I know the value of good books. You'll be impressed with Que Certification's stringent review process, which ensures the books are high-quality, relevant, and technically accurate. Rest assured that at least a dozen industry experts—including the panel of certification experts at CramSession—have reviewed this material, helping us deliver an excellent solution to your exam preparation needs.

Best Study Guides

We've also added a preview edition of PrepLogic's powerful, full-featured test engine, which is trusted by certification students throughout the world.

As a 20-year-plus veteran of the computing industry and the original creator and editor of the Exam Cram series, I've brought my IT experience to bear on these books. During my tenure at Novell from 1989 to 1994, I worked with and around its excellent education and certification department. This experience helped push my writing and teaching activities heavily in the certification direction. Since then, I've worked on more than 70 certification-related books, and I write about certification topics for numerous Web sites and for *Certification* magazine.

In 1996, while studying for various MCP exams, I became frustrated with the huge, unwieldy study guides that were the only preparation tools available. As an experienced IT professional and former instructor, I wanted "nothing but the facts" necessary to prepare for the exams. From this impetus, Exam Cram emerged in 1997. It quickly became the best-selling computer book series since "...*For Dummies*," and the best-selling certification book series ever. By maintaining an intense focus on subject matter, tracking errata and updates quickly, and following the certification market closely, Exam Cram was able to establish the dominant position in cert prep books.

You will not be disappointed in your decision to purchase this book. If you are, please contact me at etittel@jump.net. All suggestions, ideas, input, or constructive criticism are welcome!

Ed Tittel

Look for these other products from Pearson Education:

**Project Management: Best Practices for IT
Professionals**
ISBN: 0-13-021914-2
Richard Murch
Prentice-Hall PTR

Many thanks to my parents, Millard and Norma Francis, for their encouragement, development and faith through the years. Additional thanks to my brothers, Mitchell and Jeffrey Francis, for their support. Also, thanks to co-author Greg Horine and tech editor Sara Strock for their assistance with this book.

—David Francis

I dedicate this book to my personal project team: my lovely wife, Mayme, and my "fabulous five" children: Michael, Victoria, Alex, Luke, and Elayna.

—Greg Horine

About the Lead Authors

David A. Francis (PMP, MBA) has been a Project Manager and Business Analyst for more than 10 years and has worked as a consultant, instructor, and writer for the analysis, design, development, and implementation of complex projects. He has assessed and documented business requirements, prioritized modifications, scheduled and coordinated resources while being responsible for the entire project lifecycle from inception to completion. Projects have included working with clients such as Dow Chemical, EDS, Cisco Systems, SBC, and Simon Property Management. He has also assisted in the development of proposals for organizations such as the Homeland Security TASC force.

Mr. Francis is a Project Management Instructor at Indiana Institute of Technology and adjunct faculty member at Indiana University Purdue University Indianapolis. He has served as the Director of Education for the Project Management Institute (PMI) Central Indiana Chapter and is a PMI Registered Education Provider. He has provided curriculum development and delivery of Project Management educational programs to more than 1,000 students and for clients including Eli Lilly Company, Ameritech, Covance, Vifi, Conseco Insurance, and re:Member Data Services. He has also developed and taught numerous PMP certification classes and frequently sponsors new PMP study groups and programs.

Career highlights include telecommunications, utilities, supervisory management, marketing, and customer service. His educational background includes an MBA from Butler University and a BA from Indiana University. Certifications include Project Management Professional Certification (PMP), IT Programming Competency Certification, Microsoft Office Suite Certification, Project Management Certification (IUPUI), and Microsoft Project Software Certification.

Professional affiliations have included the American Society for Training and Development (ASTD), The Project Management Institute (PMI), The Organizational Effectiveness Institute, Center for Business Partnerships,

Association of Quality and Participation (AQP), Indianapolis Business and Professional Exchange, Central Indiana Quality Leadership Forum (IQLF), Indiana Quality, Productivity and Involvement Council (IQPIC), Indianapolis Ambassadors, Toastmasters, and the Indiana Labor Management Council.

Mr. Francis provides consulting, training, and development through his company, The Project Management Company (www.ProjectManagementCompany.com), and can be contacted at David@ProjectManagementCompany.com.

Gregory M. Horine (PMP, CCP) is a certified information technology professional with more than 14 years of consulting experience. His "real world" knowledge has been gained by working in a wide array of industries, including 7 years in the Life Sciences industry. His primary areas of professional expertise include

➤ Project management and leadership

➤ Enterprise solution development

➤ Business systems analysis

➤ Quality assurance and validation

➤ Software development

➤ Package implementation and integration

➤ Data analysis and transformation

In addition, Mr. Horine holds a master's degree in Computer Science from Ball State University, and a bachelor's degree in both Marketing and Computer Science from Anderson College.

Through his "servant leadership" approach, Mr. Horine has established a track record of empowering his teammates, improving project communications, overcoming technical and political obstacles, and successfully completing projects that meet the targeted objectives.

When not engaged in professional endeavors or helping managers prepare for the PMP exam, Mr. Horine hones his project management skills at home with his lovely wife, Mayme, and his five special children: Michael, Victoria, Alex, Luke, and Elayna.

About the Contributing Authors

Sara Strock (PMP) has more than 20 years of experience in IT project management. Her experiences come from a variety of business areas, including banking, telephony, consumer products, and pharmaceuticals. She is a PMP and holds an MBA in marketing and logistics, as well as a degree in programming. She is currently working as a project manager on a multiphased Global IT Security Project for a prominent Indianapolis company.

Emelee N. Mitchum is a PMP-certified IT consultant with more than 7 years of consulting experience. Her background includes 3 years in group benefits consulting and sales. Her professional focus is now concentrated in software implementation and business process reengineering. Ms. Mitchum's educational background includes an MBA from Indiana University and a bachelor's degree in Mathematics from DePauw University. In her spare time she enjoys volunteering her time to the Junior League of Indianapolis and playing the flute.

Acknowledgments

. . . .

Mr. Horine is grateful for the guidance and the challenging opportunities he has received from his mentors throughout his career. Their expectations, patience, and influence have resulted in a rewarding career that has been marked by continuous learning and improvement.

In addition, Mr. Horine is thankful for the "high-caliber" professionals he has worked with throughout his career. To walk the journey with them has made all the difference.

Mr. Francis would like to offer many thanks to his family, friends, relatives, colleagues, and co-workers. Additional thanks to Steve Rowe, Greg Horine, Sara Strock, Jerry Thompson, Emelee Mitchum, Jeffrey Riley, Elizabeth Finney, Que Publishing, and all of the talented individuals who were involved with the Exam Cram PMP book project. With their incredible assistance the authors were able to meet "on time" requirements. Special thanks to the Project Management Institute and to the Directors and members of the Central Indiana Chapter of PMI. Their guidance, volunteerism, and vision have had a major positive impact upon the world of Project Management.

Contents at a Glance

Table of Contents

Introduction

The PMP certification is considered the paramount certificate of the Project Management industry. Numerous corporations are beginning to embrace PMI methodologies and the PMP certification because it provides a consistent framework for project development, planning, and execution throughout the world. Microsoft Corporation recently acknowledged the PMP certification as its certification of choice for its employees, and we anticipate that it will be one of the most sought-after certifications as the profession continues to evolve. Many PMI chapters are seeing annual membership increase by 10% to 30% as more people become aware that project management is a discipline just like engineering, marketing, and accounting.

The term *project management* has been incorrectly used in organizations for many years, and PMI and PMP advocates want to set the record straight about the requirements of effective project management, the benefits, and the positive financial implications. Many public, private, and government entities are now seeking PMP certification as a prerequisite to employment or contract negotiations. This is indicative of the fact that PMP certification is here to stay and is a valuable addition to your career development.

The PMP Exam is internationally known within the PMI community and with practitioners of project management. It provides a framework for developing consistency and structure to the profession. Prior to PMI, the project management profession lacked uniformity across multiple disciplines. The PMP exam encourages participants to view project management in the same light as other disciplines, such as accounting, marketing, or computer science.

The Project Management Institute (PMI)

If you plan to be a Certified Project Manager, we recommend that you acquaint yourself with the *Project Management Institute (PMI)*. This is the organization that will provide support and educational opportunities for you.

Being part of this body of dedicated and learned professionals will greatly assist and support you in your own efforts as a project manager.

We also recommend that you seek out your local PMI chapter. Many of the local chapters provide study groups and seasoned professionals who can provide assistance and encouragement as you go through the certification process. The local chapters generally provide monthly or bimonthly meetings with guest speakers who can also enhance your project management knowledge. Although our book is an excellent resource guide, study groups and partners can provide you with reinforcement of the information.

The PMP Certification Process

The PMP certification process is not for new or aspiring project managers. PMI requires that any exam taker is "experienced" and emphasizes real-life situational questions on the exam.

A prospective PMP candidate is required to have a minimum of 4,500 hours of project-management experience, with an undergraduate degree, in order to begin the qualification process. Without an undergraduate degree, the experience requirements are even more stringent. Consequently, you need to be aware of the requirements before you begin the process. See the PMI International Web site, www.pmi.org, to learn about the requirements and the organization itself.

About This Book

Regardless of your exposure to *Exam Cram 2* books or the PMP certification process, the main purpose of this book is to provide you with tools and information that will assist you in passing the PMP certification exam. We will also provide background information about the PMP exam requirements, the Project Management Institute, and how you can use this certification to advance your professional development. This book will not focus on how to be a project manager. Our objective is to provide you with an understanding of the exam mechanics and how PMI views the topical areas associated with initiation, planning, execution, control, and closeout of projects.

Numerous organizations provide PMP training that costs thousands of dollars and requires weeks or months to complete. Our goal with this book is to provide you with a shortened version of training that may decrease your preparation time and allow you to get a quick overview of the program. This book may also be used in conjunction with training programs to reinforce the *Project Management Body of Knowledge (PMBOK)* materials and would be a good companion to university programs that place an emphasis on project-management certifications.

IT-Focused Project Management

Although this book can be universally utilized across multiple disciplines, we will emphasize many of the attributes of the Information Technology profession due to the fact that the majority of the *Exam Cram 2* books involve technical certifications. Because a large majority of project managers are involved in the IT field, we feel it is appropriate to focus on this area of project management.

The PMBOK: What You Need Along with This Book

Exam Cram 2 books provide a concise and focused overview of various topics. The approach of this book will center on providing you with numerous test questions and background information to reinforce the ideas and concepts of the certification program. The first step in this process is to purchase and read the *Project Management Body of Knowledge*, commonly referred to as the *PMBOK*. The PMBOK describes a framework for project-management activities and processes, and it's generally accepted as a "de facto" project-management standard. Most important to you, it serves as the principal source for PMP certification exam questions. Although several other books are useful in preparation for the test, the PMBOK is the key ingredient to your success and is required reading in order to pass the test.

You can purchase this book from PMI or several other suppliers. It is automatically provided to you when you join PMI. Because you will ultimately become a member of PMI in order to retain your certification, we recommend that you join the organization and receive a copy as part of your membership. The PMBOK is not light reading—it contains more than 150 pages and covers the complete depth and breadth of project management. Therefore, do not anticipate that you will be able to read all the material in one weekend and be prepared to take the test. Nor should you expect to read just this *Exam Cram 2* book and successfully pass the test.

Process View

The other primary advantage this book offers the prospective PMP candidate is that it covers the exam topics and the PMBOK framework from a "process" viewpoint rather than the "knowledge area" approach depicted in the PMBOK. We feel this process approach is more consistent with the natural workflow of project managers and with the nature of the PMP exam itself. Most importantly, we feel this process approach will better prepare you for the exam by providing synergy with related PMBOK processes, while bridging the gaps between the PMBOK organization and your real-life experiences.

We wish you great success with the certification process and encourage you to move forward in the profession if you choose it as a lifetime career.

PMP Exam Self-Assessment

This section of the *Exam Cram 2* book is intended to help you determine whether you are qualified to take the PMP exam. The requirements for the test are rigorous and time consuming. To achieve certification, candidates must satisfy several requirements related to education, project management experience, and project management training.

Education and Experience Requirements

There are two categories for initial eligibility requirements. The following table is a breakdown of each category, which is based on information from the Project Management Institute (PMI) Web site (www.pmi.org).

 The application process can easily be done online at the PMI Web site, which reduces the amount of approval time for the application.

Education	Project Management Experience	Educational Contact Hours
College degree (Category One)	Minimum of 4,500 hours of project management experience within the five project management process groups, with at least 3 years of experience within the 6-year period prior to the application.	35 hours of project management–related educational contact hours. These hours can be accumulated throughout your lifetime.
High school diploma or equivalent secondary school credential (Category Two)	Minimum of 7,500 hours of project management experience within the five project management process groups with at least 5 years of project management experience within the 8-year period prior to the application.	35 hours of project management–related educational contact hours. These hours can be accumulated throughout your lifetime.

Category One: Bachelor's Degree Candidates

If you feel you fit the requirements set out for a Category One candidate, you must fill out the Experience Verification forms to indicate the following:

➤ Baccalaureate or global equivalent university degree completion.

➤ A minimum of 4,500 hours of documented project management experience within the five Project Management process groups, including Initiation, Planning, Execution, Control, and Closeout.

➤ For the 4,500 hours of experience, the candidate must have at least 36 nonoverlapping months of experience within the 6-year period prior to the application.

➤ The candidate must obtain at least 35 contact hours of Project Management education. This includes seminars, workshops, classes, and any classroom instruction that includes content on project quality, scope, time, cost, human resources, communications, risk, procurement, and integration management. There is no time limitation to this requirement, but the candidate must be able to document when this requirement was fulfilled. Required supporting documentation includes educational background information, Experience Verification forms, and Project Management educational contact hours.

Category Two: Non–Bachelor's Degree Candidates

If you meet the requirements for a Category Two candidate, you must fill out the Experience Verification forms to indicate the following:

➤ High school diploma or secondary school credential completion.

➤ Minimum of 7,500 hours of documented project management experience within the five Project Management process groups, including Initiation, Planning, Execution, Control, and Closeout.

➤ For the 7,500 hours of experience, the candidate must have at least 60 nonoverlapping months of experience within the 8-year period prior to the application.

➤ The candidate must obtain at least 35 contact hours of Project Management education. This includes seminars, workshops, classes, and any classroom instruction that includes content on project quality, scope, time, cost, human resources, communications, risk, procurement, and integration management. There is no time limitation to this requirement, but the candidate must be able to document when this requirement was fulfilled. Required supporting documentation includes educational background information, Experience Verification forms, and Project Management educational contact hours.

The Application Process

The application process for the exam is time consuming. Be prepared to provide information about the time you have spent on various projects, educational diplomas, and contact hours.

Here is a checklist of the items you will need to complete or provide with the application if you meet the requirements seen for Category One:

➤ Current resume

➤ Proof of your degree

➤ Experience Verification forms for a total of 4,500 hours of project management experience that does not date back further than 6 years, but dates at least 3 years from the date of application.

➤ A completed PMP Certification Examination Application with your name written exactly as it appears on the identification that you will present when you take the exam

➤ Payment information

➤ Confirmation that the number of months on the Experience Verification forms total at least 36 months, not counting gaps or overlapping months

Here is a checklist of the items you will need to complete or provide with the application if you meet the requirements for Category Two:

➤ Current resume

➤ Proof of your degree

➤ Experience Verification forms for a total of 7,500 hours of project management experience that does not date back further than 8 years, but dates at least 5 years from the date of application

➤ A completed PMP Certification Examination Application with your name written exactly as it appears on the identification that you will present when you take the exam

➤ Payment information

➤ Confirmation that the number of months on the Experience Verification forms total at least 60 months, not counting gaps or overlapping months

We highly recommend that you apply online at www.pmi.org in order to save processing time! Applications sent via regular mail generally take 3–4 weeks to process. Online applications generally take 1–2 weeks. You will still be required to provide some additional materials via mail, but the process is much faster. If you mail the items, we recommend that you utilize a tracking number so that you can verify they were received. A tracking number also helps in case the package is lost. Make sure to keep copies of all your documents. There is nothing worse than losing documents and starting over again.

The following subsections provide a description of each of the forms and some suggestions of how to save time.

Current Resume

Update your resume, but you do not need to reformat your resume as some information suggests. This will save you a tremendous amount of time. You will provide a breakdown of project hours on the Experience Verification forms; therefore, you do not need to do this on your resume. Make sure the information is current and that you have provided enough information in case your paperwork is audited.

Examination Application

Complete the application using uppercase letters. You must complete all the areas of the application to be eligible to take the test. Examination fees are generally $150 more for non-PMI members versus members. The typical membership is approximately $140, so it is a good idea to join as a member of PMI to get the reduced rate. Plus, you receive the benefits of PMI membership with this approach. Many of the forms request your PMI ID number.

Experience Verification Forms

This is the most time-consuming part of the application process. Anticipate that you will need to review your work records, resumes, employment history, day planners, and other time-management tools to assemble these forms. You will need to indicate on the form the number of hours spent in each of the five process groups (Initiation, Planning, Execution, Control, and

Closeout) for each project you have worked on. Consequently, you may need to complete 5–10 forms to account for the time requirement. You will need to read the *Project Management Body of Knowledge (PMBOK)* to make sure you understand the differentiation between these areas so that you provide accurate information.

Proof of Degree

You will need to provide photocopies of your diploma(s) to authenticate your educational background.

Educational Contact Hours

The Education form requires you to list the classes, workshops, or training programs that constitute 35 hours of educational contact hours. These programs can include content concerning risk, procurement, integration management, human resources, scope, project quality, cost, time, or communications. The programs can be provided by any of the following:

➤ Employer/company-sponsored programs.

➤ Programs presented by a PMI Registered Education Provider.

➤ Distance learning companies, such as computer-based training.

➤ PMI Component organizations. (Chapter meetings do not qualify.)

➤ Universities, colleges, or continuing education programs.

➤ Training companies or consultants.

As you can tell, the educational contact hours are very broad and include any training, in your entire life, that fulfills the content requirements. If you attended any PMP test-preparation classes, these hours would also qualify toward the 35-hour requirement. You can list two programs per form, so make additional copies, if necessary, to summarize the 35 contact hours.

If you have any further questions concerning the application process, go to www.pmi.org or call PMI customer service at 610-356-4600.

Application Checklist

The following subsections provide some handy checklists you can use as you begin the application process. The first checklist is for Category One candidates, and the second is for Category Two candidates.

Category One (with College Diploma or Equivalent)

➤ Write your name as it appears on the identification that you will present when you take the test.

➤ Include payment information.

➤ Include your current resume or curriculum vitae.

➤ Include proof of your degree (copy of diploma or transcripts).

➤ Ensure that Experience Verification forms date back at least 3 years from the date of application.

➤ Ensure that Experience Verification forms do not date back more than 6 years from the date of application.

➤ Experience Verification forms must reflect a total of at least 4,500 hours of project management experience.

➤ When you count the months listed on the Experience Verification forms, they must total at least 36 months. This should not include gaps between projects or overlapping projects.

Category Two (Without College Diploma)

➤ Write your name as it appears on the identification that you will present when you take the test.

➤ Include payment information.

➤ Include your current resume or curriculum vitae.

➤ Include proof of your high school diploma (copy of diploma or transcripts).

➤ Ensure that Experience Verification forms date back at least 5 years from the date of application.

➤ Ensure that Experience Verification forms do not date back more than 8 years from the date of application.

➤ Experience Verification forms must reflect a total of at least 7,500 hours of project management experience.

➤ When you count the months listed on the Experience Verification forms, they must total at least 60 months. This should not include gaps between projects or overlapping projects.

When you have fulfilled all the listed requirements, send your materials to the following address:

PMI Certification Program Department
Four Campus Boulevard
Newtown Square, PA 19073-3299

 Be aware that faxes are not accepted. We recommend that you apply online at **www.pmi.org** for quicker approval. A PMP Examination eligibility letter will be sent to qualified candidates within 10–14 working days from receipt of the application at PMI.

Exam Fees

The following list gives you the pricing of the PMP exam for both PMI members and non-PMI members:

➤ Non-PMI member rate: $555

➤ PMI member rate: $405

Also, be aware that both credit cards and checks are accepted as forms of payment.

 We recommend that you join PMI to receive the reduced test rate!

Cancellations/Rescheduling and No Shows

Cancellations and rescheduling must be in accordance with the exam contractor's policy. Contact the examination site provider for more details. If you do not contact the exam contractor or do not report at the scheduled time, you forfeit the full examination fee. If this occurs, you must submit a new application and pay the full exam fee.

If you have a medical emergency, you must submit a written notification and official medical documentation to PMI within 72 hours of the scheduled appointment.

Don't be late or forget your appointment! It can be expensive and time consuming to reapply. If you must reschedule, do not wait until the last minute to contact the exam site.

Extensions

Applicants who have not taken the exam within the 6-month eligibility period may request an extension or refund. For an extension, send a written extension prior to the eligibility period, including the reason for the extension and acknowledgement that you have cancelled any exam appointments with the exam contractor.

If you meet these requirements, PMI will provide a 6-month extension at no cost. Extensions will not be allowed after the candidate's eligibility has reached 1 year.

Refunds

Refunds can be obtained by submitting a written request to PMI within 1 month of the eligibility expiration date. No refunds are provided if you have taken the test or not notified the exam contractor of any appointment cancellations or rescheduling.

A $200 processing fee will be deducted from your refund.

PMI Audit Process

PMI reviews all applications and periodically audits applications for authenticity. Make sure your documents are complete and accurate. Fraudulent information can lead to sanctions by the PMI Certification Board. Read the "PMP Certificant and Candidate Agreement and Release" for more details.

Do not endanger your certification by providing false or incorrect information on your application or documents. It is not worth the potential impact on your career or professional development.

Pre-Test

To end this Self-Assessment, we recommend that you review the following questions. These questions are intended to help you measure your experience and your knowledge of fundamental project management concepts and techniques. If your projects are rarely successful or if you are unsure of more than five of these questions, we recommend that you take official PMI project management training, find some books on fundamental project management, or spend some more time on the job to improve the skills and knowledge base you need to begin your pursuit of the PMP exam. Here's the list of questions:

➤ Do you know what a project charter is?

➤ Do you know the difference between a project charter and a project plan?

➤ Do you know the difference between initiating and planning a project?

➤ Do you understand how to use earned value to measure and control project performance?

➤ Do you know how to create a network diagram and how to find the critical path in your project?

➤ Do you understand how to crash and fast track a project schedule?

➤ Do you know how to develop a project budget and manage it?

➤ Do you understand how risk management affects your project schedule and project budget?

➤ Do you understand the role of a project manager versus the role of the project sponsor and the other team members?

➤ Do you know how to control a project against a project plan?

➤ Do you know the process for officially approving a project deliverable?

➤ Do you know who is allowed to make what types of changes to a project?

➤ Do you know what a milestone is?

➤ Do you know what a project gate is?

➤ Do you know what type of estimates provide the best accuracy?

➤ Do you know how to plan, manage, and measure quality in your project?

➤ Do you know how to plan, assess, manage, and control risks in your project?

➤ Do you know that risk management is more than a checklist?

➤ Do you know how to use a Work Breakdown Structure (WBS) to plan, execute, and control a project?

➤ Do you always follow a project management methodology?

➤ Do you understand what causes project rework and overtime?

➤ Do you understand what causes cost and schedule overruns?

➤ Do you manage projects using a communications plan?

➤ Do you know how to manage the influences that affect project scope?

➤ Do your teams always have good morale and are they clear on their assignments?

The PMP Exam

Terms you'll need to understand:

✓ PMP

✓ PMI

✓ CCRs

✓ PDUs

Techniques and concepts you'll need to master:

✓ What the PMP Exam is

✓ What PMI is

✓ What the process groups are

✓ The differences between core processes and facilitating
  processes

✓ The mapping of the 39 project management processes to the
  five project management process groups and the nine project
  management knowledge areas

The *Project Management Professional (PMP)* certification is the premier credential recognized internationally in the Project Management discipline. It signifies an individual has the process knowledge, experience, and training required to practice the methodologies prescribed by the Project Management Institute (PMI). It has become a professional standard and prerequisite for countless organizations and companies.

According to PMI, there are currently more than 50,000 PMP certifications in more than 120 countries, and the numbers continue to grow at a vigorous rate. To contrast this number, note that there were only 10,000 PMP certifications by the year 2000. As these statistics demonstrate, many individuals are just becoming aware of the certification and PMI. This incredible growth is expected to continue.

Industries that rely on PMP certification include information technology, telecommunications, construction, healthcare, government, and numerous other professions. Because project management is a relatively new discipline, the growth rate of the certification credential is incredible and will continue to expand to other disciplines, including engineering, medicine, and aerospace, among others. Many corporations are now requesting PMP certification as a requirement for career development or as a prerequisite to employment.

The requirements for PMP certification are extensive. PMI requires specific educational and experience attributes before an application can be submitted. The "PMP Certification Handbook" is a good source for explanation of the required educational and work background.

Upon completion of the requirements and passing of the exam, additional continuing certification requirements have to be fulfilled in order to maintain certification. The Continuing Certification Requirements (CCRs) mandate that you accumulate at least 60 Professional Development Units (PDUs) every 3 years after achieving your PMP certification. PDUs can be accumulated by attending various PMI programs, seminars, and educational opportunities.

What Is the PMP Exam Like?

The Project Management Professional exam is a computer-based exam composed of 200 multiple-choice questions. Each question has four answers, and the exam-taker is required to choose the best answer to the question. A total of 4 hours is allowed for the exam.

The intent of the questions is to test a thorough understanding of project management. To this end, many questions are creatively designed to check both key understanding (knowledge) and the ability to practically apply concepts at the same time. A part of this creative exam design is to utilize many different types of questions. To better prepare you for the PMP exam experience, let's review the key question types and formats you are likely to encounter:

➤ **Situational questions**—These questions require you to rely on your knowledge, real-world experience and judgment in order to answer them correctly.

➤ **Conceptual understanding**—For these questions, you must apply concepts to a new situation by using more than simple memorization. Often, PMI will intentionally use different terminology for the same concepts. This is done to test your "understanding" of the topic rather than your ability to simply recall a term.

➤ **Memorization questions**—The PMP exam will have some questions that are short and direct and can be answered in less than 20 seconds. For example, you may well encounter some fill-in-the-blank questions and factual-type questions.

➤ **Double-reverse logic questions**—A popular technique of wily test designers, these types of questions ask about a topic using reverse or double-reverse logic. Generally, you need to select the exception from the four possible options.

➤ **Story problem questions**—The long, drawn-out "story problem" questions can take several minutes (2 to 5 minutes) to process. The key to these question types is deciphering what information presented is essential and needed to answer the question.

➤ **"Use the pencil" questions**—These questions require you to perform simple calculations and/or draw simple diagrams to select the correct answer. Frequently, questions regarding earned value, financial accounting, project network diagrams, and project schedules will require the use of the pencil to get the right answer.

➤ **Non-PMBOK questions**—Estimates vary, but most people feel around 60% of the exam questions come directly from the PMBOK. The other questions originate from other reference materials, subjects related to project management, and real-world situations. In addition, past exam-takers have noted out-of-the-blue questions that test specific knowledge points. Project Management is a broad field of study, so you can never be too prepared.

➤ **"I need to change careers" questions**—A few questions are placed in every PMP exam to "rattle" the exam-taker. These questions will be difficult, if not impossible, to answer with confidence. Just expect these, and see our exam-taking strategies on how best to deal with them. This may be PMI's way of testing how you respond under pressure and when things do not go as expected.

 A common feedback point from many exam-takers is that several questions seemed to have *more than one correct answer.* Often, most, if not all, of the answers are reasonable responses to the question at hand. However, there is always one "best" response, as determined by PMI.

What Is PMI?

The *Project Management Institute (PMI)* is an international, not-for-profit, educational association. The PMI group is exclusively dedicated to expanding project management practices and excellence in areas associated with the profession. PMI sets professional standards for the project management profession and is involved with research, publishing, training, and development, as well as numerous certifications, academic scholarships, and awards.

The organization was established in 1969 by five volunteers, and is located outside Philadelphia, Pennsylvania. Membership grew to more than 2,000 by 1980, more than 8,500 by 1990, and more than 50,000 by the year 2000. PMI is a group of project managers and educators from a variety of industries who share project management experiences, applications, and concepts. PMI goals include professionalism, the development of project management educational programs, and membership growth. PMI currently has more than 100,000 members worldwide, including Europe, Latin America, the Middle East, Asia, and Africa. PMI publishes numerous books and periodicals, including *PMI Today, The Project Management Journal,* and *PM Network.*

Benefits of membership include chapter meetings, periodicals, workshops and seminars, special interest groups (SIGS), continuing certification opportunities, and PMP certification. PMI also supports an educational foundation—the PMI Educational Foundation—that promotes project management for the benefit of society. For more information about memberships and benefits, visit www.pmi.org.

Expect to feel "disoriented" at some point during the exam. This is a common feeling caused by either one of the following:

➤ A series of long questions (especially if they appear early in the exam) that temporarily have you thinking that the entire test is this way and that you'll never have enough time to complete it.

➤ The sense that the exam questions are much more difficult than the practice questions. (We hope to reduce the chance of this happening by including many "exam-like" questions.) This is the main reason why you need to understand the concepts and principles and not just memorize facts.

Study and Exam-taking Strategies

To finish your introduction to the PMP exam, let's explore some important study and exam-taking tips. Although some of these tips will not apply to everyone, this section will give you a good, general idea of how you can save time and reduce the stress of preparing for and taking the actual PMP exam.

Study Tips

The following list provides some recommended study practices that you might want to employ as you prepare for the exam. These tips have proved successful for others who have prepared for and passed the PMP exam before you. Not all these tips may suit your learning style or your particular situation, but the goal is that they help you save time, focus better, and comprehend the material you will find in this book and in other study materials:

➤ Form a study group at work or contact the local PMI chapter to determine if any study groups are available. Interacting with other exam-takers helps reinforce the information and clarify the concepts in the PMBOK.

➤ Look at several types of study guides to determine which is best for you. Some people prefer visual assistance, and some prefer straightforward reading. The *Exam Cram 2* series provides an excellent, concise overview of the material and is a good augmentation to the PMBOK.

➤ The PMBOK is not the only resource book for the certification exam. Determine exactly which books are necessary for the exam. Many study guides have a long list of required books, but you should determine whether each book is a major or minor resource for the exam. You could be overwhelmed if you read all the suggested materials. Plus, it is very time consuming.

➤ Develop a system and time frame for your studying. Set milestones and dates for completion of the chapters and review of this *Exam Cram 2* book.

➤ Spread out your reading and studying over time. Because this is complex material, it is not easy to comprehend in a short period of time. Too much reading in a short time period can be overwhelming and lead to exhaustion and frustration.

➤ Develop worksheets and short versions of the material if it is beneficial for you to write out the information. Some people study best by writing out the highlights of the chapters in their own wording. This can be time consuming, but it can also be advantageous to some people.

➤ Talk to other people who have taken the exam to get their input and suggestions. Due to PMI ethics standards, PMPs are not allowed to provide actual questions from the exam, but they can provide insight into what study habits worked best for them.

➤ Make sure you have the most current PMBOK. Do not use old copies because the information changes with each revision.

➤ Read the PMBOK first and use this *Exam Cram 2* book to reinforce and elaborate on the various sections. This book does not replace the PMBOK, although it is an excellent companion for studying with the PMBOK.

➤ Anticipate that you will spend approximately 100–200 hours on this entire process—from the time you begin the application, review the PMBOK, review study materials, and drill on practice exam questions, to when you finally take the exam.

 You cannot spend only one weekend studying for PMP certification and expect to do well on the exam.

➤ To save time, we recommend that you take practice exams to identify your knowledge gaps. Repetitive exam taking has frequently been the best method to identify knowledge deficiencies and areas to concentrate one's future studies.

➤ The PMBOK will make references to many topics outside of the book, but it will not necessarily explain these topics in full detail. Therefore, practice exams will help you identify what additional materials outside of the PMBOK are needed for you to study.

➤ Study the necessary material to close the knowledge gaps and retake the exams to determine if you have a full understanding of the material.

➤ Drill on practice exams until you are scoring 80% to 90% consistently on each part.

➤ Although the exam questions are mostly situational, you will need to memorize certain definitions and formulas. The exam is not based on simple memorization. It is based on understanding situations and choosing the best answer based on PMI's perspective.

➤ Don't let your real-life, "on the job" project management experiences interfere with your study behaviors. Remember, you must pass the exam according to the PMBOK methodologies, and not your perspectives based on your past experiences. This conflict can be very difficult to overcome, especially for seasoned practitioners of Project Management.

➤ Make sure you concentrate on the correct areas of the exam. Different quantities of questions exist for different knowledge areas, so make sure you place more emphasis on the areas that have the largest percentage of questions.

➤ The PMBOK is the main question source for the majority of the PMP exam; therefore, you should spend the majority of your study time reviewing it rather than other reference materials.

Exam-taking Strategies

Once you have completed your study and you are confident that you can tackle the exam, it will be time to schedule your exam and head to the exam center. The following list will help you on exam day before, during, and after the exam:

➤ Get to the exam site early so you can review your notes and not become stressed due to a late appointment.

➤ Take the exam within 2 weeks of completing your studies. Our research has shown that if you put off the exam any longer, you begin to lose initiative and information retention. Before you know it, a month or two has passed and you have lost the freshness of the material in your memory.

Pacing and Breaks
➤ Pace yourself and be sure to read all four answers completely. Do not just choose the first correct answer you see.

➤ You are not required to immediately take the exam when you sit down at the computer terminal. Use this time to gather your thoughts and prepare your "reference sheet." Write down all formulas, diagrams, and information that will assist you with the exam. This allows you to clear your thoughts and focus better as you begin the exam.

➤ When you begin the exam process, you will initially be provided a tutorial of how to use the terminal and how to take the exam. If you feel comfortable with the information, you can pass over this tutorial quickly and begin the exam. The clock begins as soon as you start the tutorial.

➤Take breaks throughout the exam. You have 4 hours for the exam, so allotting for periodic breaks will allow you to reenergize so that you can go back to the exam area refreshed.

➤ Do not be surprised if you are videotaped during the exam. Due to the nature of the exam and the credibility of the testing facility, many companies videotape the testing process in order to monitor the participants.

➤ Schedule your exam many weeks in advance. Some testing facilities have a waiting list, so you want to time your exam date after you have completed studying for it. This also sets a future milestone for you to anticipate and strive for as the date approaches.

What to Bring to the Test

➤ Take your driver's license or photo ID with you to the testing facility. You will be asked for identification in order to take the exam. Contact the testing facility if you have questions about approved types of identification.

➤ Don't forget to take a calculator. You can use any type of calculator except the programmable types.

➤ Take a watch with a stop-watch function and time yourself. You have 4 hours to complete 200 questions; therefore, you need to complete at least 50 questions per hour. After 1 hour, look at your watch and gauge whether you need to speed up in order to complete on time. Some exam-takers do not monitor their time and become nervous after the third hour when they realize they are behind. Then they begin to forget information and become anxious. This anxiety can lead to poor performance.

➤ Wear comfortable clothing.

➤ Take a couple pencils to take notes and develop your reference sheet.

Question Approaches

➤ Anticipate that many questions will have multiple correct answers. It is your challenge to pick the *best* answer based on how PMI feels the situation should be handled.

➤ Remember to answer questions from PMI's perspective, not from your real-life experience. Think "What should I do?" rather than "What did I do?"

➤ Be cautious of the following:

> ➤ Answers that attract the attention of less knowledgeable, less experienced professionals

> ➤ Answers that reflect common project management errors and unapproved practices

> ➤ Answers that are factually correct but are not the correct response to the question

> ➤ Answers that are sweeping generalizations (that is, *always*, *never*, and so on)

> ➤ Questions that have extraneous information not relevant to the topic or question

➤ As a key strategy, keep in mind the following points when you are actually taking the exam:

> ➤ The exam allows you to "mark" any question for later review.

> ➤ Plan on making several passes (iterations) through all 200 questions of the exam.

> ➤ On the initial pass through the exam, "mark" any question that you are not 100% sure of the answer.

> ➤ On the second pass, review all the "marked" questions. You will often find that the answer to a given question becomes clear after dealing with the other questions and/or after a second review of the question and potential answers.

> ➤ If you are now sure you have answered the question correctly, "unmark" the question. If you are still not comfortable, leave it marked.

> ➤ Continue through all the marked questions to complete your pass (iteration).

> ➤ Continue this iterative process, until the number of marked questions gets down to approximately 25 or less. This would mean you are very confident about 175 of the 200 questions. Because you only need 137 to pass, this should leave you with a comfortable margin.

> ➤ At this point, just give your best guess at the remaining questions.

➤ Look at the exam-taking and preparation process as a project. With well-thought-out, effective scheduling and planning, you will have great success!

Tips for the IT Professional

Although it is our intent to assist project managers from all disciplines in their quest for PMP certification, we do want to share a set of tips and insights that will be particularly useful to the majority of IT project managers. Why do we focus on the IT project manager? Three key reasons:

➤ Although the IT project management discipline is improving each year, a very wide range of implementation maturity levels and experiences still exist.

➤ Given the target market of the *Exam Cram 2* series, it is anticipated that most of the readers of this book have experiences from the IT field.

➤ We are both IT project management professionals.

 If your project management experience has not been in the IT world, we encourage you to read this section anyway. There are generally gaps between PMI's vision of project management and your own experiences, and this section will help you identify those gaps. More importantly, we share several key PMI insights and assumptions that will benefit you greatly on the exam.

The purpose of this section is to summarize the common gaps between the experiences of most IT project managers and what they need to know to successfully pass the PMP exam. You want to avoid the trap of thinking that you might pass the PMP exam easily because you have been managing projects for a long time. The reality may be that the way you have completed IT projects and the way you understand IT project management may not be the way that PMI sees this industry. So, when it comes to passing this exam, you will need to stay alert to what PMI says about a topic in order to answer exam questions correctly.

This section also covers several tips that will help you streamline your exam preparations. These tips are organized into the following classifications:

➤ Common "conceptual" gaps

➤ Common "experience" gaps

➤ Common "terminology" gaps

➤ What's important to PMI?

➤ Key PMI assumptions

➤ Exam topics not covered in the PMBOK

Common "Conceptual" Gaps

Because it is important to answer the questions from PMI's perspective, and not necessarily from your real-life experiences, let's first review several key, high-level differences between the PMI vision and common experiences of IT project managers:

➤ **Culture clash**—Because nearly every organization implements project management differently, we generally find that most implementations are not entirely consistent with PMI's view of the world. You will want to identify those differences for your own situation.

➤ **"The" project manager**—Given the wide range of "project manager" experiences within IT (for example, technical team leader, project administrator, project analyst, project leader, project coordinator), you may be surprised by the expectation PMI has of the project manager role and the powers that come with it.

➤ **Unapproved practices**—There are several project management practices and techniques used routinely within IT that are considered "inappropriate" by PMI (for example, the use of overtime, forcing estimates down). These will appear on the exam as incorrect options.

➤ **Bigger ballpark**—For most IT project managers, the PMI PMBOK describes a field of project management that is much broader and complex than what they have experienced in real life.

➤ **The whole story**—Most IT project managers lack experience in the complete lifecycle of project management. Generally, there is minimal exposure to the Initiating and Closing phases. You must understand the complete project management process as described by PMI.

Common "Experience" Gaps

This section reviews common gaps between the experiences and practices of most IT professionals, and their respective organizations, and what PMI expects the project manager to do:

> ➤ **Project planning**—Of the 39 PMBOK project management processes, 21 deal with planning. As you can imagine, PMI's definition is much more encompassing than the project plans routinely developed by IT project managers.

> ➤ **Developing a project schedule**—It is still rather uncommon to find IT organizations and IT professionals who build a project schedule the "right way." As you can imagine, the "right way" is much more involved than the method routinely employed within IT. If you do not use a four-step process, use network diagramming techniques (there are more than one), understand the three estimating methods, account for all Work Breakdown Structure (WBS) dictionary items, or identify all dependencies and level resources, you probably have some work in this process area.

> ➤ **Planning project management**—Yes, we still have not left this "planning" theme yet. PMI expects that all project management activities are planned and documented. So, if your project plan does not include supplementary plans, such as a staffing-management plan, a responsibility matrix, a communications-management plan, a quality-management plan, a scope-management plan, and a risk-management plan (for starters), you will want to focus on these and understand their value.

> ➤ **Tracking project performance**—"Earned value" is PMI's recommended technique for tracking and controlling project costs, schedule, and scope. Earned value analysis is not a generally applied technique across IT, and many IT professionals have limited experience in managing project costs.

> ➤ **Risk management**—Because a full-scale risk-management process, as described by PMI, is rarely implemented on IT projects, many people have not been educated in this area, either.

> ➤ **Quality management**—Quality management has the same reasons as risk management, except many organizations do have some levels of quality programs in place. The issue here is that your organization's philosophy, terminology, and processes may not match those espoused by PMI.

➤ **Procurement management**—This is not as frequent a gap as it used to be, but if your experiences have not dealt with soliciting, selecting, and managing vendors, you will have gaps to close in this area.

➤ **Project selection**—Although the practice of applying sound business principles to prioritizing and selecting IT projects is increasing each year, there are still many IT project manager types who have not been exposed to business case development and official cost-benefit analysis using financial techniques, such as NPV, IRR, and payback period. (Don't be concerned, we will explain this area further and tell you what you need to know.)

Common "Terminology" Gaps

A common revelation of many Project Management professionals, when they are first exposed to the PMBOK, is that they find terms and concepts they know in one fashion do not necessarily mean the same thing to PMI. Although a complete glossary of key PMP exam terms is included in this book, it is important to review the common terminology gaps for IT professionals now, so we can "get on the same page" early in the process:

➤ **Project charter**—To PMI, this is the document that authorizes (initiates) the project and the project manager to do his work, and is the key output from the Initiating process. In many organizations, this document is often given other names (for example, Project Initiation form, Business Case).

➤ **Project plan**—To PMI, the *project plan* is the key output of the Planning process and contains many subdeliverables (for example, the project schedule, WBS, all the supplementary project management plans). In many IT-related organizations, this document may be known as the Project Charter, Project Contract, Statement of Work, and so on.

➤ **Project plan versus project schedule**—A Gantt chart (MS Project) project schedule is not a project plan. A project plan contains the project schedule.

➤ **WBS versus Gantt chart**—To PMI, a Work Breakdown Structure (WBS) is not equivalent to a Gantt chart (MS Project) project schedule. The WBS is a key input into the schedule-development process, and the project schedule accounts for calendar time and resource leveling.

➤ **Terms to verify**—Here are several other common project management terms you use that may not have the exact same definition to PMI (these differences are less critical than the ones previously mentioned):

   ➤ Audit

   ➤ Baseline

   ➤ Corrective action

   ➤ Kickoff meeting

   ➤ Procurement management

   ➤ Risk management

➤ **Uncommon terms to notice**—Several terms used by PMI are not that well-known in the IT project management world. You will want to make sure you review these terms:

   ➤ Gold plating

   ➤ Integration management

   ➤ Project expeditor

   ➤ Project Management Information System (PMIS)

   ➤ Work Authorization System

What's Important to PMI?

To better appreciate why these common gaps exist and to better prepare for the exam, let's review some of the underlying principles guiding PMI's vision of project management:

➤ The project manager "makes it happen" and "brings it all together." The role of project manager is extremely important and extremely valuable.

➤ Planning is very important—21 of the 39 PMBOK processes are "planning related."

➤ All "management" activities should be analyzed and planned in advance. These supplementary "management" plans are part of the overall project plan.

➤ The project plan should accurately describe project activity, is based in reality, and is used as the baseline to measure progress.

➤ The Work Breakdown Structure is a very important project management tool.

➤ Communication is the most important activity of the project manager (90% of the PM's time is spent here). Other communication-based principles that are extremely important to PMI include the following:

  ➤ Coordinate with stakeholders on all project aspects.

  ➤ Clearly assign all project roles and responsibilities.

➤ The risk-management process is very important and is a continuous project management activity.

➤ All estimating should be completed by the people who will actually do the work.

➤ All projects, regardless of outcome, should complete the Closing process. The emphasized outputs from this are as follows:

  ➤ Capturing "lessons learned"

  ➤ Executing proper administrative closure

Key PMI Assumptions

To further understand these common gaps—but more importantly, to better prepare for the exam—let's review some of the key assumptions that guide PMI's vision of project management:

➤ The project manager is selected when the project is authorized—before any estimating or preliminary requirements gathering.

➤ The project manager is ultimately accountable for the project.

➤ PMI assumes you have historical records of past projects.

➤ WBS is the basis for all project planning.

➤ The project plan is the baseline that the PM uses to "control" the project.

➤ The project plan accurately describes the project activity. The project plan is realistic and can be used to measures progress.

➤ PMI assumes your organization has project management methodologies and quality-assurance procedures.

➤ The project manager does have Human Resources and team-development responsibilities.

➤ PMI assumes the project team is involved in all planning decisions and problem-solving situations.

Exam Topics Not Covered by PMBOK

Although the PMP exam is based "primarily" on the PMBOK, and the PMBOK should be a central reference in your exam-preparation efforts, several exam topics originate from general business-management knowledge or other PMI publications and are not addressed in the PMBOK.

 NOTE | This point also demonstrates one of the major values of practice exams. The questions you will encounter will help you find the topics you may need to study outside of the PMBOK.

Although this list is not meant to be exhaustive, here are some key non-PMBOK exam topics you should understand:

➤ Conflict-resolution techniques

➤ Organizational theories

➤ Problem-solving techniques

➤ Professional responsibility

➤ Theories of motivation

Project Management Framework

Terms you'll need to understand:

✓ Project
✓ Project management
✓ Progressive elaboration
✓ General management
✓ Application areas
✓ Project portfolio management
✓ Project lifecycle
✓ Product lifecycle
✓ Deliverables
✓ Stakeholders

✓ Project sponsor
✓ Functional organization
✓ Matrix organization
✓ Projectized organization
✓ Culture
✓ Process
✓ Rolling wave planning
✓ Core processes
✓ Facilitating processes
✓ Project Management Office (PMO)

Techniques and concepts you'll need to master:

✓ What a project and project management is
✓ What the project management knowledge areas are
✓ What the process groups are
✓ The differences between core processes and facilitating processes
✓ The mapping of the 39 project management processes to the five project management process groups and the nine project management knowledge areas
✓ The differences between programs and projects
✓ What a deliverable is and how it's used

✓ What a project sponsor is and how he or she is involved with the project
✓ The differences between functional, matrix, and projectized organizations
✓ The differences between leaders and managers
✓ Various communication dimensions
✓ The differences between standards and regulations
✓ Project process categories
✓ The relationship between project lifecycle and project management processes
✓ Triple constraint of project management

The Project Management Framework

This chapter explains the Project Management Framework and provides the rudimentary terms and concepts used for the rest of the book. The framework includes the first three chapters of the PMBOK, covering the introduction, project management context, and the project management processes. The rest of the PMBOK focuses on the project management knowledge areas.

 Make sure you understand these concepts before you proceed, and use them as a foundation of knowledge for the rest of the material. We recommend that you read through the exam-preparation assessment questions at the end of each section to determine whether you have understood the major highlights of the chapter and can correctly answer them.

What a Project Is and How It's Different from a Program

According to PMI, a *project* is "a temporary endeavor undertaken to create a unique product or service." This is an important definition you need to know for the test because it emphasizes that a project is temporary and has a distinct beginning, duration, and clear-cut ending. According to the PMBOK, a *program* is "a group of related projects managed in a coordinated way and includes an element of ongoing work."

 The PMP exam will not be based on memorization only. You must know the definitions and concepts and be able to utilize them in a fictitious situation.

A project is different from a program by this distinction. Processing of daily Accounts Receivable statements is not a project because it is an ongoing function. The development of an annual budget and financial report is considered a project because it is a unique activity that is not done on a daily basis. The easiest way to determine whether an event is a project is to ask yourself these questions:

➤ Does the event have a definitive beginning?

➤ Does the event have a duration in which various activities occur?

➤ Does the event have a definitive ending?

If you answer "yes" to all three of these questions, the event constitutes a project. If the event has a beginning but has stopped before the ending, it may still constitute a project. For example, suppose a military assignment is started and is supposed to end in 6 months. Due to budget cuts, all activities are ended after 4 months. These events would still constitute a project because they have a definite beginning, duration, and ending, even if the events were cut short.

Projects come in all forms and sizes and are done in the areas of government infrastructure, aerospace, pharmaceutical development, telecommunications, and a multitude of different professions. Projects are also done in our daily lives—the annual Girl Scout cookie drive, weddings, home building, and preparation of the family Thanksgiving dinner.

Projects at work may include the implementation of software on 200 computers, the introduction of a new product, or the development and distribution of a book. All these events are considered projects that involve planning and the execution of that plan. Each event is considered unique, even though it may be repeated each year.

Progressive elaboration involves various parts of projects that evolve over time. For example, a new style of automobile begins as an idea and is then transformed into blueprints. Many transformations may occur between the idea and the blueprints. The blueprints are then used to develop a prototype with additional modifications and augmentations. The prototype leads to engineering designs for the manufacturing line of the vehicle. The prototype may change as limitations of the manufacturing designs are identified. Eventually an automobile-assembly process and line will develop and cars will be manufactured. This process shows how a project can go through several or even hundreds of progressive elaborations before it becomes a reality.

What Is Project Management?

Many people define *project management* differently based on their profession or how it is utilized in their company environment. Everyone agrees it involves knowledge and the ability to make things happen. For the purposes of this book, we will use the PMI definition, which states that project management is "the application of knowledge, skills, tools, and techniques to project activities to meet project requirements." Specifically these are the tools and techniques postulated by PMI. The knowledge and skills generally come from the project manager, who has experience with managing projects. The culmination of these two areas forms the basis for effective project management.

The Project Management Knowledge Areas and Processes

The PMBOK breaks down the nine knowledge areas into 39 processes, and you will need to know all of them. The processes are organized into five groups: Initiating processes, Planning processes, Executing processes, Controlling processes, and Closing processes. We will go into further detail in the upcoming chapters. Table 2.1 is the breakdown of the nine knowledge areas according to PMI:

You will not be able to memorize all this material in one reading. Continue to read and familiarize yourself with the material before you anticipate that you will be able to understand how all the activities and processes are integrated. The PMBOK is not a study guide, but rather a project management framework reference, much like a dictionary. One of the values of this *Exam Cram 2* book is that it is a "study aid" that guides you through the PMBOK.

Table 2.1   The Nine PMI Knowledge Areas

Knowledge Area	Description
Project integration management	This area includes plan development, execution, and integrated change control. This involves input to develop the plan and the processes to keep it on track.
Project scope management	This area is composed of project initiation, scope planning, definition, verification, and change control. Initiation is where the project begins with the outline of what you want to accomplish and the processes that are required to make any alterations to the scope.
Project time management	This area encompasses activity definition, sequencing, duration estimating, schedule development, and control. Remember that time is a key element to the project and its success.
Project cost management	This area incorporates resource planning, cost estimating, budgeting, and control.
Project quality management	This area involves quality planning, assurance, and control.
Project human resource management	This area pertains to organizational planning, staff acquisition, and team development.
Project communications management	This area involves communications planning, information distribution, performance reporting, and administrative closure.

Table 2.1 The Nine PMI Knowledge Areas *(continued)*	
Knowledge Area	**Description**
Project risk management	This area describes risk management planning, identification, qualitative and quantitative risk analysis, response planning, monitoring, and control.
Project procurement management	This area focuses on procurement planning, solicitation planning, solicitation, source selection, contract administration, and closeout.

The Differences Between Core Processes and Facilitating Processes

Core processes have planning dependencies that require them to be performed in the same sequence on most projects. The core planning processes may be repeated several times during the project. For example, project work must be defined before it is scheduled and resources are assigned to it.

Facilitating processes are different from core processes because they are performed intermittently throughout the project rather than in a specific order. These planning processes are itemized later in the chapter.

 Facilitating processes are performed intermittently throughout the project; however, they are eventually utilized. They are not optional.

The Impact of Project Management on Other Forms of Management

Many of the processes, tools, and methodologies are common in other forms of general management involved with ongoing business operations and enterprises. The PMBOK views *general management* in terms of its application areas, such as functional departments, technical elements, management specializations, and industry groups. It places much emphasis on the overlap of attributes between the three knowledge areas of project management, general management, and the application areas.

Numerous other types of endeavors are related to project management, including program management. The PMBOK defines a program as "a group of projects managed in a coordinated way to obtain benefits not available from managing them individually." Consequently, many organizations have program managers to fulfill the needs of individual projects and groups of projects. Many projects are divided into subprojects to allow them to be more manageable. This frequently occurs with large, multimillion-dollar projects that take several years to complete.

Another area related to project management is *project portfolio management*, which is concerned with the choosing and managing of projects or program investments. These are closely tied with strategic plans and resources that can have an impact on the financial conditions and constraints within a company.

This concludes the first chapter of the PMBOK, which introduces you to some of the initial concepts and definitions used throughout this book. Although you need to read and comprehend a large volume of material, this *Exam Cram 2* book will help make the process shorter and the material easier to understand.

The Project Management Context

Projects can be broken down into several phases. The culmination of these phases is known as the *project lifecycle*. During each of these phases there will be some output of your work to show that the project is going forward. These outputs are known as *deliverables*. PMBOK defines a deliverable as a "tangible, verifiable work product." This could include blueprints, designs, or a prototype. It could also include all the project-related reports, such as status reports, communication plans, and reviews at the end of each phase of the project.

PMBOK refers to these phase-end reviews as *phase exits*, *stage gates*, or *kill points*, and they involve lessons learned, analysis, and providing feedback to stakeholders, team members, and other people associated with the project.

A project lifecycle includes everything from the beginning to the end of a project. It has several characteristics, which are summarized in the PMBOK. These characteristics are discussed in the following paragraphs.

Cost and staffing levels tend to increase as you begin a project, and they progress toward the end of the project and then decrease quickly as the project is completed. Consequently, the levels of activity increase gradually during the initiation phase, continue to escalate during the planning phase, and peak during the execution phase. The levels of activity then decrease as you approach the project closeout. This is diagrammed in Figure 2-1 on page 13 of the PMBOK.

 It is important to know that a project is most risky at its beginning

The risk of project failure is highest at the beginning and gradually decreases over time as the probability of success increases. This is because the uncertainty of project success is the highest at the beginning of the project. This uncertainty decreases as you proceed through the project and achieve milestones and provide key deliverables. As more milestones are achieved and deliverables provided, the confidence level increases and the success of the project becomes more inevitable.

Stakeholder impact is highest in the beginning of a project and decreases as the project proceeds. Project stakeholders are individuals and organizations actively involved in the project and have some type of vested interest. Their impact is highest at the beginning because the project is still being planned and not everyone has bought in to the project plan and set a definitive path for the project.

Functional, Matrix, and Projectized Organizations

The PMBOK identifies the differences in relation to the project manager's authority, role, titles, and administrative staff, and the percentage of an organization's personnel assigned to project work when determining whether an organization has a functional, matrix, or projectized organizational structure. Here are the PMBOK definitions of the types of organizations and the implications for the project manager:

 Most companies are functional in nature and become more projectized as the organization becomes aware of Project Management as a discipline.

➤ **Functional organization**—This is the typical corporate environment where an employee has a specific supervisor. Generally these types of organizations use hierarchies to determine the authority level of each employee. They are generally the most challenging for a project manager because resources are not fully assigned to the projects and the project manager lacks full authority to control work assignments and personnel. The organization generally starts with a CEO or president at the top of the hierarchy and utilizes pushdown management to monitor and control subordinates.

➤ **Matrix organization (strong, balanced, or weak)**—This is a mixture of functional and projectized organizations and proceeds from a weak to a strong matrix based on the allocation of resources and the level of authority the project manager exerts over project, time, and personnel scheduling. This type of organization tends to be more satisfying to a project manager because it migrates from a weak matrix organization toward a strong matrix organization.

➤ **Projectized organization**—This is generally a more rewarding type of environment for a project because most of the resources are specifically allocated to the project and the project manager has full discretion over the company's time and agenda. This allows the project manager the authority and resources to accomplish the project more effectively without conflict from the functional manager. The project manager is generally provided referent power to accomplish the goals and objectives of the project without interference from other sources. He is also allowed to escalate problems and issues to the highest levels of the organization in order to complete the project. This is the most idealistic working environment for a project manager, although he is also held fully responsible for all problems and positive or negative results.

Table 2.2 summarizes the types of organizations, their project management attributes, and some advantages and disadvantages.

Table 2.2 Organizational Structure Influences on Projects (PMBOK Figure 2-6)

	Functional	Weak Matrix	Balanced Matrix	Strong Matrix	Projectized
Hierarchy Type	Traditional. The staff reports to functional managers.	The staff reports to the functional manager with minimal project manager involvement.	The staff reports to the functional manager with moderate project manager involvement.	The staff reports to the functional manager with heavy project manager involvement.	The staff reports to the project manager.
Project Manager Involvement	Part time or limited involvement.	Part time with increased involvement.	Full-time involvement.	Full-time involvement.	Full-time involvement.
Staff Time Allocated to Projects	Part-time staff.	Part-time staff.	Part-time staff.	Full-time staff.	Full-time staff.
Authority Level of Project Manager	None or a limited level of authority.	Limited level of authority.	Low to moderate level of authority.	Moderate to high level of authority.	High to almost full level of authority.
Advantages	The functional manager is held accountable for the staff and project.	Some level of authority and staff for the project and project manager.	Increased authority and staff for the project.	Further increased authority and staff for the project.	Highest level of authority and staff allocation for the project.
Disadvantages	The project manager has little or no authority or staff for the project.	Conflicts between functional manager and project manager can occur.	Confusion about who is actually responsible for what parts of the project may develop.	The functional manager may feel left out of the process unless the project manager keeps him informed.	The project manager is held responsible for the staff and project results.

The *Project Management Office (PMO)* has become an increasingly popular fixture in many companies. This group is specifically assigned the responsibility for auditing and tracking projects. It can either provide administrative support or lead the entire project based on the corporate culture in which it operates. It is generally involved with training, development of project plans, templates, scheduling, and other areas of expertise associated with projects.

General Management Skills

General management is something that most people have encountered in their work life. It includes the daily operational aspect of running a business or contributing to a corporation. It may involve supervision, planning, time management, human resources, and accounting. These areas can have a major impact on project management and are integral to the success of a project. The following subsections discuss some of the items entailed in general management.

Managing People Versus Leading People

The PMBOK discusses the differentiation between managing people and leading them. It emphasizes that managing involves providing results to stakeholders and is process oriented. Leading people is a much broader discipline and involves a multitude of different areas, including direction, people alignment, motivation, and inspiration. As an effective project manager, you are expected to be a good manager, as well as a good leader, in order to be effective.

Communicating

The communication process involves a sender, a receiver, and information exchange. Several attributes are discussed in the PMBOK, including listening, speaking, and written and oral communication. Communication in a project can be written for internal and external forms for parties associated with the project, and the flow of communication can occur either up and down through the organization (vertical communication) or across the organization (horizontal communication).

 You need to know that project managers spend 70%–80% of their time communicating either verbally or in written form.

Negotiating

Negotiations are an important part of any project. The ability to effectively negotiate resolutions and conflicts can determine the success of your project. According to the PMBOK, negotiating "involves conferring with others to come to terms with them or to reach an agreement." The process of obtaining "buy-in" from participants is a necessary ingredient if you need to have the involvement of your team. Team members tend to support and work more diligently toward goals when they have been involved in the development process and have been allowed to give their input.

Problem Solving

This process is important to developing and working through a project. The ability to provide problem solving to situations involves creativity and can be very challenging. First, the manager must define the problem and put it into words and concepts that everyone can understand. After defining the problem, the manager must utilize creativity to develop solutions and make decisions based on her experience and input from other participants. The decision-making process involves problem analysis, feedback solicitation, and ultimately choosing the best alternative.

Influence of the Organization

The project manager is always focused on getting things accomplished. This frequently requires the ability to work through organizational influences within the organization. Understanding the politics of the organization and how the components interact can have a major impact on this ability. Formal and informal leaders frequently must be kept informed and involved in the decision-making process so that they do not push back on the project manager's authority to push the project forward.

Socioeconomic and Environmental Influences

As the world becomes more global, international, and complex in its economic perspective, a multitude of factors can influence a project. These include government regulations and industry standards, which are viewed as ways to safeguard society from inappropriate business practices. Many of these are a result of unprofessional situations that have been identified after they have occurred—for example, the Enron and WorldCom stock market problems, where investors were defrauded of millions of dollars. The PMBOK defines these attributes as follows:

➤ **Standard**—A standard is "a document approved by a recognized body that provides for common and repeated use, rules, guidelines, or characteristics for products, processes, or services with which compliance is not mandatory." Companies frequently set standards for their own products, services, and employees. These are not mandated by the government or regulatory bodies but are generally part of the culture, and many times these factors differentiate a company from its competitors in the marketplace.

➤ **Regulation**—A regulation is a "document which lays down product, process, or service characteristics, including the applicable administrative provisions with which compliance is mandatory." Government entities frequently create regulations that they feel are in the best interest of society. Examples include regulations concerning pollution levels of factories and automobiles. Fines are usually imposed on companies that do not comply with regulations to act as a deterrent to noncompliance.

Regulations, standards, and the identification of international differences are a necessary part of professional business operations. They are also constraints to a project manager who must incorporate them into the project plan as business requirements. The PMBOK emphasizes the need to acknowledge characteristics, such as cultural differences and economic climates, when developing project plans.

It is not appropriate to only think in American ideologies for the governing requirements of a project. We must think in global terms and how different cultures and economies can impact our timelines, objectives, and success factors. The world can be a volatile environment based on the implications of war, recessions, and economic downturns. Therefore, focusing on the "big picture" is a prerequisite to success and survival.

Project Management Triple Constraint

Many of the activities associated with project management can have a domino effect on the organization, as well as other projects. The interaction between time, scope, and cost can be seen as a triangle, with all the sides impacting the others as the project manager tries to maintain equilibrium among all the aspects. This triangle is known as the *triple constraint*. The concept is used as a framework to evaluate competing demands on the project, and these "demands" will vary by organization and by project. The value of the paradigm is to show the effects competing demands can have on a project.

For example, if a project is requested to be completed in a shorter time period than originally agreed upon, quality will likely be sacrificed or the price may increase, or both. If there is a request for increased quality standards after the project has begun, the project will likely take more time to complete and the cost will likely increase as well.

If a price reduction is requested, the quality will likely be impacted, although it may take less time to complete the project. The PMBOK emphasizes that project managers must set realistic expectations with the stakeholders when they change the requirements of the project after the original scope has been determined and agreed upon.

Time and resources cost money. Because project management utilizes business process improvement in order to identify redundancy and increase efficiencies, the PMBOK sees project management as interactions between linked processes. These processes are directly influenced by project budgets and the willingness of an organization to expend human or capital resources. This integration of the processes is one of the fundamentals of project management. Because projects are composed of several or hundreds of processes, they can become complex quickly. PMI defines a process as "a series of actions bringing about a result."

PMI further divides these processes into two categories:

➤ *Project management processes*—These involve all the activities that need to be done in order to finish a project.

➤ *Product-oriented processes*—These involve a lifecycle that focuses on the creation of a specific product as the outcome of the project.

Process Groups

PMI and the PMBOK divide the project management processes into five groups. Each group includes one or more processes. These groups are Initiating, Planning, Executing, Controlling, and Closing.

The following list provides the definitions of how the PMBOK interprets each of these groups of processes:

➤ **Initiating processes**—These are the processes that authorize the project or various phases of the project.

➤ **Planning processes**—The definition of *objectives* and *selection of the best alternatives* fall into this category. These processes are time consuming but very important to the success of the project.

➤ **Executing processes**—This is when you pull everything together. All your planning and refining of the scope, objectives, and deliverables come into play during the implementation of these processes. They include having all your resources in the right place at the right time with the right plan.

➤ **Controlling processes**—This group involves scope management and utilizing processes to keep the project in line with the original objectives. These processes involve a lot of follow-up to make sure everything is within the constraints mandated at the beginning of the project and in the charter.

➤ **Closing process**—The signoff process is the formalized closure of the project. This process is linked with the determination by the stakeholders that the project has fulfilled its obligations as stipulated in the original scope statement.

The Relationship Between Project Lifecycle and Project Management Processes

When evaluating processes associated with the process groups, it is important to note that the output of one group becomes the input for another group, and there is overlap between the processes in order to achieve the end result.

Many of the deliverables of one phase are needed and utilized in the following phases, and inputs and outputs for each of the processes depend on the phase in which they are ultimately carried out. The processes are ongoing activities throughout that phase of the project and are not one-time occurrences. The overlap allows the transition from the closing out of one phase and the start of another phase, while linking the results and deliverables that they produce.

Figures 2.1, 2.2, and 2.3 show the links, overlaps, and interactions of the process groups and phases. Figure 2.1 shows how the Initiating process information flow feeds into the Planning processes. This information then flows into the Executing, Controlling, and Closing processes. It also shows how the flow of information goes both ways between the processes (after the Initiating processes, through the intermediate processes, until the Closing processes).

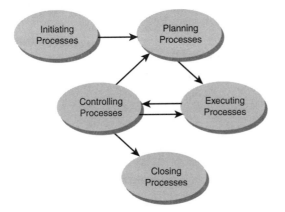

Figure 2.1   Links among process groups in a phase.

Figure 2.2 shows the relationship between time and the level of activity associated with each of the processes and how they overlap. The level of activity includes actions provided by team members or stakeholders while performing work associated with the project. When looking at the diagram, it becomes apparent that the Executing processes have the highest level of activity and the Planning processes have the second-highest level of activity.

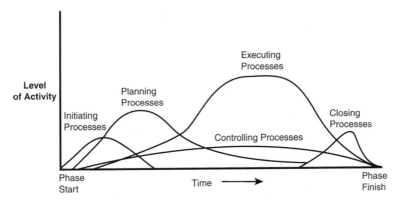

Figure 2.2   Overlap of process groups in a phase.

Although the level of activity for the Controlling processes is not the highest, it has the longest duration because the project manager is required to maintain control throughout the entire project. The Initiating processes begin the project and merge into the Planning processes. The Initiating processes are completed as the Planning processes' activity levels peak. The Planning processes then merge into the Executing processes, which have the highest level of activity.

The Planning processes continue at a diminished activity level until they merge with the Executing processes into the Closing processes as the project comes to completion. The Closing processes complete the project; as you see, the Controlling and Executing processes' activity levels also descend into the completion.

You need to know that the execution phase of a project expends the highest level of resources and has the highest level of activity.

Figure 2.3 shows how the various phases interact with each other and the flow of information as a subset of the each phase. As a project manager, you must acknowledge that the phases are interdependent but also separate entities. The inputs and outputs for each of the processes are directly affected by the phase in which they occur, and there is frequent overlapping of the actual processes.

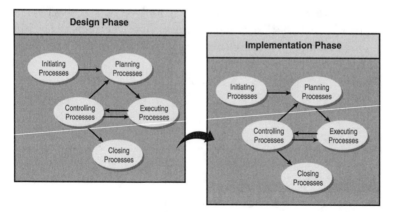

Figure 2.3   Interaction between phases.

It is easiest to think of the phases in sequential order, with one phase having an impact on the subsequent phases. This figure also shows how the closing of one phase provides the input to begin the next phase. Because the project is an ongoing process that tends to draw information and details from previous phases in order to complete the current one, the project plan uses rolling wave planning to show these details.

It is highly recommended that you involve stakeholders throughout the phases in order to gain buy-in and increase your probability of success. *Buy-in* defines the agreements between team members and stakeholders that encourage participation and elicit feedback from the participants in order to come to consensus. This tool is one of the fundamentals of effective project management and is used frequently to develop cohesiveness and camaraderie among team members and stakeholders.

The PMBOK focuses on describing each process in terms of the inputs, outputs, tools, and techniques. It defines inputs as "documents or documentable items that will be acted upon." Outputs are defined as "documents or documentable items that are a result of the process." Furthermore, tools and techniques are "mechanisms applied to the inputs to create the outputs." Thus, you can see how all these links are interrelated.

Customizing Process Interactions

The next section of the PMBOK expands on the processes, discusses some of the exceptions, and explains the fact that not all the processes are utilized on every project. Smaller projects tend to be more simplistic and may not require an extensive amount of planning or control management.

Planning processes can change or alternate due to variables such as the use of contractors and the availability of unique resources, such as physicians, computer specialists, or scientists. Because of the complexity of larger projects, more details and elaboration of tasks are required.

Consequently, the Work Breakdown Structures (WBSs) for complex projects can be huge and very elaborate. Many times the emphasis of a project plan is based on the budget for the project, and whether it is a high-profile project that has a major impact on the organization. Because many projects have time constraints, this may predefine some of the process outputs and reduce the impact of the Planning phase.

The 39 project management processes, nine project management knowledge areas, and five project management process groups are summarized at the end of Chapter 3 of the PMBOK in Figure 3-9, "Mapping of Project Management Processes to the Process Groups and Knowledge Areas." We will continue to elaborate on these areas in the following chapters.

Exam Prep Questions

Question 1

> The CIO and the head of marketing of a drug development services organization privately discuss a change to a key task in the design phase of a project. After the discussion, they tell the project manager to make the appropriate changes. This scenario is an example of:
>
> ○ A. Proactive senior management
>
> ○ B. A project-based organization
>
> ○ C. Effective decision-making
>
> ○ D. A project coordinator role

Answer D is correct. In this scenario, it is the *best* response. A project coordinator's authority and decision-making ability are generally limited to minor items. Senior management will generally make the significant decisions impacting the scope and success of the project. There is not enough information given to determine whether answer A or C are correct, and in a project-based organization, the project manager would be empowered to make these decisions. Therefore, answer B is incorrect.

Question 2

> Which of the following statements about the project expeditor or project coordinator role is true?
>
> ○ A. The project expeditor does not make decisions.
>
> ○ B. The project coordinator does not make decisions.
>
> ○ C. The project coordinator has no authority.
>
> ○ D. The project expeditor focuses on completing the project on schedule.

Answer A is correct. A project coordinator *does* make decisions on nonmajor items impacting the project and *does* have some authority to influence the project. Therefore, answers B and C are incorrect. The project expeditor is focused on coordinating communications and is not able to make decisions. Therefore, answer D is incorrect.

Question 3

> A project manager for a financial services organization is trying to complete a package application implementation project but is unable to get the planned amount of time from key resources to complete some of the critical path tasks. The key resources are focused on completing their day-to-day tasks, and the project manager does not control the work assignments for these people. This scenario is an example of what type of organization?
>
> ○ A. Balanced matrix
>
> ○ B. Tight matrix
>
> ○ C. Functional
>
> ○ D. Project coordinator

Answer C is correct. In a functional organization, the project manager has the least support and the least ability to control project resources. In a balanced matrix organization or project coordinator situation, the project manager would be empowered with more control over resources or would be able to leverage his senior management to influence resource assignments. Therefore, answers A and D are incorrect. Tight matrix deals with the colocation of project team members within a matrix organization and is not relevant to this question. Therefore, answer B is incorrect.

Question 4

> Regarding the importance of management and leadership in projects, all the following statements are false except which one?
>
> ○ A. Technical leadership is of primary importance in project management.
>
> ○ B. A project can only have one leader.
>
> ○ C. On a large project, the project manager is not expected to be the project's leader.
>
> ○ D. Managing is primarily concerned with consistently producing key results expected by stakeholders.

Answer D is correct. The statement in answer D is true. Technical leadership is not the most important element of effective project management. Therefore, answer A is incorrect. A project needs leadership at the project, team, and technical levels. Frequently, more than one person is needed to fulfill these leadership needs. Therefore, answer B is incorrect. On large projects, the project manger is expected to be the project leader. Therefore, answer C is incorrect.

Question 5

Which of the following statements is not true?

- ○ A. Cultural differences will always be an obstacle to overcome.
- ○ B. Culture is a critical lever for competitive advantage.
- ○ C. There is a common ground for people from different cultures to work from to help resolve project conflicts.
- ○ D. Only those who realize that cultural differences are a resource to leverage will survive in the twenty-first century.

Answer A is correct. The statement in answer A is not true because cultural differences are not "always" an obstacle to overcome on a project. Answers B, C, and D are all true statements and therefore incorrect answers.

Question 6

Project managers need solid communication and negotiation skills primarily because:

- ○ A. They must give presentations and briefings to senior management.
- ○ B. Getting the best deals from vendors requires these skills.
- ○ C. They may be leading a team with no direct control over the individual team members.
- ○ D. They must be able to effectively share their technical expertise.

Answer C is correct. This is a great example of where you are looking for the *best* response. Effective negotiation and communication skills are important to the other three situations, too, but the project team leadership aspect is where these skills are essential and where they will have the greatest impact on project success. Therefore, answers A, B, and D are incorrect.

Question 7

Which factors are considered to be part of the "triple constraint" paradigm used to describe the tradeoffs made when making project decisions?

- ○ A. Cost, time, scope, stakeholders, quality
- ○ B. Cost, time, scope
- ○ C. Cost, time, scope, quality, customer satisfaction
- ○ D. Cost, time, quality

Answer C is correct. This is an example of the "tricky" questions occasionally found on the PMP exam. Answer C is correct because it represents the most complete list of competing project demands. Answer A references stakeholders but does not indicate what aspect of stakeholders is important to the project's decision-making process (such as satisfaction). Therefore, answer A is incorrect. Cost, time, and scope are the three factors that originally comprised the "triple constraint" model. However, answers B and D are both incorrect because they only define a subset of the possible set of competing demands on a project team.

Question 8

Which of the following statements best describes the relationship between projects and programs?

○ A. There are no differences…just different terms for the same thing.

○ B. A project is composed of one or more related programs.

○ C. A program is composed of one or more related projects.

○ D. A project is a temporary endeavor, whereas a program is permanent.

Answer C is correct. Answer A is incorrect because it plays on a common misconception. Answer B is incorrect because just the opposite is true. Answer D is incorrect because a program is a group of projects, which are temporary endeavors.

Question 9

Which of the following statements describes the relationship between project phases and project lifecycle?

○ A. A project phase can contain one or more iterations of the project lifecycle.

○ B. The project lifecycle is known as the *sequence of project activities*, whereas phases are defined to control the overlapping activities.

○ C. The project lifecycle contains the iterative, incremental elements inside a project phase.

○ D. Collectively, the project phases are known as the *project lifecycle.*

Answer D is correct. A project lifecycle is composed of one or more phases. Answers A, B, and C do not accurately describe the relationship between project phases and project lifecycle and are therefore incorrect.

Question 10

Which of the following statements best describes the relationship between project lifecycle phases and project management processes?

○ A. Project management processes correspond one to one with project lifecycle phases.

○ B. Project lifecycle phases can repeat within a project management process.

○ C. Project management processes can repeat within a project lifecycle.

○ D. Project management processes are completely independent of project lifecycle phases.

Answer C is correct. The project management processes should be executed for each project lifecycle phase and/or iteration. Answer A is incorrect because the project management processes are used to manage the progress of the project lifecycle, and project lifecycle phases are not normally associated with Controlling and Executing processes, for example. Answer B is incorrect because it is the opposite of the correct choice. Answer D is incorrect because a relationship can exist between the Initiating, Planning, and Closing processes and traditional project lifecycle phases (such as Concept, Analysis, and Closure).

Need to Know More?

 Adams, John. *The Principles of Project Management.* ISBN 1880410303.

 Kerzner, Harold. *Project Management: A Systems Approach to Planning, Scheduling And Controlling, Sixth Edition.* ISBN 0471225770.

 Meridith, Jack and Samuel Mantel. *Project Management: A Managerial Approach, Fifth Edition.* ISBN 0471073237.

3

Project Initiation

. . . .

Terms you'll need to understand:

✓ Initiation
✓ Project charter
✓ Assumptions
✓ Constraints
✓ Management by Objectives
✓ Project charter

Techniques and concepts you'll need to master:

✓ The importance of project initiation
✓ The purpose and elements of a project charter
✓ The proper role to issue the project charter
✓ The importance of the project charter to the project manager
✓ The timing and importance of the project manager assignment
✓ The value of project selection methods
✓ The two general types of project-selection methods
✓ The sources of expert judgment
✓ The Management by Objectives (MBO) process
✓ The relationship of project initiation to planning activities

Project initiation is the first project management process to execute in the project lifecycle, and it will be the focus of approximately 8.5% of the exam questions. Although the exam questions regarding the Initiating process tend to be straightforward and involve only 1 of the 39 PMBOK processes (Initiation), many project managers have minimal real-life experience with these activities. And for the project managers with experience in project initiation, the terms and processes they use may not be consistent with PMI's expectations.

To streamline your exam preparations, we will focus on the "gotta-know" concepts and terms that are important to PMI, and the "common" gaps you may need to close to be ready for the exam questions related to project initiation.

The Importance of Project Initiation

Because many project managers have never completed activities in this phase (never completed a project charter, never signed a contract, and so on), let's quickly review why PMI considers project initiation an important process.

Initiation is the first step in the project management process, and it is the first step in the scope-management process. It authorizes (formally) a project to begin and links a project to the work and to the strategic objectives of the organization.

Be sure to understand that the Initiation step can occur more than once in a project. The Initiation process is also performed at the end of each project phase to get authorization to continue the project. A common term for this point is a *go/no-go decision*.

Per PMI, projects should be aligned with the organization's strategic direction. The project-initiation process at the beginning of each project and at the beginning of each phase helps to ensure this alignment throughout the project lifecycle.

Based on our experience, many professionals associate project initiation with some type of "analysis" effort, such as assessment, feasibility study, or business case development. To PMI, the "analysis" effort is a separate project (with its own project charter) that provides information needed to make a decision about *initiating* a new project.

The Purpose of the Project Charter

The most important result of the Project Initiation phase is the *project charter*, which formally authorizes the work of the project to begin (or continue) and gives the project manager authority to do his job. Someone external to the team and of higher organizational rank issues this authorization.

 Per PMI, a project cannot start without a project charter.

 In many organizations, the project charter document may have a different name. For instance, the terms *project initiation form* and *project authorization* are sometimes used. For the exam, make sure you are clear on what a project charter is to PMI.

 The PMBOK recognizes that a signed contract can serve as a project charter.

Elements of a Project Charter

According to PMI, a project charter should possess the following characteristics at a minimum:

➤ It should include a description of the *business need* the project will meet.

➤ It should include a description of the product resulting from the project.

➤ It should be issued by a manager external to the project who can satisfy the needs of the project.

In addition to these elements, you will generally find a section describing the key objectives and goals of the project. These objectives and goals are often the key assumptions, constraints, and/or target performance metrics for the initiative. In particular, any assumption or constraint affecting the project's schedule, budget, or quality will be listed.

As mentioned in the "Tips for the IT Professional" section of Chapter 1, "The PMP Exam," this area can be a common "gap" for project managers, because their organization may have a different definition for *project charter*. In some cases, the project charter may actually be the "project plan," or it may require details such as schedules, a Work Breakdown Structure (WBS), complete risk assessment, and so on, that are normally developed during the project plan development phase.

Also, given this definition, it should not be necessary to modify a project charter as a project executes.

The Proper Role to Issue the Project Charter

The project charter must be issued by someone external to the project team and at the appropriate organizational level to satisfy the needs of the project. For example, you need someone of the proper ranking who can acquire necessary resources, influence key stakeholders, enforce accountability on all project team members, and so on.

Generally, this "someone" is from senior-level management within an organization—someone who has authority over most, if not all, of the project team members. This also means that no one on the project team (including the project manager) can issue the project charter.

The Importance of the Project Charter to the Project Manager

The project charter is highly important to the project manager for three main reasons:

➤ **It makes the project manager's role legit.** The project charter formally recognizes the project manager role and gives the project manager the authority to "get the job done."

➤ **It makes the project legit.** The project charter formally authorizes the project to exist and/or to continue.

➤ **It sets the target for the project.** The project charter provides the high-level goals and objectives the project should achieve.

The Timing and Importance of the Project Manager Assignment

Besides the project charter, the other critical output of the Project Initiation phase is the authorized assignment of the project manager. Ideally, PMI would like to see the project manager selected, assigned, or identified at the point of project initiation. PMI advocates this practice because it feels strongly that the project manager should be a key player in any and all planning activities. PMI wants to reduce the number of real-world experiences whereby the person now responsible for the project (the project manager) does not have proper input into the key planning assumptions.

The Value of Project-Selection Methods

Outside of the project charter, the other topic that is greatly emphasized by PMI within the Initiating process is *project-selection methods*.

PMI feels strongly that organizations should have a formal process for deciding projects to sponsor and for ensuring that projects are supportive of the organization's strategic objectives. In many organizations, some type of senior management steering committee or Program Management Office (PMO) performs this project-evaluation and -selection process.

Project-selection methods are the techniques used to execute this process, and they are organized into two major categories: *benefit measurement methods* and *constrained optimization methods*.

The project-selection method(s) used by an organization should be relevant to the objectives of the company and its managers and should be consistent with the capabilities and resources of the organization.

NOTE

Project initiation is the first of many processes where PMI expects organizations to leverage historical information (such as past project-selection decisions and past project performance) when authorizing a project or the next project phase. Although this seems like common sense, the issue here is that in the "real world" the collection of reliable project data is rarely done; therefore, it is not a common practice in many organizations today.

Two General Types of Project-Selection Methods

The two methods of project selection are *benefit measurement (comparative approach)* and *constrained optimization (mathematical approach)*. Table 3.1 summarizes the key points of these two method types.

The exam will require you to know the methods of project selection, their main differences, and examples of each.

Table 3.1 Project-Selection Methods		
Method Type	**Examples**	**Notes**
Benefit measurement (comparative approach)	Scoring models, cost-benefit analysis, review board, economic models.	Benefit measurement is the most common approach.
Constrained optimization (mathematical approach)	Linear programming, nonlinear programming, integer programming, dynamic programming, multi-objective programming.	Constrained optimization makes use of math models and complex criteria and is often managed as a distinct project phase.

Using Expert Judgment for Project Initiation

Expert judgment is mentioned in this chapter because project initiation is the first PMBOK process that lists expert judgment as a primary tool or technique. In this case, as in most, expert judgment is used to evaluate the inputs into the process. Specifically, expert judgment is used to assess the product description, the project-selection criteria, and the validity of the historical information. In addition, expert judgment could be used to identify key assumptions and constraints. Anyone with specialized knowledge and/or experience relevant to the goals of the project can be used as a source of expert judgment. Common sources include the following:

➤ Subject matter experts (SMEs) within the organization

➤ Consultants

➤ Stakeholders, including customers

➤ Professional and trade associations

➤ Industry groups

Management by Objectives

Because one of the goals of *Management by Objectives (MBO)*—a business management technique you probably studied in school and/or utilize in some capacity within your organization today—is to ensure that objectives (goals) of one level within an organization are supportive of and aligned with the objectives of the other, we'll review MBO in this chapter. After all, one of the main purposes of the Project Initiation process is to ensure that authorized projects support the strategic objectives of the sponsoring organization.

MBO is not covered explicitly by the PMBOK. However, PMI expects project managers to understand this management philosophy and how it aligns with managing projects.

For the exam, you need to understand three philosophical points and three general process steps.

The management philosophy points are as follows:

➤ Because MBO uses goal setting and periodic reviews, it is a natural fit for managing projects.

➤ A project must be consistent with corporate objectives.

➤ Due to its top-down nature, MBO only works if management supports it.

And here are the MBO process steps:

➤ Establish clear and achievable objectives.

➤ Periodically check whether objectives are being met.

➤ Take corrective actions on any discrepancies.

The Relationship to Planning Activities

Because many project managers have limited project initiation experience, and because many organizations have differing views on what project initiation entails, it is not always clear how project initiation relates to project planning. When you review the following list of common project management activities performed during the Initiating phase, you can understand why the line between these two major activities is not clear:

➤ Determining business need

➤ Collecting historical info

➤ Determining project objectives and goals

➤ Resolving conflicting high-level goals

➤ Developing product descriptions

➤ Determining deliverables

➤ Determining process outputs

➤ Documenting constraints

➤ Documenting assumptions

➤ Defining strategies

➤ Identifying performance criteria

➤ Determining resource requirements

➤ Defining budgets

➤ Producing formal documentation

➤ Finalizing and gaining approval of the project charter from stakeholders

In fact, there is considerable overlap in the sets of project management activities. The main point to remember is that many of the initiation activities are further refined during project planning, especially estimating, defining assumptions, and determining deliverables.

Generally, any planning activity performed during initiation is "high level" and on the order-of-magnitude scale. In other words, the estimates are often reflected on a power-of-10 scale (10, 100, 1,000, 10,000, and so on).

Project Selection Accounting Concepts

One area, in particular, where much overlap exists between the Initiating and Planning processes is project selection. Earlier in this chapter, you reviewed the two general categories of project selection methods—benefit measurement methods and constrained optimization methods (refer to Table 3.1)—and the key elements of each that you need to know for the PMP exam.

Also, for the PMP exam, you will need to understand several cost accounting concepts that are frequently used when performing the project-selection process, especially any of the benefit measurement methods. You are not expected to be a cost accountant or even to perform the associated accounting calculations. However, you are expected to understand each of these accounting concepts and to know how to use them during the project-selection activity. Table 3.2 summarizes these accounting concepts and how they relate to project selection.

Table 3.2 Project Selection Accounting Concepts			
Accounting Concept	**Description**	**Keys for Project Selection**	**Notes**
Present value (PV)	Value today of future cash flows.	The higher the PV, the better.	$PV = FV/(1+r)n$
Net present value (NPV)	Present value of cash inflow (benefits) minus present value of cash outflow (costs).	A negative NPV is unfavorable. The higher the NPV, the better.	Accounts for different project durations.
Internal rate of return (IRR)	The interest rate that makes the net present value of all cash flow equal zero.	The higher the IRR, the better.	The return that a company would earn if it invests in the project.
Payback period	The number of time periods needed to hit the break-even point.	The lower the payback period, the better.	
Benefit cost ratio (BCR)	A ratio identifying the relationship between the cost and benefits of a proposed project.	A BCR less than 1 is unfavorable. The higher the BCR, the better.	

Table 3.2 Project Selection Accounting Concepts *(continued)*			
Accounting Concept	**Description**	**Keys for Project Selection**	**Notes**
Opportunity cost	The difference in return between a chosen investment and one that is passed up.		
Sunk costs	A cost that has been incurred and cannot be reversed.	This should not be a factor in project decisions.	

In addition to the accounting concepts directly related to project selection, PMI expects a project manager to understand other accounting concepts. Table 3.3 summarizes these additional accounting concepts.

Table 3.3 Other Relevant Accounting Concepts		
Accounting Concept	**Description**	**Notes**
Variable costs	A cost that changes in proportion to a change in a company's activity or business.	Example: fuel.
Fixed costs	A cost that remains constant, regardless of any change in a company's activity.	Example: lease payment.
Direct costs	A cost that can be directly traced to producing specific goods or services.	Example: team member salaries.
Indirect costs	A cost that cannot be directly traced to producing specific goods or services.	Example: insurance, administration, depreciation, and so on.
Working capital	Current assets minus current liabilities.	
Straight-line depreciation	A method of depreciation that divides the difference between an asset's cost and its expected salvage value by the number of years it is expected to be used.	This is the simplest method.

Table 3.3 Other Relevant Accounting Concepts *(continued)*		
Accounting Concept	**Description**	**Notes**
Accelerated depreciation	Any method of depreciation that allows greater deductions in the earlier years of the life of an asset.	Double declining balance. (DDB).
Lifecycle costing	This includes costs from each phase of a project's or product's lifecycle when total investment costs are calculated.	

The material on accounting concepts is an example of the non-PMBOK knowledge that is tested for on the exam.

Exam Prep Questions

Question 1

> Which of the following must be included in the project charter?
>
> ○ A. Risk analysis
>
> ○ B. Budget estimates
>
> ○ C. Product description
>
> ○ D. Scope statement

Answer C is correct. The product description is one of the three requirements of the project charter, as described by the PMBOK. The other alternatives may appear in some organization's charters, but these vary and are not mandated by PMI. Therefore, answers A, B, and D are incorrect.

Question 2

> An organization is starting a PMO. For the initial phase, the PMO director has decided to roll out the use of project charters. As a project manager, why would you be encouraged by this plan?
>
> ○ A. The project charter allows you to establish the business need for the project.
>
> ○ B. The project charter ensures that a preliminary budget and schedule are developed.
>
> ○ C. The project charter authorizes you to use organizational resources to accomplish the objectives of the project.
>
> ○ D. The project charter allows you to get senior management buy-in for your project management approach.

Answer C is correct. Answer A is incorrect because the project manager cannot establish the business need alone. Remember that the charter is issued by someone external to the team. Answer B is incorrect because the project charter does not require a preliminary schedule and budget. Answer D is incorrect because the project management approach would be defined in the project plan.

Question 3

> You have created the project charter but could not get it approved by senior
> management. Your manager and his boss have asked you to begin the project
> anyway. Which of the following actions is the *best* thing to do?
>
> ○ A. Focus on other projects that have a signed charter.
>
> ○ B. Start work on critical path tasks.
>
> ○ C. Update your Project Risk Log.
>
> ○ D. Show your manager the impact of proceeding without approval.

Answer D is correct. Remember the importance PMI places on effective communications and on "doing the right thing." Answers A and D are incorrect because these would not be the best actions to take next. Answer B is incorrect because you have not dealt with the "lack of senior management approval" issue yet.

Question 4

> What is the most important criterion when an organization chooses a project-
> selection model?
>
> ○ A. Organizational fit
>
> ○ B. Flexibility
>
> ○ C. Cost
>
> ○ D. Capability

Answer A is correct. The most important factor is that the project-selection method be "realistic" for the organization. It needs to be consistent with its goals and objectives, and it needs to account for the capabilities of the organization. Answers B, C, and D are all incorrect because although they are key criterion when choosing a project-selection model, they are irrelevant if the model is not first an effective organizational fit.

Question 5

A project is an ideal environment in which to apply the technique of MBO because:

- ○ A. Top management policy and goals should flow down through the management hierarchy.
- ○ B. Project management involves setting organizational objectives.
- ○ C. All projects should be strongly oriented toward goals and objectives.
- ○ D. Projects are generally handled in a matrix management environment.

Answer C is correct. The approach of goal/objective setting and periodic evaluations are common to both MBO and project management. Answer A is incorrect because projects use more than functional management hierarchy structures. Answer B is incorrect because project management is focused on executing organizational objectives and not on setting them. Answer D is incorrect in much the same way that Answer A is incorrect. You cannot rely on a top-down organizational flow in project environments.

Question 6

All of the following are examples of benefit-measurement methods of project selection except which one?

- ○ A. Scoring models
- ○ B. Multi-objective programming
- ○ C. Economic models
- ○ D. IS steering committee review

Answer B is correct. Multi-objective programming is the only constraint optimization method listed. Answers A, C, and D are all incorrect because they are not constraint-optimization methods.

Question 7

The project charter should by issued by whom?

- ○ A. One or more functional managers
- ○ B. The head of the performing organization
- ○ C. A manager external to the project
- ○ D. The CFO

Answer C is correct. The other answers could be accurate in specific situations, but their role alone does not meet the key criterion of being "external" to the project team. Answers A, B, and D are incorrect because these individuals are not external to the project.

Question 8

Which of the following is not a scope-management process?

- ○ A. Scope planning
- ○ B. Scope reporting
- ○ C. Initiation
- ○ D. Scope verification

Answer B is correct. Answers A, C, and D are incorrect because they are explicitly defined by the PMBOK as scope-management processes, including Initiation, which is the first step in the scope-management process.

Question 9

In which scope-management process are SMEs first used?

- ○ A. Scope planning
- ○ B. Scope definition
- ○ C. Initiation
- ○ D. Scope verification

Answer C is correct. Initiation is the first step in the scope-management process, and expert judgment is one of the techniques routinely utilized. Answers A, B, and D are incorrect because they would come after the Initiation process.

Question 10

From the point of initiation, why should assumptions be documented?

- ○ A. Assumptions limit the project team's options for decision making.
- ○ B. Assumptions might prove to be incorrect. The ability to identify these assumptions allows for baseline adjustments in case of project crisis.
- ○ C. Assumption analysis is a key technique of risk identification.
- ○ D. In case of schedule or budget overruns, the documentation of assumptions provides an accountability trail.

Answer C is correct. Answer A is incorrect because "constraints" limit your options. Answer B is incorrect because it's not the correct process for adjusting project baselines. Answer D is incorrect because, although it's a tempting answer based on real-world experience, it's not the answer PMI is looking for, and it would be more applicable to project controlling.

Need to Know More?

 Project Management Institute. *A Guide to the Project Management Body of Knowledge (PMBOK Guide), 2000 Edition*. ISBN 1880410230.

 The PMI Bookstore (www.pmibookstore.org)

Offers general project management reference materials *and* other self-study texts.

 PMI eLearning Connection (www.pmi.org)

Offers virtual, online seminars and study programs.

 Commercial PMP Prep Courses

Search PMI (www.pmi.org) for a listing of PMI Registered Education Providers that offer PMP exam-prep courses. Many of the courses are now offered "online" and better support your lifestyle.

Project Planning—Core Processes

Terms you'll need to understand:

✓ Scope planning and definition
✓ Schedule development
✓ Cost estimating and budgeting
✓ Scope statement
✓ Work Breakdown Structure (WBS)
✓ Precedence Diagramming Method and Arrow Diagramming Method
✓ Chart of Accounts
✓ Milestones
✓ Activity list, definition, and sequencing
✓ Activity Duration Estimate
✓ Resource pool
✓ Scope, cost, and risk management plans
✓ Decomposition
✓ Project network diagram
✓ Resource requirements
✓ Reserve time
✓ Crashing
✓ Fast tracking
✓ Graphical Evaluation and Review Technique (GERT)
✓ Program Evaluation and Review Technique (PERT)
✓ Critical Path Method (CPM)
✓ Project Management Information System (PMIS)
✓ Duration compression
✓ Resource leveling
✓ Cost baseline
✓ Project plan
✓ Project schedule
✓ Work package
✓ WBS
✓ Analogous, Bottom-up, and Parametric estimating

Techniques and concepts you'll need to master:

✓ The core planning process steps, including inputs, outputs, techniques, relationships, and differences
✓ The differences between project charter, scope statement, WBS, activity list, project schedule, and project plan
✓ The differences between project initiation, scope planning, and scope definition
✓ The difference between scope definition and activity definition
✓ The process of building a project schedule
✓ The types of task dependencies
✓ The three different types of network diagram techniques
✓ Time estimating guidelines and methods
✓ Scheduling techniques
✓ Critical path, lag, slack, and other scheduling concepts
✓ The criteria for completing the schedule-development process
✓ The techniques for shortening the schedule
✓ The key cost-estimating factors
✓ The role of risk management in the core planning process

Project planning is the second project management process to execute in the project lifecycle, and it will be the focus of approximately 23.5% of the exam questions. Because project planning comprises 21 of the 39 PMBOK processes, we decided to "decompose" this section into two chapters. This chapter will review the "core" project planning processes, and the following chapter will review the "facilitating" project planning processes.

Although the exam questions regarding the core project planning processes tend to be straightforward, and many project managers have considerable experience performing these activities, this is a subject area not to be taken lightly. The techniques and terms utilized in real-life project planning are not always consistent with PMI's methodology. In addition, the PMBOK organization and definition of Project Time Management, Project Scope Management, Project Cost Management, and Project Integration Management can make the project planning process seem much more difficult and complex than it really is.

To streamline your exam preparations, we will focus on the "gotta-know" concepts and terms that are important to PMI and the "common" gaps you may need to close to be ready for the exam questions related to the core project planning processes.

Core Planning Process

Unfortunately, there's no way to really avoid this. You will need to understand how PMI defines the project planning process. In general, PMI defines the project planning process as the development and maintenance of the project plan. That's straightforward. However, it is the 11-step breakdown of core project planning and the inter-relationships among those 11 processes that may be "less than straightforward."

The PMBOK definition of project planning is accurate, complete, and logical. The confusing element is that in our real-life experiences, we simply have not thought about each of these steps in the same way as PMI. It is also possible that we, as project managers, simply execute these steps naturally (or in rare circumstances, perhaps this level of diligence is not always exercised during project planning).

Table 4.1 describes how PMI defines the core project planning process, and the content in this table describes what Figure 4.1 depicts. Note that Table 4.1 provides references back to where these processes can be found in the PMBOK. Pay particular attention to the PMBOK reference terminology.

Table 4.1	Translation of PMI Core Project Planning Process	
Step	**Planning Step Description**	**PMBOK Process Reference**
1	Perform a detailed assessment of the requested product and project alternatives. Determine the objectives, products, and deliverables for the project.	5.2: Scope Planning
2	Break down (decompose) the project deliverables and products into logical chunks (work packages) that can be estimated, resourced, and managed.	5.3: Scope Definition
3	Once you have the work of the project broken down, you can determine what resources you need to accomplish the work and begin to estimate the effort required.	7.1: Resource Planning 6.1: Activity Definition
4	For each logical chunk of work (WBS work package), identify each key activity that is required to complete the work.	6.1: Activity Definition
5	For each activity, estimate the effort to perform the activity.	6.3: Activity Duration Estimating
6	Once you know your resource requirements and your estimated work efforts, estimate your project costs.	7.2: Cost Estimating
7	Once you know your key work activities, determine the logical relationships and dependencies between them.	6.2: Activity Sequencing
8	Once you know the estimated effort/ duration for each work activity and the logical relationships between them, a project schedule.	6.4: Schedule Development
9	Once you know the estimated costs (by resource and work activity effort) and the project schedule, develop the project budget and cost baseline.	7.3: Cost Budgeting
10	Include the project schedule and cost baseline in the project plan.	4.1: Project Plan Development

To succeed on the exam, you must know the definitions, relationships, key inputs, and outputs for each of the core planning processes detailed in Table 4.1.

The process flow diagram shown in Figure 4.1 illustrates how the steps in Table 4.1 relate to each other. This diagram also demonstrates how the key results (output) from one step are used by the other steps.

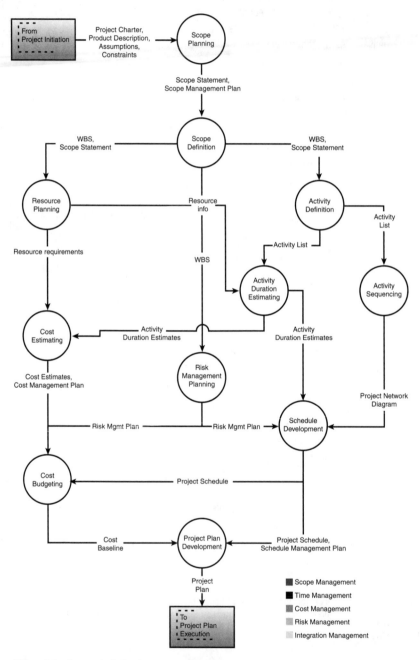

Figure 4.1 Core project planning process flow.

The process flow in Figure 4.1 corrects an inconsistency in the PMBOK. The project planning process flow depicted in Section 3.3.2 of the PMBOK does not show a flow from schedule development to cost budgeting, although the information in Section 7.3.1, "Inputs to Cost Budgeting," clearly indicates that the project schedule is a key input to the cost budgeting step.

Key Analysis of the Core Planning Process

At this point, we've described the core planning process, and we've noted the importance of understanding each process step and the corresponding outputs for the exam. Our experience has shown us that this learning process can be accelerated, if there is clarity on a few key definitions and on the differences among these process steps. These next subsections will review these key learning points.

Project Plan—It's Not a Microsoft Project File

Because the end goal for the entire project planning activity is a project plan, let's review the standard PMI definition. A *project plan* is the document (or set of documents) that describes the complete project, including work, costs, resources, performance baselines, and project management processes. Recommended components of a project plan include the following:

➤ Assumptions and constraints

➤ Project charter

➤ Scope statement

➤ Work Breakdown Structure (WBS)

➤ Cost estimates and cost baseline

➤ Key resources and team members

➤ Major milestones and target dates

➤ Project schedule

➤ Project Management Approach

➤ Risk management plan

➤ Open issues and pending decisions

➤ Communications plan

➤ Cost management plan

➤ Scope management plan

➤ Schedule management plan

➤ Quality management plan

➤ Staffing management plan

➤ Risk response plan

➤ Procurement management plan

Many organizations use the term *project charter* to describe the PMI definition of a project plan. What's more, many organizations use the term *project plan* to refer to a work plan, schedule, or task list. All of these usages are incorrect.

Differences Among the Project Charter, Scope Statement, WBS, Activity List, Project Schedule, and Project Plan

Given the PMI definition of a *project plan*, and the assumption that this definition may not be consistent with your experiences, let's review the PMI definitions of all the key scope and work-related project planning outputs and the key differences between them. Table 4.2 describes these definitions and differences.

A Microsoft Project file (or anything else resembling a project schedule or WBS) is not a project plan.

Table 4.2 Summary of Scope and Work-Related Project Planning Outputs		
Tool	**Definition**	**Notes**
Project charter	A project charter authorizes the project and PM role. It includes a high-level product description and project objectives.	Results from project initiation.
Scope statement	A scope statement lists the product and major subproducts of the project. It is also used as a basis for future scope decisions.	An MS Word document. Results from scope planning.

Table 4.2 Summary of Scope and Work-Related Project Planning Outputs *(continued)*		
Tool	**Definition**	**Notes**
Work Breakdown Structure (WBS)	The WBS is a deliverable-oriented grouping of project components. The lowest level items of a WBS are known as *work packages*.	Usually presented in a hierarchical chart. Results from scope definition.
Activity list	An activity list details the steps required to complete each work package listed in the WBS.	Each activity normally lasts between 4 and 80 hours.
Project schedule	A project schedule applies the activity list, duration estimates, and activity relationships to a calendar with certain dates for completion.	Presented using a project-scheduling tool such as MS Project.
Project plan	A project plan is an all-encompassing document that is used as the basis for project controlling and executing.	Normally an MS Word document with references to other files/documents.

Differences Among the Project Initiation, Scope Planning, and Scope Definition

Another common source of confusion for project managers new to the PMBOK is understanding the differences between the three project scope management processes: project initiation, scope planning, and scope definition. Two of these happen to be part of the core project planning process. The main reason for the confusion is in the "real world" these activities are frequently performed in combination. Logically, the PMBOK processes make sense:

➤ First, authorize the project (initiation).

➤ Second, perform an assessment on the targeted product and project alternatives (scope planning).

➤ Third, decompose the approved work scope into work packages that can be assigned, estimated, and managed (scope definition).

For many project managers, their organizations' processes may combine some or all of these steps into one activity. Therefore, the PMBOK definition is not always "intuitive" at first.

Differences Between the Scope Definition and Activity Definition

Another common area of confusion for project managers studying the PMBOK and the core project planning process is the difference between the scope definition (PMBOK 5.3; subdividing the major project deliverables into smaller, more manageable components) and the activity definition (PMBOK 6.1; identifying the specific activities that must be performed to produce those deliverables). At first glance, these processes seem to be very similar, because both involve breaking down something large into smaller, more manageable components (decomposition) and both provide similar benefits.

The similar benefits of scope definition and activity definition are as follows:

➤ They improve accuracy of cost, duration, and resource estimates.

➤ They define a baseline for performance measurement and control.

➤ They facilitate clear responsibility assignments.

However, the "key difference" is the target of the decomposition. In scope definition, the scope statement is decomposed and captured in the WBS. The WBS may actually represent a "program" rather than just a single project. In activity definition, the WBS work packages are decomposed into a list of activities that can be used for project scheduling:

1. Identify major deliverables, including project management.

2. Decide if adequate costs and duration estimates can be made. If yes, proceed to step 4 (verifying correctness).

3. Break down each deliverable into subcomponents; repeat step 2.

4. Verify the correctness of the decomposition using the following questions:

   ➤ Are lower-level items necessary and sufficient?

   ➤ Are items clear and complete?

   ➤ Can each item be scheduled, budgeted, and assigned to a responsible party?

When decomposing work packages into activities, you should ask additional questions to verify the correctness of the decomposition. These include the following:

➤ Can this activity be logically subdivided further?

➤ What does this activity "deliver?"

➤ Can this activity be performed within the "rule of thumb" duration used for project activities (less than 80 hours, 4–40 hours, 8–80 hours, and so on)?

Know the "80-hour rule." This heuristic (rule of thumb) recommends that each lowest-level task/activity on a project schedule (or WBS) should take no more than 80 hours to complete.

Now that we've reviewed the steps and the key terms involved in the core project planning process, let's move on to a few other key concepts related to core project planning that you'll need to know for the exam. The first key concept to discuss is the WBS.

Work Breakdown Structure (WBS): You Shall Manage No Project Without It

The major output of the decomposition processes mentioned previously is the project's *Work Breakdown Structure (WBS)*. The WBS is a hierarchical representation and definition of the project's work as it relates to project objectives and provides the structure for managing this work through completion. As a result, it is a key tool for the project manager and is highly valued by the PMI organization.

Understand that PMI places great value and priority on the WBS. It may be the most important tool to the project manager.

Download the PMI document **Practice Standard for Work Breakdown Structures** from the PMI Web site (www.pmi.org) for additional insights into PMI's view of the WBS.

Effective Techniques for Developing a WBS

Here are a few "guidelines" regarding the development of the project WBS that you will want to know for the exam:

➤ *All* the work of the project is included in the WBS.

➤ The WBS should be "deliverable focused."

➤ The WBS should be developed "with the team."

➤ The lowest level of the WBS is the work package or activity level.

➤ Unique identifiers are assigned to each item in the WBS to allow for better management reporting of costs and resources.

➤ Review and refine the WBS until all key project stakeholders are satisfied.

The level of granularity for the work package level in a WBS will vary. It depends on what level of detail the project manager plans to manage to. In other words, the level of detail that is needed for effective management and control.

In a program, or on large projects, the work package level may represent efforts in the hundreds of hours. In these cases, it is expected that the teams assigned to these work packages (or subprojects) will define the detail activities and tasks (and schedule) needed to complete the work package.

Benefits of a WBS

For good reason the WBS is given tremendous importance by PMI. More than any other project management tool, it best communicates the work of the project to all stakeholders. As a result, it offers these key benefits:

➤ It facilitates understanding and buy-in of the project scope and the work effort involved from all stakeholders.

➤ It enables identification of all necessary work for the project. It also reduces the number of items that "slip through the cracks," as well as the "Oh, I didn't think of that!" moments.

➤ It allows each team member to easily understand how his or her work fits into the overall project, and how it impacts the work of other team members.

➤ It provides a basis for staffing, cost and time needs, and decisions made for the project.

➤ It keeps team members focused on the deliverables.

➤ It provides a basis for future projects. A good WBS can be used as a template for future projects.

Different Types of Breakdown Structures

Although not a common problem in the IT industry, many industries utilize other breakdown structures and related acronyms that can confuse this subject. Therefore, you should be familiar with these other types of breakdown structures, as listed in Table 4.3, and how they are different from a WBS.

Table 4.3   Different Types of Breakdown Structures

Acronym	Description	Notes
CWBS	Contractual WBS	Defines the level of reporting between the seller and buyer. The CWBS is not as detailed as the WBS used to manage the actual work.
OBS	Organizational Breakdown Structure	Maps work components to organizational units.
RBS	Resource Breakdown Structure	Maps work components to individuals.
BOM	Bill of Materials	Describes the physical components needed for the project.
PBS	Project Breakdown Structure	The PBS is actually the same as the WBS. This term is only used in areas where the term *WBS* is incorrectly used to refer to a BOM.

The Process of Building a Project Schedule

The next important concept related to core project planning we need to review is "the process of building a project schedule." As mentioned at the beginning of this chapter, people often think they know how to plan a project and develop a project schedule. However, when they review the PMBOK and learn of PMI's methods for doing these items, many of these project managers realize they have "holes" in their skill sets (according to PMI) that could prove detrimental on the PMP exam. There are four main reasons why the PMBOK can create this doubt in project managers:

➤ The breakdown of the Time Management component into four distinct steps (activity definition, activity sequencing, activity duration estimating, and schedule development) is not familiar.

➤ Project managers have never thought about the "logical" steps involved in building a project schedule. They just instinctively know and do this.

➤ Project managers were never taught how to build a project schedule correctly and/or have never worked in organizations where a project schedule is used properly to manage a project. (See the prior sections that describe a project schedule.)

➤ Project managers were never taught how to use their project planning tools properly to actually build a project schedule in this way.

For the exam, it's important that you understand the logical steps involved in building a project schedule, regardless of whether you physically complete each step in real-world practice. Plus, if you understand this, you may actually improve the quality of the project schedules you develop for future projects. Table 4.4 describes the purpose of each PMBOK time management process involved in developing a project schedule.

Table 4.4	Building a Project Schedule
PMBOK Process	**Translation**
6.1: Activity Definition	In this process you identify all tasks to be scheduled.
6.2: Activity Sequencing	In this process you identify the relationships (dependencies) between these tasks.
6.3: Activity Duration Estimating	In this process you estimate the effort and duration for each task.
6.4: Schedule Development	In this process you apply the tasks, their relationships, and their estimated durations to a calendar, assign resources, level resources, account for risk factors, and look for ways to compress the schedule.

Another discrepancy between the expectations of PMI and the real-world experiences of many project managers regarding the project schedule is the criteria for completing this important planning activity. Per PMI, the project schedule must possess the following key attributes to be considered complete and ready to be used as a baseline for project performance:

➤ **Buy-in**—The schedule must have acceptance from team members and stakeholders.

➤ **Achievable and realistic**—The schedule must represent all the work to be done and must be realistic with regard to time expectations.

➤ **Formal**—The schedule must be documented and formalized.

Types of Task Dependencies

Now that we've reviewed the key steps and the key completion criteria for schedule development, let's get into a few of the important details of this process that you'll need to know for the exam. After the project's work has been decomposed into activity lists (tasks), you are ready to identify the relationships between tasks. Understanding task dependencies (the relationships between the activities) enables a project manager to build a more realistic, achievable schedule, and it helps to identify the focal points for any type of schedule-compression activity.

For the exam, you will need to be familiar with the various types of task dependencies and relationships detailed in Table 4.5 and be able to identify examples of each.

Table 4.5	Types of Task Dependencies and Relationships		
Type	**Description**	**Example(s)**	**Notes**
External	Dependencies on events outside the project	A permit must be granted by the local government to start construction.	A dependency can be both external and mandatory.
Mandatory	Logical dependencies due to the nature of the work	The foundation of the house must be built before the first floor construction can start.	Also known as "hard logic."
Discretionary	Dependencies defined by the project team	An internal QA review should be conducted before the deliverable is presented to the client.	Also known as "soft logic." This type is often based on "best practices" and needs to be fully documented.
Predecessor	When one activity must occur "before" the other	"Software selection" is a predecessor of "software implementation."	These relationships are captured in the network diagram and then in the project schedule.
Successor	When one activity must occur "after" the other	"Software implementation" is a successor of "software selection."	These relationships are captured in the network diagram and then in the project schedule.

Table 4.5	Types of Task Dependencies and Relationships *(continued)*		
Type	Description	Example(s)	Notes
Concurrent, parallel	When one activity can occur "at the same time" as the other	"User acceptance test case design" can be performed concurrently with "software module design."	Generally, tasks can be concurrent if they are not dependent on each other.

Benefits of Network Diagrams

As mentioned in Table 4.5, the task relationships are usually captured in a network diagram, as well as later in the project schedule. A network diagram (or project network diagram) is one of the best mechanisms available to help you identify task relationships in your project. By creating a visual representation of the project activities and tasks, it is much easier for you to see how they are related to each other. Depending on the schedule development process you were taught or expected to follow, you may or may not have much experience with constructing network diagrams.

For the PMP exam, you will need to know the following about network diagrams:
➤ How to use network diagrams
➤ The benefits of network diagrams
➤ The three different types of diagrams

In addition to highlighting relationships among activities, here are some other advantages offered by a network diagram:

➤ It helps to identify the time and resources for each activity.

➤ It helps to identify schedule development constraints.

➤ It identifies the critical path.

➤ It illustrates total and free float.

Three Different Types of Network Diagrams

For the exam, you need to be familiar with the three different types of project network diagrams and how they compare to each other. Table 4.6 summarizes this information.

Table 4.6	Types of Project Network Diagrams				
Network Diagram Type	Also Known As	Key Characteristics	Example	Notes
Activity-on-Node (AON)	Precedence Diagramming Method (PDM)	*Nodes* represent activities, and arrows represent relationships. AON does not use "dummy" activities, and it can use four types of dependency relationships: ➤ Start-to-finish ➤ Start-to-start ➤ Finish-to-finish ➤ Finish-to-start	See Figure 4.2	AON is the most popular network diagram type. Nodes are displayed as boxes or rectangles. Finish-to-start is the most common dependency relationship.
Activity-on-Arrow (AOA)	Activity Diagramming Method (ADM)	*Arrows* represent activities, and nodes connect activities to represent relationships. AOA uses dummy activities and only uses finish-to-start relationships.	See Figure 4.3	Dummy activities are shown as dashed arrow lines. AOA is rarely used in IT.
GERT	Conditional Diagramming Method (CDM)	GERT uses loops and conditional branches and is also a scheduling technique.	See Figure 4.4	Used to represent repeated activities such as "test cycles" or conditional activities such as updates to validation documents after QA inspection.

NOTE   A "dummy activity" is an activity arrow that does not represent any actual work. It is needed to represent a logical dependency only in an AOA network diagram.

Figures 4.2, 4.3, and 4.4 provide graphical representations of network diagrams.

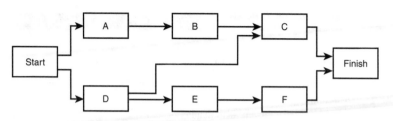

Figure 4.2 Activity-on-Node network diagram example.

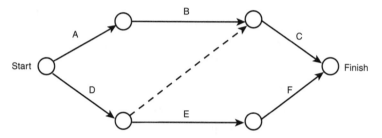

Figure 4.3 Activity-on-Arrow network diagram example.

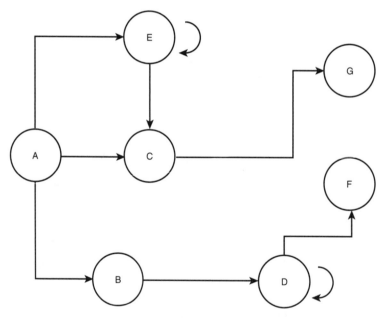

Figure 4.4 GERT network diagram example.

PDM network diagrams are often referred to as *PERT diagrams*. This was the term used by MS Project for network diagrams in the past. However, Microsoft now uses the term *network diagram*. Technically, and for the PMP exam, "PERT" has a distinct definition.

You must be able to assess and draw a network diagram to answer some of the exam questions.

Time Estimating Guidelines and Methods for Schedule Development

With network diagrams, we can clearly see the "relationships" among the various activities. A corresponding step to review in schedule development is the critical process of "estimating" the activity durations. This section summarizes the key activity duration estimating guidelines and methods that you need to know for the exam.

First, let's start with the "Golden Guidelines" of estimating activity duration by PMI:

➤ Estimating should be performed (or approved) by the person doing the work.

➤ Estimating should be based on the work breakdown detailed in the WBS.

➤ Estimating should be based on historical information and expert judgment.

➤ Estimates are influenced by the capabilities of the resources (human and materials) allocated to the activity.

➤ Estimates are influenced by the known project risks.

➤ All bases and assumptions used in estimating should be documented.

➤ Estimates should be given in specific time ranges.

 Per PMI, estimating should be performed (or approved) by the person doing the work. The two main reasons: more accurate estimates and higher commitment levels to the project.

Next, you need to understand several estimating methods, techniques, and terms for the exam. These are summarized in Table 4.7.

Table 4.7	Estimating Methods, Techniques, and Terms	
Estimating Topic	**Key Characteristics**	**Notes**
Expert judgment	Needed due to various factors that influence actual durations. Should be guided by historical information and not just "memory" (see the next entry).	Delphi technique, heuristic estimating, rule of thumb.
Historical information	Critical to improving estimate accuracy. The three types are project files, commercial databases, and project team members.	Recollection of project team members is the least reliable source.
Bottom-up	Starts at the lowest level of the WBS and provides accurate time and cost estimates.	Takes longer to develop and is more costly to develop.
Analogous (top-down)	Utilizes actual duration periods from previous projects to form estimates. Reliable if activities from previous projects mirror activities needed for this . project	Used in early planning phases and project selection. This method costs less to develop because you are leveraging historical information. It's a form of expert judgment because it's based on historical information.
Parametric estimating	Uses historical data and statistical relationships and is 25% to 75% accurate. Estimates are developed by identifying the number of work units and the duration/effort per work unit.	Also known as quantitative-based estimating. Examples include: ➤ Lines of code for software development ➤ Square footage for construction ➤ Number of sites for network migration
Phased estimating	Estimates the project phase by phase. This method is simple and accurate.	Helps stakeholders decide whether to continue the project.

Project Management Guidelines Related to Estimating

In addition to the key concepts and definitions related to the "estimating" activity itself, several "project management" guidelines regarding estimating are emphasized by PMI throughout the PMBOK and the PMP exam. Here's a list of those guidelines:

➤ A project's time and cost estimates (requirements) should be based on project needs and not dictated by senior management. The project manager should work with senior management to reconcile any differences.

➤ Reserve time (contingency, buffer) should be added to either the project schedule or to individual activity duration estimates to account for the level of risk and any uncertainty that exists.

We have no doubt that these first two guidelines are common, everyday practice in your "real-world" experience!

This is a clear example of why leadership, negotiation and communication skills are so important.

➤ Historical information is vital to improving estimates.

➤ Key project success factors (cost, time, scope, resources) should be managed to baselines and only changed when an approved project change has been executed.

➤ All assumptions used in estimating should be documented.

➤ The scheduling technique to be used will impact the estimating effort (see the section titled "Scheduling Techniques" for an additional discussion of this topic).

Improving the accuracy of activity duration and project costs estimates is a key reason why PMI emphasizes the importance of historical project records and information.

Critical Path, Lag, Lead, Slack and Other Scheduling Concepts

Before we review the key scheduling *techniques*, let's review some fundamental scheduling concepts and terms. You'll need this knowledge to effectively answer many questions on the exam related to schedule development. The best way to review these fundamentals is by walking through an example of a question type you may see on the exam.

Table 4.8 lists a set of project activities, their predecessor relationships, and their estimated durations.

Table 4.8	Network Diagram Sample Question		
Activity	**Predecessors**	**Duration (Days)**	**Earliest Start Date**
A	None	5	8/1/03
B	A	2	

Table 4.8	Network Diagram Sample Question *(continued)*		
Activity	**Predecessors**	**Duration (Days)**	**Earliest Start Date**
C	A	3	
D	B	7	
E	C	4	
F	D	1	
G	E, F	2	

Now that you've reviewed Table 4.8, follow along with these steps:

1. From this table, draw an Activity-on-Node network diagram, using the node template depicted in Figure 4.5.

Early Start	Duration	Early Finish
	Task Name	
Late Start	Slack	Late Finish

Figure 4.5 Activity Node template.

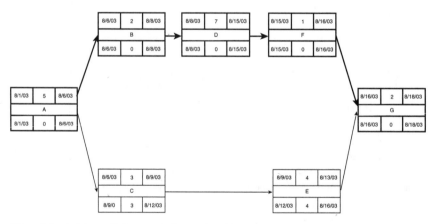

Figure 4.6 Activity-on-Node network diagram for table.

2. From this network diagram, which activities make up the critical path and how long is the critical path?

The critical path represents the longest sequence of activities in the network diagram and is characterized by zero float or slack at each node (activity) in the path.

Given this understanding, the critical path is the combination of activities A, B, D, F, and G and has a total duration of 17 days (5+2+7+1+2 = 17).

> Any delay in the critical path delays the project. You must decrease this path time to shorten the project. Also, keep in mind that a schedule may have multiple critical paths.

3. From this network diagram, what are the earliest start and earliest end times for each activity?

   Earliest start time (EST) is the sum of the durations for all *predecessor* activities. Earliest finish time equals EST plus the activity duration.

   See the earliest start and end time values listed for each activity node in Figure 4.6. Do you see how these were calculated?

> Earliest start times and earliest end times for project activities are calculated by starting at the first activity and moving forward through the network diagram. This is known as the *forward pass*.

4. Now, calculate the latest start and latest end times for each activity.

   Latest finish time (LFT) equals the project EFT minus the expected duration of the *successor* activities, and latest start time (LST) equals LFT minus the activity duration.

   See the latest start and end time values listed for each activity node in Figure 4.6. Do you see how these were calculated?

> Latest start times and latest end times for project activities are calculated by starting at the last activity and moving backward through the network diagram. This is known as the *backward pass*.

5. Now that you know the latest finish time (LFT) and the earliest finish time (EFT) calculated for each activity, what is the slack (or float) time for each activity?

   Mathematically, activity slack (or float) is calculated as follows:

   Float = LFT – EFT

However, the key to remembering this is understanding what slack represents. *Slack* is the amount of time an activity can be delayed without impacting the start time of the successor activities.

Given this definition, do you see how the slack values were calculated for each activity in Figure 4.6?

 There is no slack along the critical path.

 You may see the terms *free slack* and *total slack* on the exam.

Free slack refers to the time the activity can be delayed without affecting the start of the successor activity. This is what you normally think of when you hear the term *slack* or *float*.

Total slack refers to the time the activity can be delayed without affecting the project completion date.

Two additional scheduling and task relationship concepts that are frequently misunderstood are *lead* and *lag*. In many cases, project managers also confuse *lag* with *slack* (or *float*).

Let's start with the lag. Lag is the amount of delay time before the successor activity can start. In other words, once Activity A is complete, how soon can Activity B start? If the lag is zero, Activity B can start immediately after Activity A is complete. Generally, "lag" times are captured when there are external dependencies on a task that are not being captured in the project schedule.

Note that slack time (or float) is concerned with the amount of time an activity can be delayed without impacting the successor activity; it's not an attribute of the dependency relationship.

Lead is described as the amount of advance notice that is required for the successor activity to begin. This is most frequently used when a successor activity can be started before the predecessor is completely finished.

 Most scheduling software calculates EFT, EST, LFT, LST, total float, free float, and the critical path, if the following information is provided for each activity:

➤ Activity name
➤ Activity duration
➤ Dependency relationships

Scheduling Techniques

The PMBOK categorizes these scheduling techniques as *mathematical analysis techniques* that calculate theoretical early/late start and finish dates. In other words, these techniques will give you a preliminary schedule. The final schedule may be different, depending on the application of any resource leveling and/or schedule-compression techniques (discussed later in this chapter).

For the exam, Table 4.9 summarizes the key facts about these scheduling techniques.

Table 4.9 Scheduling Techniques			
	CPM	**PERT**	**GERT**
Full name	Critical Path Method	Program Evaluation and Review Technique	Graphical Evaluation and Review Technique
Key features	Identifies the critical path as well as identifies the least flexible activities based on float calculations. Used for crashing. Uses the most likely estimate.	Uses three estimates for each activity (weighted average). Used mainly on large scale projects. Incorporates risk management. Can be used for crashing and can develop four types of schedules.	Illustrates loops in an activity sequence, branches between activities, and different project outcomes.
Shows alternative paths?	No	No	Yes
Looping?	No	No	Yes
Estimating	Uses one estimate for each activity (most likely). Does not allow for risk events.	Uses three estimates for each activity: optimistic, most likely, pessimistic. $ET = (O + 4M + P) / 6$ This technique is time consuming.	Multiple

All schedules are "assumption based." The activity duration estimates are based on staffing and project execution assumptions.

In addition to the three mathematical analysis techniques, you should also be familiar with *simulation scheduling techniques*. In particular, you need to know what the Monte Carlo simulation technique is all about.

In summary, a preliminary project schedule can be submitted to a simulation tool to validate its feasibility. The Monte Carlo simulation technique is the most popular one used. In addition, a project scheduling simulation tool is often used in risk management to perform "what-if" analysis.

The Monte Carlo Simulation Technique

The Monte Carlo simulation technique was indeed named after Monte Carlo, Monaco—specifically, after the casinos and games of chance located in Monte Carlo. The random behavior that we find in "games of chance" is similar to how the Monte Carlo simulation technique selects variable values at random to simulate a model.

When you roll a die, you know that either a 1, 2, 3, 4, 5, or 6 will come up, but you don't know which value for any particular roll. It's the same with the variables that have a known range of values but an uncertain value for a specific time or event (such as interest rates, staffing needs, stock prices, inventory, and phone calls per minute).

The Monte Carlo simulation technique randomly generates values for uncertain variables corresponding to every node in the model (or in our case, random duration times for every activity in the project schedule) and combines these event outcomes with each other until a statistically accurate representation of all possible combinations has been created. This allows a project manager to make better decisions by understanding what's most likely to happen and by understanding the impact individual event outcomes can have.

Here are the key facts to understand about the Monte Carlo simulation technique:

➤ It's the most common simulation technique.

➤ It uses specialized software.

➤ It allows multiple project durations to be calculated.

➤ It figures duration probability for each activity.

➤ It assesses the feasibility of the schedule under adverse conditions.

➤ It allows for "what-if" (risk) analysis.

A schedule is considered "preliminary" until resource assignments are confirmed.

Various Methods of Presenting a Project Schedule

One element of project planning and project management that is often over-looked is effectively communicating the project schedule to the various project stakeholders. Although presenting a detailed, tabular view of the schedule to the core team is acceptable, PMI favors the use of visual, summary representations when presenting the schedule to other stakeholders. For the exam, you should be familiar with the common methods of presenting a project schedule summary, as detailed in Table 4.10, and the benefits of each.

Table 4.10	Methods for Presenting a Project Schedule Summary		
Method	**Key Attributes**	**Benefits**	**Notes**
Milestone chart	This is a bar chart that shows start and end dates, major deliverables, and key external dependencies.	Highlights key decision and completion points, as well as any external dependencies.	Milestone tables are also used (same information, no bar chart).
Gantt chart	This is a bar chart that shows the various levels of the WBS.	Easy to read, incorporates the WBS, and can easily show actual progress against estimates.	Does not generally show interdependencies.
Network diagram	A network diagram uses nodes and arrows. Date information is added to each activity node.	Highlights the critical path and shows project logic (flow).	For presentations, the summary task level of the WBS is generally used. Otherwise, a network diagram is best suited for wall display.

Techniques for Shortening the Schedule

As mentioned previously, the scheduling techniques result in a theoretical schedule. On most projects, this will not be the schedule presented to the stakeholders for approval. Due to either stakeholder expectations or an external deadline that must be met, an effort must be made to compress or "shorten" the schedule without reducing the scope of the project. For the exam, you will need to understand the techniques detailed in Table 4.11 and the key issue(s) with each.

The only way to shorten a schedule is to compress the critical path time.

Table 4.11	Techniques for Compressing the Project Schedule	
Technique	**Definition**	**Key Issue(s)**
Crashing	Adding resources to critical path activities only	Certain activities cannot be completed faster by adding resources. Additional resources often add overhead that can negate any time savings. Crashing can increase project costs.
Fast tracking	Performing critical path activities in parallel	Fast tracking is a high-risk technique that increases the probability of rework.
Process improvements	Gaining productivity increases based on different work processes, technologies, and/or machinery	New approaches can increase project risks. Process improvements are not always available.
Limited overtime	Increasing the number of hours per day or week available to work on project tasks	Overtime is most effective when used for limited periods of time. Overuse can lead to team morale and quality of work issues.

Techniques to shorten the project schedule can also be deployed during project execution as a corrective action to a schedule variance.

The project schedule is a critical component of the project plan, and it is a critical input for the creation of the cost baseline. In addition to this fact, you should review several other important points related to project cost estimating to help with your exam preparation.

Key Cost Estimating Factors

A great deal of overlap exists between the "time" estimating topics covered earlier in this chapter (and in the PMBOK) and the "cost" estimating and budgeting topics you need to know for the exam. The key difference is that *cost estimating* is focused on the cost of the resources needed by the project, whereas *activity duration estimating* is focused on the time duration of the project's work activities.

Another key point to remember is that you need to have the activity duration estimates to do cost estimating. In total, three main factors affect project cost estimating:

➤ Activity duration

➤ Resource rates

➤ Risk

With a cost estimate for each work activity, a time-phased budget or cost baseline can be developed to measure and monitor project cost performance.

 Memorize the estimate accuracy levels listed in Table 4.12.

Table 4.12   Estimate Accuracy Levels

Level	Accuracy Range	Generally Used During
Order of magnitude	–25% to +75%	Initiating phase
Budget	–10% to +25%	Planning phase
Definitive	–5% to +10%	Planning phase

 Although a *chart of accounts* is more of a controlling technique, it needs to be set up during planning. You should understand that a chart of accounts is a list of accounting codes assigned to the project's work packages that are used to monitor project costs.

One of the key cost estimating factors not explicitly mentioned by the PMBOK—but one you need to be aware of for the exam—is the "common pitfalls" factor with project cost estimating. Although most of these pitfalls are intuitive, a quick review of them will be helpful to your exam preparation:

➤ Basing cost estimates on poorly defined work definitions (such as scope statement and WBS)

➤ Basing cost estimates on a poorly developed schedule

➤ Not utilizing estimating techniques properly

➤ Not accounting for inflation, overhead costs, or all lifecycle costs

Although obvious to those who "sell" project work to clients, there is a difference between a project's *costs* and a project's *price*.

The Role of Risk Management in the Core Planning Process

Although all but one of the project risk management processes is defined as a "planning" process, only one is defined as a "core" planning process: risk management planning (11.1 PMBOK). The remaining risk management planning processes will be covered in the next chapter.

Here are the key points to recall about the risk management planning process:

➤ PMI considers risk management planning a "core" planning process because it *plans* the critical risk management process and should *always* be done as part of project planning.

➤ A risk management plan is not a risk response plan.

To PMI, a risk management plan does not identify the project risks and document the response strategies (this is the *risk response plan*).

Exam Prep Questions

Question 1

All the following statements about a WBS are true except which one?

- ○ A. It provides a framework for organizing and ordering a project's activities.
- ○ B. It breaks down a project into successively greater detail by level and can be similar in appearance to an organizational chart.
- ○ C. It's a scheduling method.
- ○ D. It's a planning tool.

Answer C is correct. A WBS is *not* a scheduling method. Instead, it provides input into the scheduling process. Therefore, answers A, B, and D are correct.

Question 2

All the following statements are false about the scope statement except which one?

- ○ A. It provides a documented basis for preparing the PERT/CPM network.
- ○ B. It's not the basis for the contract between the buyer and seller.
- ○ C. It includes a description of project objectives such as cost, schedule, and quality measures.
- ○ D. It's not developed by functional managers during the concept phase of a project.

Answer C is correct. The question is made more difficult by negating otherwise correct choices, which is a common technique on the PMP exam. Answer A is incorrect because the activity list is used as the basis for preparing the PERT/CPM network. Answer B is incorrect because the scope statement is the documented basis for the contract between buyer and seller. Answer D is incorrect because functional managers *do* develop the scope statement during the concept phase.

Question 3

Which statement best describes the proper way to develop the initial project schedule?

○ A.   Create a new MS Project file, enter key deliverables, enter start and end dates for each, and assign resources.

○ B.   Create a new MS Project file, enter the WBS structure and work packages, break down work packages into activities, enter the estimated duration and resource assignments for each activity, and enter the logical dependencies between the activities and work packages,

○ C.   Create a new MS Project file, enter the WBS structure and work packages, break down work packages into activities, enter start and end dates for each activity, and compress the schedule to meet the deadline.

○ D.   Find an MS Project file with a proven WBS and activity list template, review the estimated duration and resource assignments for each activity, and review the logical dependencies between the activities and work packages.

Answer D is correct. This question can be difficult because it provides common, but incorrect, practices as options, and it incorporates some of the important PMI principles. Answer A is incorrect because it does not refer to the WBS or to activity durations. Answer B is tempting, but it's not the *best* response. In this case, answer D is a better response because of the use of "historical information" in the process. Answer C is incorrect because it does not refer to activity durations.

Question 4

A precedence diagram and an arrow diagram are both examples of networks. Which statement best describes the primary difference between them?

○ A.   The arrow diagram does not indicate critical path.

○ B.   The precedence diagram uses float as part of the activity duration.

○ C.   The arrow diagram incorporates PERT in the activity duration.

○ D.   The precedence diagram represents activities on nodes.

Answer D is correct. Answer A is incorrect because both types can represent the critical path. Answer B is incorrect because float is associated with scheduling techniques, not network diagrams. Answer C is incorrect because it is GERT that uses PERT for activity duration.

Question 5

Activity A has a duration of 4 days and begins on the morning of Wednesday the 4th. The successor activity, Activity B, has a finish-to-start relationship with Activity A. The finish-to-start relationship has a lag of 3 days, and Activity B has a duration of 3 days. Saturday isn't a workday. What can be determined from this data?

- ○ A. The total duration is 11 days.
- ○ B. The finish date of Activity B is Sunday the 15th.
- ○ C. The total duration is 14 days.
- ○ D. The finish date of Activity B is Tuesday the 17th.

Answer B is correct. Activity A completes on Sunday the 8th because Saturday isn't a workday. The 3-day lag occurs Monday, Tuesday, and Wednesday. Activity B starts on Thursday the 12th and completes on Sunday the 15th because Saturday isn't a workday. The total calendar duration is 12 days.

Question 6

"I cannot test the software until I code the software." This expression describes which of the following dependencies?

- ○ A. Mandatory
- ○ B. Discretionary
- ○ C. External
- ○ D. Preferential

Answer A is correct. Mandatory or "hard logic" dependencies are ones where one task *must* occur before another can start.

Question 7

Which of the following is a schedule development technique that provides early and late start and finish dates for each activity?

- ○ A. GERT
- ○ B. PERT
- ○ C. CPM
- ○ D. Monte Carlo

Answer C is correct. See the PMBOK definition (PMBOK, page 75) of the critical path method scheduling technique.

Question 8

All the following statements about analogous estimating are true except which one?

- ○ A. It has an accuracy rate of ±10% of the actual costs.
- ○ B. It supports top-down estimating and is a form of expert judgment.
- ○ C. It's used to estimate total project costs when a limited amount of detailed project information is available.
- ○ D. It involves using the cost of previous, similar projects as the basis for estimating the cost of the current project.

Answer A is correct. Analogous estimating has a –25%/+75% accuracy level.

Question 9

What is the purpose of resource planning?

- ○ A. To determine the physical resources needed to perform the project activities.
- ○ B. To provide quantitative assessments of the costs of resources required to complete project activities.
- ○ C. To approximate the costs of resources needed to complete the project.
- ○ D. To determine the resources that are potentially available.

Answer A is correct, per the PMBOK definition of resource planning. Answers B and C are incorrect because they describe cost estimating. Answer D is incorrect because it is focused on availability of resources, not on what is required to perform the project activities.

Question 10

What is the purpose of cost budgeting?

○ A. To allocate cost estimates to individual work items to establish a cost baseline against which project performance can be measured.

○ B. To monitor cost performance to detect variances from the plan.

○ C. To determine the cost of the resources needed to complete the project activities and allocate them to the proper chart of accounts for the organization.

○ D. To provide a quantitative assessment of the likely costs of the resources required to complete project activities.

Answer A is correct, per the PMBOK definition. Answer B is incorrect because it describes cost control, not cost budgeting. Answer C is incorrect because it describes cost estimating, not cost budgeting. Answer D is incorrect because it describes estimating activity as well.

Need to Know More?

 Project Management Institute, *PMBOK Guide 2000.*

 Project Management Institute, *Practice Standard for Work Breakdown Structures*

 PMI Bookstore (www.pmibookstore.org)

The PMI Bookstore provides general project management references materials and other self-study texts.

 PMI eLearning Connection (www.pmi.org)

The PMI eLearning Connection offers virtual, online seminars and study programs.

 Commercial PMP prep courses

Search the PMI Web site (www.pmi.org) for a listing of PMI Registered Education Providers that offer PMP exam prep courses. Many of the courses are now offered "online" to better support your lifestyle.

 Other Internet resources

Search the Web for other PMP exam materials available. It is not uncommon to find free sample exam questions available from training companies and PMI user groups.

 Amazon.com (www.amazon.com)

Search for "project management" to find general project management reference materials and other self-study texts.

Project Planning—Facilitating Processes

Terms you'll need to understand:

- ✓ Quality, organizational, and communication planning
- ✓ Staff acquisition
- ✓ Risk management
- ✓ Quality management
- ✓ Procurement and solicitation planning
- ✓ Risk identification
- ✓ Qualitative risk analysis
- ✓ Quantitative risk analysis
- ✓ Risk response planning
- ✓ Risk event
- ✓ Resource pool
- ✓ Procurement management plan
- ✓ Responsibility matrix
- ✓ Risk rating matrix
- ✓ Contingency plan
- ✓ Fallback plan
- ✓ Decision tree
- ✓ Avoidance
- ✓ Mitigation
- ✓ Acceptance
- ✓ Transference

Techniques and concepts you'll need to master:

- ✓ The impact of the core and facilitating planning processes on the core processes
- ✓ The differences between risk management planning and risk response planning
- ✓ The differences among resource planning, organizational planning, and communications planning
- ✓ The purpose and key elements of each supplemental project plan
- ✓ Key factors for communications planning
- ✓ HR responsibilities of the project manager
- ✓ Quality management principles and the PMI quality definition philosophy, and quality principles
- ✓ In what ways quality management and project management are similar
- ✓ Costs and responsibilities of quality management
- ✓ How quality management impacts project success
- ✓ What the differences among quality planning, quality assurance, and quality control are
- ✓ Who the pioneers in quality management are and what they are known for
- ✓ The key PMI risk management principles and risk management tools
- ✓ The different types and the common sources of project risk and risk response strategies
- ✓ The key PMI procurement management principles and project management skills used in procurement management
- ✓ Key *contract* facts
- ✓ The purpose, risk, and advantages of each contract type
- ✓ Key factors in the "build versus buy" decision
- ✓ Advantages of centralized versus decentralized contracting organizations

Project planning involves more than the scope, time, and cost elements we reviewed in the last chapter. The project planning process also sets the stage for project communications, project quality, project risk management, procurement management activities, and the project team. The PMBOK refers to these activities as the *facilitating* processes of project planning. These facilitating planning processes are depicted in Figure 5.1.

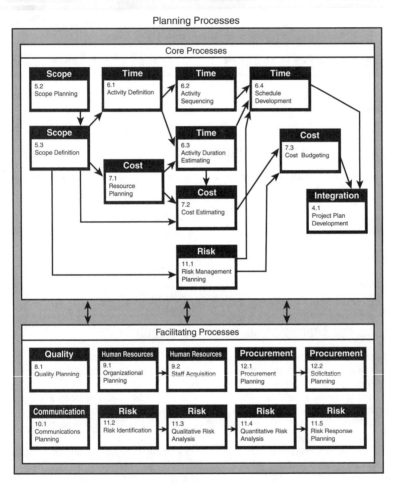

Figure 5.1 Facilitating project planning processes.

This subject area, more than any other we discuss in this book, may best illustrate PMI's philosophy that effective project management is proactive, that the project manager should be in control of the project (and not the other way around), and that all project management activities should be planned.

All project management activities should be "thought about" and planned.

Communications, risk, and quality project management are excellent examples of *proactive* project management.

Although most project managers have considerable experience with the core planning steps, there is a much wider range of experience with the facilitating planning processes. Depending on your industry, the mission-critical level of your projects, and the project management methodology of your organization, your exposure to disciplined risk management, quality management, and procurement management procedures may be quite limited. In addition, even when people are experienced in these areas, they often find that the techniques and terms they have utilized are not always consistent with PMI's methodology or philosophy.

On top of all this, the PMBOK coverage of the core and facilitating planning processes tends to make the project planning process seem less intuitive and much more complicated than it really is.

To streamline your exam preparations, we will clarify these process relationships, emphasize the "gotta-know" concepts and terms that are important to PMI, and identify the "common" gaps you may need to close to be ready for the exam questions related to the facilitating project planning processes.

The Differences Between the Core and Facilitating Planning Processes

A common confusion point for project managers and readers of the PMBOK is understanding the differences between "core" and "facilitating" planning processes. Common questions include the following:

➤ Does "core" mean that the processes are *always* performed, whereas "facilitating" indicates *optional?*

➤ Why is risk management planning considered a "core" planning process, but communications planning, quality planning, and risk response planning are not?

These are good, insightful questions. In order to answer them and improve your understanding of the distinction between the planning process types, let's review a couple points:

➤ The distinction between core and facilitating planning processes is more of an "academic" distinction.

The *core* processes are those that must be done in a specific sequence. The *facilitating* processes can vary in sequence, are often performed in parallel with each other, and have a two-way feedback loop with many "core" processes.

➤ The facilitating planning processes are always performed.

The effort to perform these processes will vary greatly depending on the nature of the project and the project management maturity level of the performing organization.

 Facilitating planning processes are always performed. They are not optional.

Although these points help to explain the difference between core and facilitating processes, they do not clarify why risk management planning is considered a core planning process. Only PMI can completely explain this distinction, but here is our attempt:

➤ The risk management plan is the only supplemental project plan with its own budget estimate. This budget estimate is needed to feed the "core" cost budgeting process. Therefore, it meets the "sequence" criteria for a core process.

➤ PMI places high importance on the risk management process.

The Impact of the Facilitating Processes on the Core Processes

The PMBOK illustrates a two-way feedback loop between the core and facilitating planning processes (refer to Figure 5.1). Although most experienced professionals naturally understand this two-way feedback loop, this "natural" understanding can get lost if you are not accustomed to seeing this activity described this way, if you do not have considerable experience with many of these facilitating processes, and/or if you are trying to understand the individual process-to-process relationships between the two groups. To clarify the relationships between the facilitating and core planning process groups and to improve your context understanding of the facilitating planning processes, review Table 5.1 for common situations in which the results from a facilitating planning activity can impact a core planning activity.

Table 5.1 Facilitating Planning Process Impact on Core Planning Processes		
Facilitating Planning Process	**Impact Description**	**Impacted Core Planning Area(s)**
8.1: Quality Planning	Cost and schedule adjustments may be needed to meet quality standards. Quality assurance and quality control activities must be staffed and added to the project schedule.	Cost baseline, WBS, resource plan, network diagram, and project schedule
9.2: Staff Acquisition	Not able to get resources that meet all the skill requirements. Must acquire staff externally at rates higher than estimated.	Cost baseline, activity duration estimates, and project schedule
10.1: Communications Planning	Communications management plan details must be added to project schedule.	WBS, activity list, network diagram, and project schedule
11.5: Risk Response Planning	Risk response strategies may entail the allocation of additional resources, tasks, time, and costs.	Resource requirements, budget reserves, cost baseline, schedule contingency, WBS, project schedule, and project plan
12.1: Procurement Planning	If a decision is made to "buy," the remaining procurement management tasks must be added to project schedule.	WBS, activity list, network diagram, and project schedule
12.2: Solicitation Planning	Constraints of scheduling procurement activities with third-party vendors may impact the project schedule.	Project schedule

The risk management process can impact the project plan throughout the project because it is a continuous, proactive project management activity.

 Solicitation planning is closely aligned with the project schedule.

Solicitation planning is only performed if a "buy" decision is made during procurement planning.

The Relationships Among Quality, Risk and Procurement, and HR Management

In addition to the interactions between the facilitating and core planning processes, there are significant relationships among the facilitating planning processes themselves. Specifically, strong logical links exist among project quality management, project risk management, and project procurement management. Again, to improve your context understanding of the facilitating planning processes and to clarify the relationships within the facilitating planning process group, review Table 5.2 for common situations in which these interactions occur.

Table 5.2   Relationships Among Facilitating Planning Processes

Facilitating Process	Relationship Description	Related Facilitating Process(es)
8.1: Quality Planning	Quality management resources need to be reflected in the project organization.	9.1: Organizational Planning 10.1: Communications Planning
	The communications plan should reflect QA and QC communications.	11.2: Risk Identification
	A detailed risk analysis may be needed if the cost and/or schedule impact to meet a quality standard is high.	
9.2: Staff Acquisition	A decision is made to acquire external staff resources.	12.1: Procurement Planning
9.1: Organizational Planning	The information and communication needs of project stakeholders.	10.1: Communications Planning

Table 5.2 Relationships Among Facilitating Planning Processes *(continued)*		
Facilitating Process	**Relationship Description**	**Related Facilitating Process(es)**
11.5: Risk Response Planning	Whenever the risk response strategy is transference, the resulting action usually involves outsourcing either all or part of the project scope and/or obtaining insurance policies.	12.1: Procurement Planning

Although not a project planning scenario, it is worth noting that *procurement*-based issues can affect project quality management, too. Here are some of those issues:

➤ Cost of materials

➤ Contractor (seller) qualifications

➤ Contractor's (seller's) bid

➤ Contractor's (seller's) quality policy

➤ Amount of lead time needed for delivery

➤ Actual delivery time

The Differences Between Risk Management Planning and Risk Response Planning

Because the PMBOK itself is not consistent when describing the contents of a risk management plan (see the note after Table 5.3), and because many project managers have used risk management methodologies that differ from the one described by PMI, some project managers are initially confused by the distinction that PMI makes between risk management planning and risk response planning. Table 5.3 summarizes the key differences between these two risk management processes to ensure this is not an issue for you on the exam.

Table 5.3 Key Differences Between Risk Management Planning and Risk Response Planning		
Category	Risk Management Planning	Risk Response Planning
Step number in PMI risk management process	First	Fifth
Purpose	To plan the risk management process	To plan the responses to the identified and analyzed risks
Budget impact	For the risk management activity	As part of the response strategy for each applicable risk
Key output	Risk management plan	Risk response plan

Be aware that the PMBOK is not consistent in its description of a risk management plan. On page 45 of the PMBOK, where the elements of a project plan are described, the risk management plan is described as *including* key risks, constraints, and planned responses. However, in Section 11.1.3, page 130, the risk management plan is explicitly described as *not* including identified risks and their responses.

The latter description is regarded as the official one. It appears the description on page 45 may have not been edited out from the 1996 edition of the PMBOK. The 2000 edition of the PMBOK included a complete "rewrite" of the risk management section.

The risk management plan and the risk response plan are not the same thing.

Due to the wide variations in risk management methodologies, you will want to *memorize* the PMBOK risk management process and definitions.

The Differences Among Resource Planning, Organizational Planning, and Communications Planning

One last area to cover in our analysis of the core and facilitating planning processes is the differences among resource planning, organizational planning, and communications planning. The differences among these three PMBOK processes are not always intuitive to project managers—mainly because activities or elements of these activities are routinely performed in tandem with each other, and we are not accustomed to thinking about them in their logical parts. Plus, it is not always obvious why PMI places resource planning in the Project Cost Management knowledge area and not in the Human Resources knowledge area with the rest of the "project team" type processes. To clarify the distinctions among these three planning processes and prepare yourself for the exam, review Table 5.4.

Table 5.4 Key Differences Among Resource Planning, Organizational Planning, and Communications Planning			
Category	Resource Planning	Organizational Planning	Communications Planning
Purpose	Determine what resources are needed and at what quantities they are needed.	Determine roles, responsibilities, and reporting relationships.	Determine information and communication needs of each project stakeholder.
Knowledge Area	Cost.	Human resources.	Communications.
Why?	Types and quantities of resources are key inputs into the project budget.	The focus is on the specific roles and responsibilities of the project human resources.	The focus is on the information and communications needs.
Type of Planning Process	Core.	Facilitating.	Facilitating.
Why?	Needed for budget determination. Sequence is important.	The exact sequence can vary. The magnitude and formality of the effort will vary.	The exact sequence can vary. The magnitude and formality of the effort will vary.
Notes	Closely linked with scope definition, activity definition, and cost estimating.	Often initiated during resource planning. Often finalized during communications planning.	Closely linked to organizational planning.

The Purpose and Key Elements of Each Supplemental Project Plan

Before we get into some of the specific details of the facilitating planning processes, let's review all the key supplemental project plans referenced by the PMBOK. Given the breadth of subject material covered by these 21 project planning processes, as well as the wide range of experiences project managers have had with these supplemental plans, it may be helpful for your exam preparations to see all these in one place. This may be especially helpful if you are still coming to terms with the fact that a project plan and a project schedule are not the same thing. In Table 5.5, each supplemental project plan, its main purpose, and a few key elements are listed.

Table 5.5 Summary of Supplemental Project Plans		
Supplemental Plan	**Purpose**	**Key Elements/Notes**
Communications plan	Describes how the information and communication needs of project stakeholders will be met	Often documented and presented in tabular form.
Configuration management plan	Describes how changes to project deliverables and work products will be controlled and managed	Should include both technical work products and project documentation.
Cost management plan	Describes how cost variances will be managed	The output of cost estimating. Documents planned responses to different variance levels.
Procurement management plan	Describes how the procurement process will be managed	Results from procurement planning. Contract types. Roles of project team and procurement department.
Quality management plan	Describes the project quality system	Should address both project work products and the project processes.
Responsibility matrix	Lists the project roles and responsibilities; cross-references roles with assigned resources	RACI matrix.
Risk management plan	Describes how the risk management process will be structured and performed	Describes the process to be used. Can include a budget. Can include a cost contingency.
Risk response plan	Describes the response strategies for identified risks	Risk register. Details action steps to be taken if risk event occurs.
Schedule management plan	Describes how changes to the schedule will be managed	Output of schedule development.

Table 5.5 Summary of Supplemental Project Plans *(continued)*		
Supplemental Plan	**Purpose**	**Key Elements/Notes**
Scope management plan	Describes how the project scope will be managed and how scope changes will be integrated	Can include assessment of expected stability of the project scope.
Staffing management plan	Indicates when team members are needed on the project (start and end dates)	Can include resource histograms.

As noted by PMBOK, the formality and detail of each supplemental plan will vary depending on project need.

If an exam question asks about where you would find certain planning information, and both the project plan and the supplemental plan are answer options, the supplemental plan is regarded as the *better* response because it is more specific.

Key Factors for Communications Planning

A great example that illustrates that a *facilitating* process does not mean "optional" is communications planning. Given that project success depends on the quality of communications and that 90% of a project manager's time is (or should be) spent communicating, *communications planning* is an essential activity on any project.

Ninety percent of a project manager's time is spent communicating. Communication is the most important project management skill.

The goal of communications planning is to ensure that all the stakeholders involved in the project have the information they need, when they need it, to fulfill their responsibilities. The key factors that affect communications planning and the communication requirements for a project include the following:

➤ Sponsoring organizational structure

➤ Results of stakeholder analysis

➤ Reporting relationships

➤ Functional areas involved in the project

➤ The number of people involved in the project

➤ Location of the project stakeholder

➤ Information needs of each stakeholder

➤ Experience level of project team members

➤ Availability of technology

➤ Immediacy and frequency of information needs

➤ Desired form of project communications

➤ Expected length of the project

➤ Level of "external" communications needed

➤ Procurement contracts

➤ Any constraints advised by legal counsel

Techniques for Better Project Communications

In addition to testing your understanding of the communications planning process, the PMP exam will also test your understanding of basic techniques for better project communications. Although most of these are "common sense," you'll find it helpful to review them for the exam.

Guidelines for Effective Communications

The first points to review are the basic guidelines for effective communications. These guidelines apply to all types of communications, but in project management they are often the key differentiators between average and superior project managers:

➤ Think about your message in advance.

➤ Choose the best form for your message.

➤ Send all necessary information.

➤ Indicate whether a response is needed.

➤ Be clear, concise, and courteous.

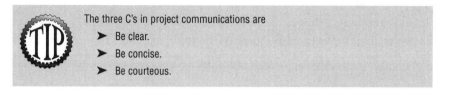

The three C's in project communications are

➤ Be clear.

➤ Be concise.

➤ Be courteous.

Recommended Project Communication Mechanisms

In addition to effective status reporting (including the use of earned value techniques), the other communication mechanisms favored by PMI include the following:

➤ Work Breakdown Structure (WBS)

➤ Kickoff meetings

➤ Mini kickoff meetings (each phase)

➤ Responsibility matrix (RACI)

➤ Project organization chart

Essential Information for Team Members

One area of project communications that is often overlooked is the importance of providing the right information to the core project team members. The following list of essential information for team members is valid over the entire project lifecycle, but it is especially important to remember anytime a new person joins the project:

➤ Project context

➤ Project goals

➤ Team members' roles and responsibilities

➤ Team members' assignments

➤ Project schedule

➤ Chain of command and reporting relationships

HR Responsibilities of the Project Manager

In addition to the extraordinary communications responsibilities of a project manager, he or she is also expected to fulfill several Human Resources department–type responsibilities during a project. These responsibilities include the following:

➤ Negotiating with resource managers

➤ Assigning roles and responsibilities

➤ Developing detailed project job descriptions

➤ Identifying training needs for all stakeholders

➤ Implementing training for all stakeholders

➤ Creating a project organization chart

➤ Creating a project team directory

➤ Developing a staffing management plan

Understand the roles and responsibilities of the project manager.

Quality Management Principles and the PMI Philosophy

To best prepare for exam questions on quality planning, you need to understand some key quality management principles and the PMI quality management philosophy. Specifically, you should be able to answer the following questions:

➤ What are the key PMI quality principles and how does PMI define *quality*?

➤ In what ways are quality management and project management similar?

➤ Who has responsibility for quality?

➤ What are the costs associated with quality?

➤ How does quality management impact project success?

➤ What are the differences among quality planning, quality assurance, and quality control?

➤ Who are the pioneers in quality management and what are they known for?

Key PMI Quality Principles

The PMI quality management philosophy is a generalized approach that remains consistent with the industry quality standards (such as ISO 9000 and ISO 10000) and popular quality methodologies (such as Total Quality Management, Continuous Improvement, and the Deming Cycle). To PMI, *quality* equals "conformance to requirements and fitness of use." Simply translated, this means that the project produces what it said it would, and that what it produces satisfies real customer needs.

Here are the key principles to remember about the PMI quality management approach:

➤ Quality is doing what you said you would do.

➤ Quality is planned in, not inspected in.

➤ Quality is "prevention over inspection."

➤ Quality management addresses both *product* (goods and services) quality and *project management* quality.

➤ The project manager has ultimate responsibility for the project *product* quality.

➤ Effective quality management is consistent with effective project management.

➤ A work package should be verified and tested before submission.

PMI also emphasizes that quality is *not* giving the customer "extras" or doing more than promised.
PMI refers to this practice as "gold plating" and consistently discourages it.

Memorize PMI's definition of quality: "conformance to requirements and fitness of use."

Similarities Between Quality Management and Project Management

As mentioned before, PMI believes strongly that there is a natural partnership between effective quality management and effective project management. To better illustrate this, the following list highlights the similarities between the two disciplines:

➤ Both focus on customer satisfaction.

➤ Both generate requirements from customer needs.

➤ Both focus on the project accomplishing its goals.

➤ Both emphasize prevention over inspection.

➤ Both emphasize accountability.

➤ Both emphasize activity verification.

➤ Both leverage lessons learned from the past.

➤ Both use processes within phases.

➤ Both advocate management responsibility.

➤ Both focus on keeping the project on schedule (to avoid the temptation to sacrifice quality steps in the interest of meeting target dates).

➤ Finally, the project manager has the ultimate responsibility for the *product* quality and *project management* quality for the project.

Quality Responsibility

Per PMI, the project manager has the ultimate responsibility for the product quality of the project. However, he or she shares the responsibility for quality with the sponsoring organization and other project team members. Refer to Table 5.6 for a summary of the project quality responsibilities.

Table 5.6 Summary of Project Quality Responsibilities

Stakeholder	Quality Responsibility	Notes
Senior management	Has the ultimate responsibility for quality in the *organization*	The entire organization has quality-related responsibilities.
Project manager	Has the ultimate responsibility for the *product* quality of the project	Establishes quality procedures for the project.
Individual team members	Responsible for self-inspection	Work should be verified and tested before submission.

Quality Costs

Another attribute of quality management that is consistently tested on the exam is costs. As reported in the PMBOK, 85% of the costs associated with quality management is the direct responsibility of management (both project and senior). For the exam, you need to understand that there are three types of quality costs—prevention, appraisal, and failure—and that costs are associated with conformance to requirements, as well as with nonconformance to requirements. Table 5.7 summarizes these quality cost categories.

Table 5.7 Summary of Project Quality Cost Categories			
Category	**Type**	**Examples**	**Impact on Project**
Conformance	Prevention costs and appraisal costs	Cost of quality management, quality training, studies, surveys and inspections	Increased productivity, increased cost effectiveness, and decreased cost risk
Nonconformance	Failure costs; internal and external	Rework, scrap, inventory costs, warranty costs, and goodwill costs	Increased costs, lower morale, lower customer satisfaction, and increased risk

The Differences Among Quality Planning, Quality Assurance, and Quality Control

To better understand the role of quality planning in the quality management process, it is important that you review how this step fits in with the other quality management processes. In addition, because many project managers have not had extensive experience with disciplined quality management, the distinctions between the processes are not always obvious. To bring clarity to these matters and to help prepare you for the exam, Table 5.8 details the differences among quality planning, quality assurance, and quality control.

Table 5.8 Key Differences Among Quality Planning, Quality Assurance, and Quality Control			
	Quality Planning	**Quality Assurance**	**Quality Control**
Process Group	Planning	Executing	Controlling
One Word Description	Plan	Implement	Measure

Table 5.8 Key Differences Among Quality Planning, Quality Assurance, and Quality Control *(continued)*			
	Quality Planning	**Quality Assurance**	**Quality Control**
Key Questions	What quality standards apply? How will we meet those standards?	How can we improve quality? Are the standards still appropriate?	Did we meet the specific standard? What are the measurements?
Key Output	Quality management plan	Quality audit results and quality improvements	Inspection results and corrective actions

Quality Pioneers

Frequently the exam will reference material outside the PMBOK for quality management–related questions. A common technique is for the exam not to ask specifically about this "outside" material but rather to mention this material as part of the project context with the assumption that you *know what the exam is talking about*. If this assumption is not true, you'll find yourself less than confident on those questions. To assist in this area, we summarize the key facts regarding the pioneers of the quality management field in Table 5.9. You can count on references to one or more of these guys on an exam question.

Table 5.9 Pioneers of Quality Management Summary		
Pioneer	**Best Known For**	**Notes**
Dr. W. Edwards Deming	The Plan-Act-Do-Check Cycle The Deming Cycle	The cycle is repeated within a phase, much like the project management processes.
Dr. Joseph Duran	The Duran Trilogy: quality improvement, quality planning, and quality control The Ten Steps to Quality Improvement The concept of "fitness for use"	Quality is the set of product features that meets the needs of the customers and provides the most satisfaction.
Philip Crosby	The Fourteen Steps to Quality Improvement The Four Absolutes Meeting all requirements Error prevention Zero defects Done right the first time	Focused on the consequences. Doing the right thing properly the first time is less costly.

Exam questions concerning quality management frequently reference material outside the PMBOK.

Risk Management Principles and the PMI Philosophy

To best understand how risk management affects project planning and to better prepare yourself for exam questions on risk management, you need to understand some key risk management principles and the PMI risk management philosophy. Specifically, you should know the following:

➤ The key PMI risk management principles

➤ The common gaps with implementing risk management

➤ The different types and the common sources of project risk

➤ Key risk management tools

➤ *Data precision* and other uncommon risk terms

➤ How to use decision tree analysis to determine the best alternative

➤ The types of risk response strategies

If you only read one chapter in the PMBOK, read the "Project Risk Management" chapter.

This area often has more differences between "real-life" experiences and the PMI methodology, and the exam questions concerning risk management are generally based on the PMBOK material.

Key PMI Risk Management Principles

The PMI risk management philosophy is an approach that remains consistent with PMI's core beliefs that project management is *proactive* and that the project manager should be and remain in control of the project at all times. PMI supports the belief that effective risk management can reduce project risks by up to 90%. Not only will effective risk management reduce project risks, but it will also lead to much better project decision making and to a higher degree of project success.

The key principles to remember about the PMI risk management approach include the following:

➤ The level, type, and visibility of risk management should be consistent with the level of risk and the importance the project has to the organization.

➤ The organization must be committed to risk management for the entire project lifecycle.

➤ Any factor or risk that could impact the project should be identified, quantified, and assessed for possible impacts to the project.

➤ For each identified risk, both the probability that it will occur and its possible impact to any project objective are determined

➤ The identification of risks is an iterative process. Risk identification is repeatedly performed throughout the project, not just at the beginning.

➤ The identification of risks is a continual process throughout the project.

➤ Quantitative analysis is generally reserved for high-probability, high-impact risks.

➤ Risk management will change the project plan during the Planning, Executing, and Controlling phases.

➤ The risk response plan is updated whenever a risk occurs.

➤ A risk can be good (opportunities) or bad (threats).

➤ Five of the six risk management processes are in the Planning process group.

➤ Risk management planning and risk response planning are two distinct activities.

 Project risks can be reduced by up to 90% if they are properly managed.

 A risk can be good or bad. Good risks are *opportunities*, and bad risks are *threats*.

The Common Gaps with Implementing Risk Management

The PMI risk management process is generally much more involved and disciplined than what most project managers use in "real-world" situations.

One of the best ways to learn the steps in the PMI risk management process is to review the common differences noted by many project managers, as detailed in Table 5.10.

Table 5.10 Summary of Common Risk Management Gaps		
Risk Management Process	**Slogan**	**Common Gaps**
11.1: Risk Management Planning	Plan the activity.	No risk management plan. Risk management plan equals risk response plan. Separate budget not allocated for risk management.
11.2: Risk Identification	Identify.	Performed only once and not proactively managed. Process is incomplete. Missing a review of key deliverables. Missing entire types/categories of risk. Only assessing critical path activities. The process does not use multiple tools/methods. Confusing issues with risks.
11.3: Risk Qualitative Analysis	Prioritize.	The organization has not established standard practices/tools. The probability of occurrence is not calculated for each risk. The impact of each risk is not determined. Risks are not prioritized. Data precision is not determined.
11.4: Risk Quantitative Analysis	Measure implications.	Not performed at all. Usage is not limited to high-priority risks. No experience with Monte Carlo simulation.
11.5: Risk Response Planning	Create a plan of attack.	Response strategies are not documented. No risk response plan. Response strategies are not appropriate for risk severity. The project plan is not updated to implement and monitor responses.
11.6: Risk Monitoring and Control	Keep it going.	The risk response plan is not maintained. Risk identification is not continued. The project plan is not updated to implement and monitor responses. Responses are not reevaluated.

The Common Sources of Project Risk

An activity that can help prepare you for the risk management exam questions is to pretend you have been asked to perform a risk assessment on a troubled project. Where would you start? What would you look for? In Table 5.11 we list some of the common sources of project risk to help you get in the proper mind set.

Table 5.11 Common Sources of Risk	
Risk Source	**Examples**
Project management	Improperly defined project deliverables
	Incomplete planning
	Improper procedures
	Poor leadership
	Poor communications
	Not clearly assigning tasks
	Lack of contingency plans
	Inadequate risk management
Organization	Changes to project objectives
	Lack of priorities
	Lack of project management "buy-in" and support
	Inadequate project funding
	Misallocation and mismanagement of resources
Stakeholders	All key stakeholders not identified
	Missing "buy-in" from a key stakeholder
	Stakeholder needs not completely identified
Project charter	Not approved by a single person
	Nature of objectives
Scope statement	Incomplete scope definition
	Inconsistent scope definition
WBS	Not reviewed and approved by stakeholders
	Missing tasks
	Lack of team understanding
	Missing project management activities
	External dependencies not identified and understood
Project schedule	Incomplete schedule
	Unrealistic schedule
	Resources not balanced
	Resources over-allocated
	Missing dependencies
	No contingency allowances (reserves)
	Not reviewed and approved by stakeholders

Table 5.11 Common Sources of Risk *(continued)*	
Risk Source	**Examples**
Cost baseline	Poorly developed cost estimates
Requirements	Unrealistic or aggressive performance standards
	Poorly defined requirements
	Incomplete requirements
Product design	Incomplete product description
	Unrecognized design errors
Team	Lack of skills
	Lack of commitment
	Personal issues
Technology	Missing technical data
	Use of unproven technology
Network diagram	Missing task dependencies
Assumptions	Not completely defined
Constraints	Not completely defined
External dependencies	Changing weather conditions
	Changes in legal and regulatory environment
	Approvals from governmental agencies

Key Risk Management Tools

One aspect of the risk management process described in the PMBOK that many people find difficult to grasp initially is the reference to *unfamiliar tools and techniques*. Table 5.12 summarizes many of these tools and techniques to assist your learning and review process.

Table 5.12 Summary of Risk Management Tools		
Risk Tool	**Description**	**Notes/Examples**
Risk impact matrix	Used to establish the impact score to assign to the risk.	Refer to Figure 11-2 in the PMBOK.
	Measures the level of impact against standard project objective areas.	Generally developed at the organizational level to improve the consistency of risk rankings.
Probability/impact matrix	Used to establish general High, Medium, and Low classifications for a risk factor.	Refer to Figure 11-3 in the PMBOK.
	Cross-references the probability score with the impact score.	Generally developed at the organizational level to improve the consistency of risk rankings.

Table 5.12	Summary of Risk Management Tools *(continued)*	
Risk Tool	**Description**	**Notes/Examples**
Overall risk ranking	A project-level score used to compare the relative risk of one project with another.	Output of Qualitative Risk Analysis
Decision tree analysis	Uses a decision tree to determine the best alternative path. Based on risk probabilities and cost/reward of each path step.	Refer to Figure 11-6 in the PMBOK.
Simulation	Captures risk probabilities at the detailed task level to determine potential impacts at the overall project level.	Refer to Figure 11-7 in the PMBOK. Monte Carlo is the most common simulation technique.

Data Precision and Other Uncommon Risk Terms

Another aspect of the PMI risk management process that many people find difficult to understand is the reference to uncommon terms or the use of terms in an unfamiliar context. Table 5.13 summarizes and explains many of these terms to assist in your learning and review process.

Table 5.13	Uncommon Risk Management Terms	
Risk Mgmt Term	**Description**	**Notes/Examples**
Data precision	Describes the extent to which the risk is known and understood	Accounts for the amount of available data, the reliability of that data, and the source of the data
Residual risks	Risks that remain after the risk response has been implemented	
Secondary risks	New risks that occur as a direct result of an implemented risk response	Should be managed like any other project risk
Risk trigger	An indication that a risk has occurred or is about to occur	Warning signs and risk symptoms
Sensitivity analysis	A technique used to determine which risks could have the greatest impact on the project	Focuses on the uncertainty level of the individual risk factor when all others are held constant

How to Use Decision Tree Analysis

Decision tree analysis, also known as *risk tree analysis* or *probability tree analysis*, is a technique that graphically represents the costs associated with decision alternatives and potential risks. For the exam, you will need to be able to do three things to answer decision tree analysis questions correctly:

➤ Draw a decision tree to represent the situation described.

➤ Calculate any missing outcome values or probabilities.

➤ Figure the expected monetary value (EMV) of each decision path.

The best way to quickly review this technique and to prepare for these types of exam questions is to walk through a typical decision tree scenario. Let's take a look at such a creature.

A Sample "Decision Tree" Problem

You are managing a strategic software development project, and are attempting to "sell" to the executive sponsor the benefit of adding 3 months onto the project timeline for thorough design and testing processes. You decide to use a decision tree to illustrate your case.

The values to the organization of good, fair, and poor market reactions to the new software application are $2M, $500K, and –$200K, respectively.

You determine the following probabilities of the market reactions based on the use of both thorough and rapid software engineering practices:

Market Reaction	Thorough	Rapid
Good	.4	.1
Fair	.5	.2
Poor	.1	.7

Here are the questions you'll need to answer:

➤ What is the expected monetary value of using *thorough* software engineering practices?

➤ What is the expected monetary value of using *rapid* software engineering practices?

➤ If the cost of an additional 3 months is $100K, which decision should be made?

To begin, let's draw the decision tree. The tree should have a path for each decision alternative, and the total probabilities of each uncertain outcome should equal 100%. Figure 5.2 shows what the decision tree for this problem should look like.

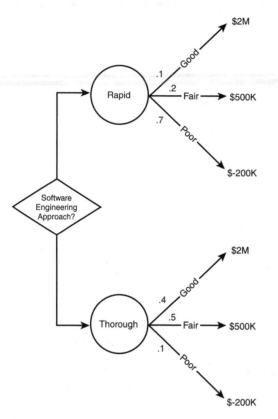

Figure 5.2 Decision tree example.

Now, let's calculate the value of each outcome:

Market Reaction	Value	Thorough	Outcome Value	Rapid	Outcome Value
Good	$2M	.4	$800K	.1	$200K
Fair	$500K	.5	$250K	.2	$50K
Poor	–$200K	.1	–$20K	.7	–$140K

Next, we can calculate the expected monetary value of each decision alternative:

Market Reaction	Value	Thorough		Rapid	
		%	Outcome Value	%	Outcome Value
Good	$2M	.4	$800K	.1	$200K
Fair	$500K	.5	$250K	.2	$50K
Poor	−$200K	.1	−$20K	.7	−$140K
EVM			**$1.03M**		**$110K**

So, let's take a look at the original questions:

➤ What is the expected monetary value of using thorough software engineering practices?

Answer: $1.03M

➤ What is the expected monetary value of using rapid software engineering practices?

Answer: $110K

➤ If the cost of an additional 3 months is $100K, which decision should be made?

Answer: The use of thorough software engineering practices. ($1.03M minus $100K equals $903K, which is greater than $110K.)

You will see at least one decision tree risk analysis question on the exam. You should be able to determine the expected monetary value (EMV) of each alternative path.

Types of Risk Response Strategies

Unless you have utilized a risk management methodology or have taken a risk management course, you may not have realized there are four recognized risk response strategies. Most people tend to think "mitigation" strategy when they think of how to manage a risk factor. For the exam, you will need to completely understand the four risk response strategies described in the PMBOK and be able to identify examples of each response type. Table 5.14 summarizes each response strategy and provides examples of each.

You should be able to identify examples of the four types of risk response strategies.

Table 5.14	Summary of Risk Response Strategies	
Risk Response	**Description**	**Examples/Notes**
Avoidance	Avoiding the risk. Changing the project plan to eliminate the risk. Changing the project plan to protect a project objective from the impact.	Reducing the scope to remove high-risk tasks. Adding resources or time. Adopting a proven approach rather than a new one. Removing a "problem" resource.
Acceptance	"Accepting" the consequences of the risk. The project plan is not changed to deal with the risk. A better response strategy cannot be identified.	Active acceptance. Contingency allowance (reserves). Contingency plan. Fallback plan. Passive acceptance. No action. Notifying management that there could be a major cost increase if this risk occurs.
Mitigation	Taking action to reduce the likelihood the risk will occur. Taking action to reduce the impact of the risk. Reducing the probability is always more effective than minimizing the consequences.	Adopting less complex approaches. Planning on more testing. Adding resources or time to the schedule. Assigning a team member to visit the seller's facilities frequently to learn about potential delivery problems as early as possible. Providing a less-experienced team member with additional training. Training the team on conflict-resolution techniques. Deciding to prototype a high-risk solution element.
Transference	Transferring ownership of the risk factor. Shifting the consequence of a risk and the ownership of the response to a third party. Does not eliminate the risk.	Outsourcing difficult work to a more experienced company. Fixed price contract. Contracts, insurance, warranties, guarantees, and so on. Used most often for financial risk exposure.

Procurement Management Principles and the PMI Philosophy

The last two remaining facilitating planning processes to review come from project procurement management. Those processes are procurement planning and solicitation planning. In order for you to best understand these processes, we need to review how they fit into the overall procurement management structure. In addition, to best prepare for exam questions on these steps, you need to understand some key procurement management principles and the PMI procurement management philosophy. Specifically, you should know the following:

➤ The overall procurement management process

➤ The key PMI procurement management principles

➤ The project management skills used in procurement management

➤ The key elements of the procurement management plan

➤ Key *contract* facts

➤ The purpose, risk, and advantages of each contract type

➤ Key factors in the "build versus buy" decision

➤ Advantages of centralized versus decentralized contracting organizations

If you only read two chapters in the PMBOK, read the "Project Risk Management" and the "Project Procurement Management" chapters.

Both subject areas often represent experience gaps for many professionals, and the exam questions concerning both risk and procurement management are generally based on the PMBOK material.

The Overall Procurement Management Process

Although this process depends largely on the industry you work in, many project managers lack considerable exposure to procurement management. Often, this is due to organizational structures and the common use of procurement specialists due to the legal and contractual nature of this activity. Given the limited experience with formal procurement procedures, this subject area can be more difficult for many professionals. In many industries, it is standard practice to use a "selection" methodology when a significant investment will be made to procure products or services. Our guess is that you've had some exposure to organized, planned selection activities. We'll use that experience in our review of the overall procurement management process to help you better understand how procurement planning and solicitation planning fit together. Table 5.15 provides this summary.

		Common Selection	
Step	**Slogan**	**Phase(s)**	**Key Deliverables**
12.1: Procurement Planning	Build or buy.	Plan Project startup	Build or buy decision, contract types, draft scope of work(s), and procurement management plan.
12.2: Solicitation Planning	Define Requirements.	Requirements definition	Requirements docu ment, RFI, and RFP.
12.3: Solicitation	Facilitate responses.	Vendor analysis	Seller proposals and RFP response ratings.
12.4: Source Selection	Pick a winner.	Evaluation Selection	Signed contracts.
12.5: Contract Administration	Oversee.	Not part of the "selection" phase Implementation phase	Reviews, reports, change requests, and payments. (See Chapter 7, "Project Control.")
12.6: Contract Closeout	Finish.	Not part of the "selection" phase Closeout phase	Formal acceptance. (See Chapter 8, "Project Closing.")

Table 5.15 Summary of Procurement Management Process

After procurement planning, the other steps are only performed if a "buy" decision is made.

Solicitation planning does not actually produce a project management *planning* output.

Key PMI Procurement Management Principles

Now that you have a better understanding of the overall procurement management process, let's review the key PMI procurement management principles you need to know to be better prepared for procurement-focused exam questions.

Here are the key principles to remember about the PMI procurement management approach:

➤ The procurement management process is based on the buyer's perspective.

➤ The procurement management process is based on a formal contractual process that's most common in the United States.

➤ A contract is a formal agreement.

➤ All requirements should be specifically stated in the contract.

➤ All contract requirements must be met.

➤ Changes must be in writing and formally controlled.

➤ Project communications dealing with procurement management should always be formal and written.

➤ Incentives should be used to align the seller's objectives with the buyer's.

 The PMI perspective of project procurement management is from the *buyer's* perspective.

The Project Management Skills Used in Procurement Management

To help you prepare for the procurement management–based questions on the exam, we'll review the type of skills and knowledge a project manager should possess to be effective at procurement management. The key project management skills needed for procurement management include the following:

➤ Proficient negotiating

➤ Effective verbal and written communications

➤ The ability to identify risks and develop appropriate responses

➤ Contract knowledge

➤ The ability to manage to a contract

➤ Understanding when and how to use legal assistance

The Key Elements of the Procurement Management Plan

To further improve your understanding of the scope and context of procurement management, let's review the key components of the procurement management plan, which include the following:

➤ The types of contracts to be used on the project

➤ The need for independent estimates in evaluation criteria

➤ The criteria for evaluating estimates

➤ The roles and responsibilities for the procurement department versus the project team

➤ The plans to manage the sellers

➤ The use of standard procurement forms

➤ The coordination of procurement with performance reporting and scheduling

 The procurement management plan is considered part of the project plan.

Key Contract Facts

We mentioned earlier that contract knowledge is a key project management skill for procurement management. So, what exactly do we mean by *contract knowledge*? The following list details what you need to understand concerning contract knowledge:

➤ The purpose of a contract

➤ Common contract components

➤ Contract classifications

➤ Common contract types

➤ The common contract clauses and conditions that have the most impact on the project

➤ The common source of contract conflict for a project manager

➤ The benefit of using incentives in a contract

➤ When a contract is legally enforceable

Although there is no substitution for actual experience, in-depth study, and formal training, here is a quick synopsis of key contract facts. These will improve your contract knowledge and assist your PMP exam preparations:

➤ A contract is a legally binding agreement.

➤ The common contract components include the following:

  ➤ Responsibilities of each party

  ➤ Identification of the person authorized to make changes

  ➤ The change/configuration management process

  ➤ Penalties for ending the contract

  ➤ Financial arrangements

➤ The two contract classifications are as follows:

  ➤ Completion

  ➤ Term

➤ The three common contract types are as follows:

  ➤ Cost reimbursable (CR)

  ➤ Fixed price (FP)

  ➤ Time and materials (T&M)

➤ The three variations of cost-reimbursable contracts are as follows:

  ➤ Cost Plus Fixed Fee (CPFF)

  ➤ Cost Plus Percent of Cost (CPPC)

  ➤ Cost Plus Incentive Fee

➤ The four conditions that make a contract legal are as follows:

  ➤ It must be voluntarily entered into.

  ➤ It must contain mutual considerations.

➤ It must be created for legal purposes.

➤ It must be signed by authorized parties.

➤ Generally, a natural conflict exists between the contract administrator and the project manager. There are three reasons for this:

  ➤ The contract administrator is the only one authorized to change the contract.

  ➤ The contract includes the statement of work (SOW).

  ➤ The project manager manages the SOW.

➤ The motivation to use incentives in a contract is to align the objectives of both parties.

The motivation behind incentives is to align the seller's objectives with the buyer's.

The Purpose, Risks, Advantages, and Disadvantages of Each Contract Type

In the previous section, we mentioned the three key contract types. For the exam, you will need to understand the following about each type:

➤ Its advantages and disadvantages

➤ What situation is best for its use

➤ Who owns the risk

➤ The required project management tasks

Table 5.16 summarizes these key facts about each contract type.

You should understand the contract types, as well as the purpose, advantages, disadvantages, and risk elements of each.

Table 5.16	Summary of Contract Types		
	T&M	**FP**	**CR**
Advantages	Quick to create. Brief duration. Good choice when hiring "people" to augment your staff.	Less work for buyer to manage. Seller has strong incentive to control costs. Buyer knows total project price. Companies are familiar with this type. Includes incentives.	Simpler scope of work. SOW is easier than an FP one. Lower cost than FP because the seller does not need to add as much for the risk. Includes incentives.
Disadvantages	Profit in every hour billed. Seller has no incentive to control costs. Good only for small projects. Requires most day-to-day oversight by the buyer.	Seller may underquote and make up profits with change orders. Seller may reduce work scope if it is losing money. More work for the buyer to write the SOW. Can be more costly than CR if the SOW is incomplete. Seller will increase the price to cover risk.	Must audit seller's invoices. More work for buyer to manage. Seller has only moderate incentive to control costs. Total project price is unknown.
Best to use when...	You need work to begin right away. You need to augment staff.	You know exactly what needs to be done. You don't have time to audit invoices.	You want to buy expertise in determining what needs to be done.
Who has the risk?	The buyer.	The seller (cost), or both the buyer and seller if not well defined.	The buyer.
Scope of work detail	Brief. Limited functional, performance, or design requirements.	Extremely complete. Seller needs to know *all* the work. "Do it."	Describes only performance or requirements. "How to do it."

Table 5.16	Summary of Contract Types *(continued)*		
	T&M	**FP**	**CR**
Project management tasks	Providing daily direction to seller. Striving for concrete deliverables. Close monitoring of project schedule. Looking for a situation to switch the contract type.	Establishing clear acceptance criteria of deliverables. Managing change requests. Monitoring project task dependencies. Managing risks. Monitoring project assumptions.	Auditing seller's costs. Monitoring seller work progress. Ensuring added resources add value to the project. Watching for shifting resources. Watching for unplanned seller charges. Rebudgeting.

Key Factors in a "Build Versus Buy" Decision

Because the "build versus buy" decision is a key component of procurement planning, let's review a few points about this process:

➤ There are three possible outcomes:

  ➤ Buy/procure *all* of the solution.

  ➤ Buy/procure *none* of the solution.

  ➤ Buy/procure *a part* of the solution.

➤ When evaluating a "buy" decision, make sure to factor the indirect costs of procurement management.

➤ Understand the key factors that influence this decision.

Table 5.17 summarizes the key reasons why an organization would "build" the solution itself or "buy" solution elements from outside the organization.

Table 5.17	Key "Build Versus Buy" Decision Factors
"Build" Reasons	**"Buy" Reasons**
Existing resources are idle (plant, workforce, and so on).	A need to decrease risk (cost, time, performance, scope).
More control is needed. Proprietary information or procedures are involved.	The required resources, skills, or expertise are not available. "In-house" processes are not efficient.

Advantages of Centralized Versus Decentralized Contracting Organizations

A frequent procurement-related question that has appeared on the exam involves how organizations structure their contracting or procurement functions. Overall, the general advantages of centralized versus distributed or decentralized functions of any type apply to contracting, too. A quick summary of the advantages is provided in Table 5.18.

Table 5.18 Advantages of Organizational Contracting Structures	
Centralized Advantages	**Decentralized Advantages**
Increased expertise	Easier access to resources
Better use of expertise and resources	Increased project commitment and loyalty
Standard company practices	
Career path for contracting/procurement staff	

Exam Prep Questions

Question 1

> The ultimate responsibility for identifying and managing project risks rests with the _____.
>
> ○ A. Project sponsor
> ○ B. Project manager
> ○ C. Manager and sponsor
> ○ D. Project team

Answer B is correct. Although the project manager shares this responsibility with all project stakeholders, the project manager has "ultimate" responsibility for this task. Therefore, answers A, C, and D are incorrect.

Question 2

> A decision to augment the staff with independent consultants is an example of the interaction between which two project planning processes?
>
> ○ A. Resource planning and risk response planning
> ○ B. Organizational planning and procurement planning
> ○ C. Risk identification and procurement planning
> ○ D. Staff acquisition and procurement planning

Answer D is correct. Staff acquisition deals with acquiring the proper human resources for the project, and procurement planning is the first step in acquiring these external resources. Answer A is incorrect because resource planning is not when the "source" of the human resources is determined, and there is no "procurement" process mentioned. Although answer B is very tempting, organizational planning deals with the relationships among the project team members. Therefore, answer B is incorrect. Answer C is somewhat tempting, because the decision to use external, independent consultants could be part of a risk response strategy, but this is not the best answer. Therefore, answer C is incorrect.

Question 3

The most important aspect of risk from a management point of view is _____.

○ A. causes

○ B. effects

○ C. costs

○ D. probability

Answer A is correct. Remember the importance PMI places on proactive management and preventing risks. Answers B and C are incorrect because they emphasizes minimizing the consequences rather then reducing the probability of risk occurrence. Answer D is tempting, but it's not correct either. Management is more concerned with understanding the causes than measuring the specific probability the risk may occur.

Question 4

To be effective, the risk management process should _____.

○ A. be applied throughout the project and at all levels of system decomposition and project organization

○ B. focus on risks that senior management finds most critical

○ C. include a meeting with key stakeholders to identify risks and develop response strategies

○ D. be applied primarily during concept and closeout and to some extent during planning and implementation

Answer A is correct. It emphasizes the need to apply risk management for the entire project lifecycle and in all areas. Although answer B is true, and something a project manager should understand, it is not the only risk type to focus on. Therefore, answer B is incorrect. Answer C is part of risk identification, but it's not the best answer. Therefore, answer C is incorrect. Answer D violates the concept that risks must be managed consistently throughout the project. Therefore, answer D is incorrect.

Question 5

> You are leading a project to select a new enterprise resource planning system, and you have just completed gathering your functional, technical, and vendor require-ments. Which procurement management process step are you engaged in?
>
> ○ A. Requirements definition
> ○ B. Solicitation planning
> ○ C. Source selection
> ○ D. Procurement planning

Answer B is correct. Solicitation planning is focused on defining require-ments for both the product and the vendor. Therefore, answers A, C, and D are incorrect.

Question 6

> The best place to find information about the immediacy and frequency commu-nication needs of the project stakeholders is the _____.
>
> ○ A. organizational chart
> ○ B. project plan
> ○ C. communications management plan
> ○ D. responsibility matrix

Answer C is correct. The communications management plan documents the "immediacy" and "frequency" communication needs of the project stake-holders. Answer A is incorrect because the organizational chart denotes reporting relationships among project team members. Although answer B is valid, because the communications management plan is part of the project plan, it is not the *best* answer. Therefore, answer B is incorrect. Answer D is incorrect because it defines the points and levels of responsibility by each project team member and does not address communication needs.

Question 7

The responsibilities of the project manager include all the following except which one?

- ○ A. Developing detailed project job descriptions
- ○ B. Negotiating with functional resource managers
- ○ C. Conducting kickoff meetings
- ○ D. Updating the project contracts

Answer D is correct. In most cases, the procurement manager or legal department has responsibility for updating project contracts. Therefore, answers A, B, and C are incorrect.

Question 8

The best time to use a time and materials (T&M) contract is when _____.

- ○ A. you know exactly what needs to be done
- ○ B. you have a good relationship with the vendor
- ○ C. you need help in determining what needs to be done
- ○ D. you need to enhance your existing project team with specialized skills

Answer D is correct. T&M contracts are best suited for resolving gaps in skills or expertise levels on projects. Answer A would be correct for fixed price contract arrangements. Therefore, answer A is incorrect. Answer C would be correct for cost-reimbursable contract arrangements. Therefore, answer C is incorrect.

Question 9

All the following statements are true regarding fixed fee contract arrangements except which one?

- ○ A. The seller shares the primary cost risk.
- ○ B. The buyer shares the cost risk if the scope is not well defined.
- ○ C. It requires the least amount of work for the buyer's project manager.
- ○ D. The detail of the scope of work is focused on how to do the work.

Answer D is correct. The detail regarding the scope of work is focused on "what to do," not "how to do" the work. Therefore, answers A, B, and C are incorrect.

Question 10

All the following are key factors to consider during procurement planning except which one?

- ○ A. Are there advantages to a CPFF contract for this scope of work?
- ○ B. Which vendors have given us the best deals in the past?
- ○ C. How will we manage the sellers?
- ○ D. What will be key criteria for evaluating the responses from the prospective sellers?

Answer B is correct. This would be a factor for *solicitation planning*. Instead, procurement planning is focused on the overall procurement process. Identifying the appropriate contract types, defining the process for managing the sellers, and establishing the key evaluation criteria are all part of that. Therefore, answers A, C, and D are incorrect.

Need to Know More?

 Project Management Institute, *PMBOK Guide 2000*.

 PMI Bookstore (www.pmibookstore.org)

Offers general project management references materials and other self-study texts.

 PMI eLearning Connection (www.pmi.org)

Offers virtual, online seminars and study programs.

 Commercial PMP prep courses

Search PMI (www.pmi.org) for a listing of PMI Registered Education Providers that offer PMP exam prep courses. Many of the courses are now offered "online" to better support your lifestyle.

 Other Internet resources

Search the Web for other PMP exam materials available. It is not uncommon to find free sample exam questions available from training companies and PMI user groups.

 Amazon.com (www.amazon.com)

Search for "project management" to find general project management references materials and other self-study texts.

Project Management Executing Processes

Terms you'll need to understand:

- ✓ Organizational policies
- ✓ Preventive action
- ✓ Corrective action
- ✓ Status review meetings
- ✓ Quality assurance
- ✓ Quality audits
- ✓ Quality improvement
- ✓ Collocation
- ✓ War room
- ✓ Solicitation
- ✓ Qualified seller lists
- ✓ Bidder conferences
- ✓ Source selection
- ✓ Weighting system
- ✓ Contract administration
- ✓ Change requests
- ✓ Contract change control system

Techniques and concepts you'll need to master:

- ✓ How a project plan is used to execute a project
- ✓ What performance-measurement baselines are key inputs to the project plan execution
- ✓ What project quality controls are and how they impact the success of a project
- ✓ How often a project plan should be monitored
- ✓ What a quality assurance audit is and how it can help your project
- ✓ How lessons are learned related to quality assurance
- ✓ What the difference is between quality planning and quality assurance
- ✓ How team development impacts the project performance
- ✓ Who can do team building and how it affects a project
- ✓ What the five conflict-resolution techniques are
- ✓ What Maslow's Hierarchy of Needs is
- ✓ What Herzberg's Hygiene Theory is
- ✓ What the difference is between the Expectancy Theory and the Achievement Theory
- ✓ What McGregor's X and Y Theories are
- ✓ What a war room is and how it can help a project
- ✓ What solicitation is used for
- ✓ When a contract between the buyer and seller should be developed
- ✓ What ensures the seller's performance meets the contractual requirements

The project management executing processes include the following sections from the PMBOK:

➤ 4.2: Project Plan Execution

➤ 8.2: Quality Assurance

➤ 9.3: Team Development

➤ 10.2: Information Distribution

➤ 12.3: Solicitation

➤ 12.4: Source Selection

➤ 12.5: Contract Administration

Topics such as team development, information distribution, source selection, and others all contribute to executing project management processes. This chapter will cover the processes associated with executing aspects of a project.

Because project execution requires the most resources and time, there is a heavy emphasis on the PMP exam on questions that pertain to this topic. Make sure you are familiar with the concepts and terms associated with project execution and how it is related to the stages of a project.

Project Plan Execution

The *project plan* is one of the key deliverables necessary to carry out the project, and the *plan execution* is the main process associated with it. The project plan is covered in Section 4.1.3.1 of the PMBOK, but it is important enough to reiterate in this chapter. The definition of a project plan according to PMI is "a formal, approved document used to manage project execution."

The organizational policies affect project plan execution by potentially putting limitations on execution options. For example, a company may state that it will only allow a certain group of people to work on the project. This may limit resource options for the plan execution. The organizational policies associated with the plan are constraints for the project and have a direct impact on the project plan execution.

You should be familiar with these variables for the PMP exam. Another one of the inputs to the project plan execution is *preventative actions*, which include any actions taken to reduce, eliminate, or transfer the risks of the project. These are frequently identified during the risk analysis of the project.

Many times, *corrective actions* are utilized by the project management team to bring the project back on track with the plan. Corrective actions are outputs of the control mechanisms and are a necessary ingredient to effectively manage the project.

Without corrective actions, a project has the potential to go astray, causing problems that can be difficult or impossible to resolve. Consequently, the project could be a major failure.

You must know that the project plan, supporting details, organizational policies, preventative actions, and corrective actions are all inputs to the project plan execution. Consequently, the outputs of the project plan execution are work results and change requests.

For the exam you will need to know the six sets of tools and techniques for project plan execution.

The execution processes, tools, and methodologies are emphasized on the test since they have numerous implications for effective project management. Therefore, almost 25% of the questions are related to the execution phase of the project. These items are summarized in the Table 6.1.

Table 6.1 Execution Tools and Techniques	
Project Execution Tool or Technique	**What Does This Mean?**
General management skills	These are the skills that are routinely used for various types of management, including leadership and communication.
Product skill and knowledge	This involves how well you know your product.
Work authorization system	Coordination and timing of work.
Status review meetings	Effective tool to keep everyone informed.
Project Management Information System (PMIS)	The interactive processes that occur during the evolution of a project.
Organizational procedures	Guidelines and rules of a company or organization.

The first set of tools is *general management skills*, which include universal skills, such as communication, negotiation, and leadership needed to work effectively with your team and stakeholders for fulfillment of your project objectives. General management skills are further explained in the Framework section of the PMBOK.

The second set of tools applicable to the plan execution is *product skill and knowledge*. A well-trained and developed project team is knowledgeable about the products it represents. Knowledge is power and is developed during the planning and staff-acquisition processes of the project.

Another procedure that is used to make sure the work is completed, in the proper sequence and time, is the *work authorization system*. This system is considered the third tool and is usually triggered by a written or verbal authorization to begin the work and encourages control of the work processes. The intent is to have only the work that is supposed to be done worked on. A big problem with some projects is keeping human resources focused on the tasks they need to do as opposed to the tasks they want to do.

Because project managers are constantly providing updates to team members and stakeholders, it is appropriate that the fourth set of tools for project plan execution is *status review meetings*. The official definition, according to the PMBOK, for status meetings is "regularly scheduled meetings held to exchange information about the project."

As you would expect, consistent and timely scheduling of status meetings is a necessity for the team and stakeholders to allow the continual flow of information among the participants. These meetings typically identify problem areas and encourage discussions related to action items, deliverables, deadlines, and expectations. You need to know the purposes and participants of the various meetings for the PMP exam.

You will likely see questions related to the *project management information system (PMIS)* and how it is used to gather, integrate, and distribute the process outputs. Therefore, the PMIS is considered the fifth tool for the project plan execution process. Although it sounds complex, the PMIS is actually utilized throughout the entire project as a means to communicate how the team is going to accomplish the project while also providing updates and direction as the team advances toward project completion.

 The PMIS is used throughout the entire project.

The sixth and final set of tools utilized for project plan execution is the *organizational procedures* frequently linked with organizational policies. These include informal and formal procedures that may be associated specifically with the organization facilitating the project or are mandated by the stakeholders.

Project Plan Execution Outputs

The PMBOK encapsulates two outputs from the project plan execution: work results and change requests. *Work results* are simply the byproducts of events and activities related to the project. These results are interpreted and evaluated to provide an input for the performance-reporting process. It is also important to realize that work results are generally deliverables that are outputs from the tasks associated with the project.

Change requests are frequently responses to scope creep, project alterations, or changes to project objectives and goals. The change request process is elaborated further in the Change Control Management section of the PMBOK; however, it is important to note that change requests generally have a direct influence on the work results.

 For the exam, you should be familiar with the two outputs to the project plan execution: work results and change requests. Change requests are very common and can significantly impact the direction of the project. Also, you should fully understand the change-control management process for the exam.

Quality Assurance

The PMBOK spends a significant amount of time on quality assurance, and you should be familiar with the impact of quality on a project, both for the exam and for your own projects. When looking at the triumvirate of project aspects—time, price, and scope—you should note that quality is at the center of the three elements and is paramount to the understanding of the PMBOK. *Quality assurance* involves following up to make sure everything is done correctly and fulfills the requirements of the project.

Quality assurance may be provided by the project team or any other stakeholder responsible for maintaining or assisting with the maintenance of quality for the project. Alternatively, an external organization may be utilized to provide quality assurance assistance.

The project manager is ultimately responsible for the quality of the project.

 The costs of nonconformance to quality standards tend to increase over time; therefore, the project manager should adhere to the quality conformance requirements of the project from the onset.

Two terms regarding quality assurance are *quality planning* and *quality control*. Quality control concerns auditing of the project to make sure it adheres to the guidelines that are required in the quality management plan. Quality planning involves the setting of these standards, which will later be controlled.

Another term you should know concerning quality is *probability*, which is the likelihood that an event or activity will occur. Probabilities are frequently assigned to risks and outcomes that can have a direct impact on quality.

Six Sigma is a combination of philosophy and tools involved with quality improvement. Many companies use Six Sigma methodologies for improvements, ranging from manufacturing to inventory management and design. Process engineering and business process improvement are also closely tied with the Six Sigma strategies.

 The charting of quality is frequently done to isolate variances that impact the quality of the project. You need to know that variances are abnormalities in the quality of a project.

Inputs to Quality Assurance

Quality assurance is an integral part of a project and the PMP exam. PMI constantly emphasizes that unless a high-quality project is provided, it does not matter if the project arrives on time and on budget. PMI's philosophy is that the project should be on time and on budget and that high-quality standards should be maintained through the use of control mechanisms. Projects of sloppy quality are not successful projects, according to the methodologies of PMI.

The three inputs to project quality assurance are the quality management plan, the results of quality control measurements, and the operational definitions. The quality management plan and the operational definitions are defined and detailed further in Chapter 8 of the PMBOK as outputs from quality planning.

The results of the quality control measurements are the reports, records, and test results concerning quality testing. These allow readers to perform analysis of the quality standards and see whether they are met. This includes analysis of variances and explanations for patterns of quality irregularity.

Tools and Techniques for Quality Assurance

Quality assurance and quality planning use the same set of tools and techniques. These are summarized in Table 6.2.

Table 6.2 Quality Assurance Tools and Techniques	
Technique	**Description**
Benefit/cost analysis	Answers the question: How much did the project cost monetarily in comparison to the benefits of the project?
Benchmarking	Comparing similar projects to determine feasibility.
Flowcharting	Using cause-and-effect diagrams to show where problems occur.
Design of experiments	An analytical technique that shows the elements that affect project outcomes.
Cost of quality	Asks the question: How much does it cost to maintain our quality standards?

 These techniques are described in Section 8.1.2 of the PMBOK, and you should know them for the exam.

Another tool for measuring and assuring quality in a project is *quality audits*. The reason for the audits is to document and explain the strengths and weaknesses associated with the project. The summary of the audit should include what was learned from the project for future reference to make other projects more successful.

The PMBOK refers to "lessons learned" in this section. You should understand that *lessons learned* describes the knowledge the team and stakeholders gain by actually performing the project. The experience and knowledge development gained from lessons learned is referenced throughout the PMBOK, and you must understand this concept for the test. These lessons are frequently used to set quality assurance standards for the current project or future projects.

Quality Assurance Outputs

The only output to quality assurance is *quality improvement*, which involves any actions taken to improve the quality of the project in response to quality deficiencies or irregularities. In order words, if quality is not up to the standards set, corrective action is taken to bring it back in line with the quality requirements for the project. Frequently, such corrective actions will require a change order request and will utilize the change control integration processes referenced in other sections of the PMBOK.

Team Development

Team development involves the development of competencies to increase the performance of the project. This could include individuals, stakeholders, or group development, which occurs as the project team progresses through the project. As the project evolves, so does the team. Consequently, the team members' knowledge and expertise also increase. Therefore, team development can have a significant positive impact on project performance.

The inputs to team development include project staff, the project plan, staffing management plan, performance reports, and external feedback. All these inputs are covered in other sections of the PMBOK but are listed in this section, too. You must understand these concepts and recognize these terms for the test. Because team development is a general management concept, the majority of workers in today's workplace have experienced it first-hand.

Team development occurs throughout the entire project.

Tools and Techniques for Team Development

Team development encompasses a multitude of activities and events that increase knowledge, team cohesiveness, effectiveness, and efficiency. According to the PMBOK, these include team-building activities, general management skills, reward and recognition systems, collocation, and training.

The effective management of a dual reporting relationship between the functional manager and the project manager is often a critical success factor for a project.

Team building involves activities that develop camaraderie in order to enhance team performance. They could include conflict-resolution exercises, interpersonal communication skills development, sponsor and stakeholder brainstorming activities, and other group activities that emphasize team development. A key way to create team building is through participation in planning activities. Team building can be provided by individuals or organizations that operate internally or externally to the organization.

You must be aware that if a project team does not work together, this will have a negative impact on the project. Positive team building plays an integral role in the success of a project.

General management skills are discussed in Chapter 2 of the PMBOK and are an important facet of the team development process. Reward and recognition systems are defined in the PMBOK as "formal management actions that promote or reinforce desired behavior." Managers frequently use rewards in the workplace (or should) and understand the importance of providing positive feedback to their teams and stakeholders. Providing linkage between positive outcomes and rewards is the key to reinforcing constructive performance on a project. The PMBOK also discusses how cultures can make a difference on a project and the implications of rewards based on different individuals.

The PMBOK states that traditional reward systems do not generally fulfill the requirements for a project. Therefore, specialized reward systems will need to be developed to provide ample coverage to the needs of the project and team.

Collocation occurs when team members are physically located within a close proximity of each other. The advantages of collocation include the following:

➤ Enhanced communication among team members

➤ An intense focus on the project

➤ Emphasis on successful project completion

Many times a *war room* is set up so that team members can be collocated in a single room. Here, they can focus on the project without external interference and complications. The main purpose of a war room is to provide collocation, with a heavy emphasis on the project, and to supply the appropriate tools, such as whiteboards, bulletin boards with schedules, and other project-related materials.

 You must know the definition of a *war room* for the exam. This is where the team is collocated in a specific area and utilizes the space to post reports, schedules, and other pertinent project-related information.

Although you will not likely be asked to provide the definition of *training* for the PMP exam, you could be provided examples concerning the effectiveness of training and the implications on the project and the fact that the cost of training is usually paid by the organization that performs the project management.

Outputs to Team Development

Team development has only two outputs—performance improvements and input for performance appraisals—but these can involve a lot of results. Performance improvements can originate from several sources, including individual skills or group behaviors, by increasing competency levels of individuals, teams, or both. The performance of individuals or teams is an element to the overall performance appraisal process for the team or team members.

Problem Solving

The role of the project manager and the team in problem solving includes identifying problems and determining the various options for resolution. After the options have been determined, the project manager must make a decision to choose the best alternative. The project manager should solicit feedback from the team members and encourage their buy-in so that everyone takes part in the process.

Problems generally get elevated to senior management when the team cannot resolve the matter itself by utilizing referent power and needs the assistance of a sponsor or upper management. This process involves the identification of the problem, the source or sources of the problem, and recommendations for resolution.

 You will encounter several situational questions on the exam dealing with problem-solving scenarios.

Types of Power

Team development frequently involves utilization of power for resolution of issues. This involves the use of some type of influence to make a decision and determine how to proceed with a project. Power and authority will be covered extensively on the PMP exam. You need to know the types of power and how they can be utilized in various situations. The types of power are detailed in Table 6.3.

Table 6.3	Formal and Informal Types of Influence
Type of Power	**Description**
Legitimate	Formal authority based on a title or position within an organization. For example, a CEO has power based on his or her position in the corporate hierarchy.
Coercive	Power that is based on intimidation or use of force to push one's issue or decision.
Reward	Power based on the ability to provide or withhold rewards to or from a participant. For example, a supervisor might say, "Do as I ask or you will not get a pay increase."
Expert	Power based on a person's knowledge or expertise.
Referent	"Borrowed" legitimate power that is transferred from a formal leader to a project manager. For example, a vice president might say, "Whenever the project manager speaks, it is just like me speaking."

 Referent power is one of the most important types of power for project managers because they generally have all the responsibility for a project without the authority to get everything done.

Conflict Resolution

Part of building and maintaining a project team is the ability to handle conflict and resolve conflict issues. You need to know and understand five conflict-resolution techniques for the exam. You will encounter situational questions on the exam that require you to determine which type of conflict-resolution technique is best suited for a particular situation, and whether it is a win-win, win-lose, or lose-lose conflict-resolution technique. In a win-win scenario, both parties win. In a win-lose situation, one party wins and the other party loses. In a lose-lose scenario, both parties lose. The five conflict-resolution techniques are detailed in Table 6.4.

Table 6.4   Conflict Resolution Methods

Conflict Resolution Technique	Description	Best Used When...
Confronting	Also known as *problem solving*. This involves approaching an issue straight on in order to discuss it for a win-win resolution.	The time for fact finding is available to develop the best solution. This is the preferred way to resolve conflict.
Compromising	Utilizing negotiation to come to a resolution by each party giving in. Neither party loses or wins.	Team involvement is encouraged and positive relationships need to be maintained. Neither side is 100% satisfied, but the conflict is generally resolved.
Withdrawal (avoidance)	Ignoring a conflict in an attempt that it will disappear or decrease over time. This approach does not provide resolution because it results in a lose-lose outcome.	The issue is very hot and someone refuses to discuss the matter any further.
Smoothing	This is just a temporary solution and not a final resolution. The conflict is downplayed for the time being until it reappears at a later time. This is a lose-lose resolution technique because the conflict is not resolved.	The conflict needs to be put on the "back burner" until someone brings it up again.
Forcing	Formal power is generally utilized in this situation to emphasize the resolution by saying "I have the authority to say this is the final decision." This is a win-lose conflict-resolution technique.	Time is short or the conflict cannot be resolved through problem-solving techniques.

Team Development Theories

You will need to know these theories for the PMP exam, which are detailed in the following subsections. Table 6.5 consolidates this information for you, summarizing the theories for the team development section.

Table 6.5 Theories Summary Table	
Theory Name	**Description**
Maslow's Hierarchy of Needs	The pyramid of hierarchical needs, from basic physical needs to self-actualization.
Fredrick Herzberg's Hygiene Theory	Asserts that people are motivated by hygiene factors that deal with the work and satisfaction people get by performing the actual functions of the job. This includes the ability to learn new skills and get promoted, among other attributes.
Expectancy Theory	Asserts that people are motivated in their work with the expectation of being rewarded.
Achievement Theory	Asserts that people are motivated by power, affiliation, or achievement.
McGregor's X Theory	Theory X managers believe that people are mostly lazy and need close supervision.
McGregor's Y Theory	This Theory postulates that Y managers believe that people are mostly hard workers and do not need close supervision.
Contingency Theory	A combination of the Y Theory and the Hygiene Theory. It asserts that people strive to become competent and are motivated after the competency is developed.

Maslow's Hierarchy of Needs

The first theory is Abraham Maslow's Hierarchy of Needs. This hierarchy is seen as a pyramid with the first level, Physical Needs, at the base of the pyramid. The contents of the pyramid are described in Table 6.6.

This popular theory is included in the PMBOK team development area because it emphasizes how team members can strive to achieve their peak performance. After a person has risen to the highest levels of the hierarchy, this provides him or her with the ability to communicate effectively and provide results to difficult situations that require creativity in a team setting. The exam will likely have some questions associated with this well-known theory.

Table 6.6	Maslow's Hierarchy of Needs	
Level	Needs Title	Examples
First	Physical Needs	Food, water, clothing, shelter
Second	Safety and Security	Physical welfare and personal belongings
Third	Social Needs	Love, friendship, acceptance
Fourth	Self-Esteem	Self-respect and feelings of accomplishment
Fifth	Self-Actualization	The ultimate of self-potential

 You will likely see at least one or two questions concerning Maslow's Hierarchy of Needs on the PMP exam.

Herzberg's Hygiene Theory

Also know as the *Motivation-Hygiene Theory*, Herzberg's theory states that motivation is based on two factors: motivators and hygiene factors. Benefits, pay, and work conditions are examples of hygiene factors. Motivators are related to the challenge and satisfaction associated with actually performing one's job.

Motivators help provide job satisfaction and hygiene factors are job attributes that help prevent job dissatisfaction. The necessity to keep your team satisfied is an important part of maintaining good productivity levels and team development.

 Herzberg felt that pay was not a motivator and that hygiene factors only prevent job dissatisfaction. They do not motivate.

Motivating factors include your actual work and the satisfaction you get from doing the work. These involve learning new skills, getting promotions, and facing work-related challenges.

Expectancy Theory

The expectation of being rewarded is the driving motivation behind the Expectancy Theory. Therefore, there is a linkage between behavior and a positive outcome. This positive outcome is what motivates us to respond in a certain way.

The theory also involves a self-fulfilling prophecy aspect in regard to positive reinforcement. In other words, if you praise your team as high performers, they tend to become high performers. Conversely, if team members are repeatedly told that they are low performers, they tend to become low performers.

Achievement Theory

The need for power, affiliation, and achievement are the only three motivating factors for people, according to the Achievement Theory. Let's examine these factors further. The *power* of motivation includes the ability to influence others. *Affiliation* is a feeling of belonging to a team and involves developing relationships. *Achievement* is the feeling of satisfaction you receive from advancing in your career or completing a project.

According to the Achievement Theory, if a person is not motivated by any of these three factors, that person is not motivated in his or her job.

McGregor's X and Y Theories

These theories describe how different managers respond to their employees. The X Theory asserts that workers are generally lazy and need an autocratic type of manager to get their work completed; whereas, the Y Theory maintains that employees are generally hard workers and do not need constant supervision in order to complete their duties. Y Theory–type managers provide limited supervision and feel that most employees want to positively contribute to the organization.

X Theory managers and Y Theory managers are generally opposites of each other concerning how they view the motivation behind employee productivity.

Information Distribution

Project managers usually spend 70%—80% of their time communicating in one form or another. Information distribution must be "timely" and provide the "needed information." Both of these components are necessary for the message to be effective.

You must know that the inputs to information distribution include work results, the communications plan, and the project plan. The outputs include project records, project reports, and project presentations.

The work results (outcomes of project activities) and the project plan (document for project execution) are detailed in Chapter 4 of the PMBOK, and the communication management plan (the who, how, and when of project communicating) is described in Chapter 10.

The most common communication model, which you will need to know for the PMP exam, breaks down communication in terms of a sender, a receiver, and the message. The *sender* is the person providing the message, and the *receiver is* the intended recipient of the message. The message can be any of the following:

➤ Written

➤ Oral

➤ Nonverbal

➤ Internal

➤ External

➤ Formal

➤ Informal

➤ Transmitted vertically, up and down the organization

➤ Transmitted laterally, across the organization

Tools and Techniques Associated with Information Distribution

The tools and techniques for information distribution include communication skills, information retrieval systems, and information distribution methods. The PMBOK elaborates further concerning the responsibilities and methodologies associated with the senders and receivers of information. It specifically states that the sender must provide information that is clear and complete. In response, the receiver must reciprocate by indicating that he or she understands the information completely. This can be done by restating the information or paraphrasing it.

Communication Skills

Good communication skills can come in several forms, including speaking, listening, and writing. There is also a differentiation between internal communications, which involve communications with people in the project, such as other stakeholders and team members, and external communications, which occur outside of the project, including non-stakeholders or non–team members.

The PMBOK also discusses formal communication, which may include structured plans and reports, versus informal communication, which takes the form of memos, notes, or short correspondence. *Horizontal communication*, which extends across peers, is contrasted with *vertical communication*, which flows up and down through the organization. You need to know all the various types of communication for the exam.

 The communication types are an important part of the PMP exam.

Information Retrieval Systems

Information retrieval systems come in a multitude of forms. One of the more cutting-edge technologies is the use of a database system and an FTP site to allow participants to download and upload information 24 hours a day, 7 days a week by logging on through the Internet. This is frequently referred to as an *electronic project management office (EPMO)*. Another technique includes the use of a manual project notebook, which is a repository for all documents, communications, status reports, and other various documents associated with the project.

Information Distribution Techniques

The last tool and technique for information distribution involves methods for getting the information to people so they can stay updated. There's no limit to how information is provided to the team and other stakeholders. Some common methods include the following:

➤ Conference calls

➤ Email messages

➤ Reports

➤ Videoconferencing

Information distribution tools and techniques will likely be covered somewhere on the PMP exam because they are important aspects of any project.

Outputs from Information Distribution

Information distribution has only three project outputs, so they are relatively easy to remember: records, reports, and presentations. *Project records* is just another term for information and documents. Therefore, it includes any formal or informal documentation associated with the project. The PMBOK recommends that this information be kept in the project notebook.

The *project reports* include the team status reports, the deliverables, and the action item updates, which are formal documents associated with the project. These are different from records because they are strictly formal documents.

Project presentations involve a speaker or facilitator and the presentation of information in a formal or informal setting. These presentations comprise a key, frequent method for keeping everyone informed, and they encourage buy-in from the participants.

Project records are informal types of communication for the project. *Reports* are formal documents utilized for the project. *Presentations* may use one or both of these communication formats for providing information.

Project Procurement Management

Another important set of project management executing processes are those dealing with project procurement management. We reviewed key concepts for procurement planning and solicitation planning in Chapter 5, "Project Planning—Facilitating Processes." We will now review the important aspects of the executing processes of procurement management. The first procurement management executing process to review is solicitation.

Inputs to Solicitation

Solicitation has two inputs: procurement documents and qualified sellers lists. The *procurement documents* are the instruments used to request bids, proposals, or quotes from the potential sellers. Bids and quotes are used for selecting a proposal based on pricing. A proposal is used when skills, knowledge, and expertise are more important.

A *preferred vendor list* is an example of a qualified seller list because it provides information about positive past business relationships with vendors and provides individuals and other departments within the organization with a foundation of knowledge concerning suitable and legitimate vendors. This reduces search time for vendors and provides a network of previously successful relationships to continue rather than dealing with an unknown entity.

Without a qualified seller list, the team will be required to investigate the professionalism and legitimacy of a vendor before the proposal is accepted. Sources for these background checks can include the following:

➤ The Better Business Bureau

➤ The Chamber of Commerce

➤ Personal references

➤ Business references

➤ Industry benchmarking

➤ Internet rating systems

 For the exam, you should be aware of the various types of resources that are useful for verification of vendor business transactions. This includes professional references and ratings.

Tools and Techniques for Solicitation

Solicitation has two tools and techniques: bidder conferences and advertising. Bidder conferences can also be referred to as *pre-bid conferences*, *vendor conferences*, and *contractor conferences*.

 There are several terms for bidder conferences, including *pre-bid conferences*, *vendor conferences*, and *contractor conferences*. You should be aware of all these terms because they may be used interchangeably on the exam.

Bidder conferences are meetings that are held with potential vendors prior to the proposal-development phase. This activity allows the vendors to ask questions and be aware of all the requirements for the proposal development and to incorporate them into the pricing. Advertising is used by the customer to expand its vendor selection pool by soliciting potential vendors to submit bids or proposals.

The important negotiation principles involve clarification and mutual agreement on the requirements and contract structure prior to the signing of the contract. Consequently, the final contract should include all agreements discussed during the negotiations. At a minimum, these agreement should include the following:

➤ Price

➤ Applicable terms and laws

➤ Technical and business management approaches

➤ Contract financing

➤ Responsibilities and levels of authority

Solicitation Outputs

There is only one output to the solicitation process: proposals. Although almost everyone is familiar with proposals, the definition according to PMI is "seller-prepared documents that describe the seller's ability and willingness to provide the requested products."

You must know that the inputs of the solicitation process are procurement documents and qualified seller lists and that the output is proposals.

Source Selection

After the proposals and bids have been submitted by the vendors, the next step in the process is to select a vendor that can fulfill the needs of the project. This process is known as *source selection*. Several determining factors are associated with source selection, including pricing and technical aspects. The process frequently involves the use of a weighting system to determine the best vendors based on numerous criteria.

A weighting system is a multiple-step process and initially involves the identification of several attributes, such as the following:

➤ Pricing

➤ Availability

➤ Quality

➤ Shipping time

➤ Previous history with the company

➤ Other relevant aspects of the product or service

After these attributes have been identified, a weight is assigned to each category based on the importance of that attribute.

> The weighting system is a tool used to eliminate or reduce bias by quantifying the attributes of the vendors.

For example, if pricing is a very important issue, you might give that aspect a weight of 5. If shipping time is not very important, you might give that aspect a weight of 1 or 2. You then multiply the weight by the rating of each category to calculate a total for that attribute. You would then prepare a matrix for all the attributes, and total each category based on the vendor's ability to fulfill that attribute's requirement (see Table 6.7 for an example).

After each of the vendors is rated, all the attribute ratings are totaled to provide a summary of the vendors. Then they are ranked to determine the best source selection. This process may be repeated several times as new variables are identified, vendors are added, or priorities change. This process allows the customer to quantify qualitative aspects of the vendors to minimize bias.

Table 6.7 Vendor Weighting Analysis			
Attribute/Weight	Vendor #1	Vendor #2	Vendor #3
Lowest price (5)		5	
Overnight shipping (10)	10		10
24/7 customer service (8)	8	8	8
90-days-same-as-cash billing (8)		8	8
Total	18	21	26

In this case, vendor #3 has the highest weight (26) based on these criteria, although vendor #2 has the lowest cost. Vendor #1 has the lowest weighting.

You need to understand the source-selection weighting process concepts for ' PMP exam.

Inputs to Source Selection

The source-selection process has three inputs: proposals, evaluation criteria, and organizational policies. Proposals were covered in the previous section. *Evaluation criteria* are the attributes analyzed and rated during the source-selection process. *Organizational policies* can have a major impact on the source-selection process. These formal policies frequently involve constraints to which the vendors must comply in order to be part of the proposal-submission and source-selection processes.

Tools and Techniques for Source Selection

The four tools and techniques for sources selection include contract negotiation, a weighting system, a screening system, and independent estimates.

According to the PMBOK, *contract negotiation* involves "clarification and mutual agreement of the structure and requirements of the contract prior to the signing of the contract." In other words, everyone has to understand and agree to the contract; otherwise, the contract is not valid. As expected, many variables are involved in the negotiation process and frequently involve some negotiation by both parties before the final agreement is reached.

A *screening system* sets minimum standards that must be met in order for the vendor to proceed within the source-selection process. For example, the ability to accept a purchase order as a means of payment would be a constraint that is required of all vendors for submitting an initial proposal. If the vendor cannot fulfill the initial requirements, it should not continue through the process.

"Should cost" estimates is another term for *independent estimates*. These estimates are periodically prepared by the customer as a sanity check to the vendors' cost estimates. This allows benchmarking so that the customer can determine whether its needs are being correctly fulfilled and everyone has a full understanding of the project details. This could include every aspect of the project.

Outputs from Source Selection

The only output from the source-selection process is the actual contract, which can be subject to remedy in the courts, if necessary. Besides *contract*, it may also be called an *agreement, subcontract, purchase order*, or *memorandum of understanding*. If an organization has any policies concerning who can sign these contracts, this is called *delegation of procurement authority*.

Approved and signed contracts are generally critical success factors to a large project.

A scope statement defines what the project is trying to accomplish. It outlines the requirements and constraints while providing milestones and objectives. The difference between a contract and a scope statement lies in the legal ramifications. A scope statement is not legally binding unless it is incorporated into a contract. Contracts are legally binding and subject to all the aspects associated with legal instruments, including penalties and liabilities.

Incentives are frequently used in contracts to keep the project to the originally agreed baseline. If a project manager is financially rewarded for maintaining the timeline or penalized for exceeding it, this gives him or her a lot of incentive to properly manage the project within the original constraints agreed upon in the contract.

The project manager should ensure that the contract has the provisions to address project risks.

Contract Administration

The monitoring of the seller's performance and making sure that they fulfill their requirements is known as contract administration. For the test you should realize that contracts are legally binding and therefore there may be legal issues associated with monitoring them. The processes that are applicable to contract administration include project plan execution, performance planning, quality control and change control.

Inputs to Contract Administration

For the test, you will need to know that contracts, work results, change requests, and seller invoices are inputs to contract administration. You will likely see some questions concerning changes that are contested that can result in claims, disputes or appeals.

The decision to terminate a contract because the seller's work is unsatisfactory would be handled as a change request.

Tools and Techniques for Contract Administration

Like other aspects of project management, there are several types of change control systems and contract administration is no different. The three tools and techniques for contract administration include a *payment system, performance reporting* and a *contract change control system*.

As expected, the contract change control system describes how changes to the contract are to be made. Performance reporting is a way that the seller is kept in line with the requirements of the contract by keeping everyone informed. The payment system simply describes how the vendor gets paid.

The term "fait accompli" has been seen on the PMP test. This term describes when one party tries to convince another that one or more of the contract terms are not important in order to distract them or coerce them into the contract.

Outputs from Contract Administration

Contract administration has three outputs: correspondence, contract changes, and payment requests. The easiest way to remember these outputs is to acknowledge that all contracts have some type of written communication that originates from them. This correspondence is necessary for any type of changes to occur. After everyone is satisfied with the results, payment is made to complete the transaction.

A contract can be terminated if the seller's work is unsatisfactory or violates the terms. However, this may be debated through the legal system. Contested changes are called *claims, disputes,* or *appeals.*

Contract closeout will be discussed later in this book, but it is important to note that a completed contract is different from a closed contract, because a closed contract may not be fully completed in regard to the requirements of the contract. Early termination of a contract is an example of contract closeout.

The contract can only be changed by utilizing change-control processes to make sure that any changes are properly approved and that everyone is aware of the changes. This type of contract affects the project manager because it may involve review by some public or government agencies.

The contract terms and conditions impact the project manager because they are the constraints in which the project manager must fulfill the project requirements. Changes in the contract and undefined work are handled through change requests, and the change-control management process is utilized to review and implement these changes.

Exam Prep Questions

Question 1

Which of the following statements does not describe what a project plan is?

○ A. Formal and approved

○ B. A document or collection of documents that change over time

○ C. Only used by the project manager to execute the project

○ D. A method for identifying milestones

Answer C is correct. Project plans are used by the entire project team and help to communicate the tasks needed during that timeframe. Project plans are distributed to the project staff according to the communications plan. Further a project plan is formal and approved. Answers A, B, and D are all true statements and are therefore incorrect answers.

Question 2

Which of the following is not true during project execution?

○ A. The majority of the budget is spent.

○ B. The product of the project is actually produced.

○ C. Project performance against the plan is monitored.

○ D. Decisions on when and with whom to communicate are made.

Answer D is correct. Although certain ad hoc communications and information requests are handled during project execution, decisions on how, when, and with whom to communicate are defined in the planning stage in a Communications plan. Answers A, B, and C are all true of the project execution phase and are therefore incorrect answers.

Question 3

How often should a project plan be monitored?

○ A. Weekly.

○ B. Monthly.

○ C. Never. Once the plan is done, the team knows what to do and can do it.

○ D. Continuously.

Answer D is correct. Answers A and B are incorrect because although some projects may have tasks that can be monitored monthly or weekly and depend on the project itself, the *best* answer per the PMBOK is *continuously*, so that a project manager can ensure budget adherence and timeliness of the project. Answer C is incorrect because a project plan is a "living" document and as such is modified often to reflect change within the project.

Question 4

What is the difference between quality planning and quality assurance?

- O A. None. Prior to ISO 9000 they were considered the same thing.
- O B. Quality planning is where the tools and techniques of cost-benefit analysis, benchmarking, flowcharting, and design of experiments are used to determine how quality should be assessed. Quality assurance does not use these.
- O C. Quality assurance is the totality of characteristics of an entity that bear on its ability to satisfy stated or implied needs. Quality planning is planning those characteristics.
- O D. Quality planning focuses on identifying which quality standards to use, whereas quality assurance focuses on planned and systematic activities to ensure the standards.

Answer D is correct. Answer A is a true statement, but it isn't the *best* answer and is therefore incorrect. Answer B is incorrect because both quality planning and quality assurance use the same tools and techniques. Answer C is the definition of *quality*, not quality planning or quality assurance, and is therefore incorrect.

Question 5

What is the best project team environment?

- O A. A team in the same room that reports directly and only to the project manager
- O B. A team that meets frequently face to face but has other functional duties
- O C. A loosely connected group of functional experts who help direct the project
- O D. A team that resides offsite

Answer A is correct. Collocation and a projectized environment is the best situation for a project team. Although answer B can work effectively, team members with other functional duties will have conflicts of priorities. Therefore, answer B is incorrect. Answer C is the definition of subject matter experts. Therefore, answer C is incorrect. Answer D is tricky because off-site team building is often encouraged in team literature. However, it's not the *best* answer and is therefore incorrect.

Question 6

> Which of the following is a good team-building technique?
> - A. Involving the team in the planning process
> - B. Having a barbeque
> - C. Doing a "lessons learned" session
> - D. Letting individual team members operate independently

Answer A is correct. Involving the team in the planning of the project helps all members develop a better understanding of the project and helps to provide buy-in. Having a barbeque can be a team-building technique, but it isn't the *best* one. Therefore, answer B is incorrect. "Lessons learned" sessions are typically done at the end of phases or the end of a project. These can become team-building events by airing difficulties, but they are intended to correct project direction, not to build the team. Therefore, answer C is incorrect. Allowing individuals to operate independently is a good management technique in general; however, without supervision or project control, it could actually cause team problems. Therefore, answer D is incorrect.

Question 7

> What is the key purpose of distributing project information?
> - A. To create an archive of project information that can be used by other projects
> - B. To inform stakeholders in a timely manner of work results
> - C. To make sure the project continues to have sponsorship
> - D. To resolve conflicts between project members

Answer B is correct. Project information is important so that stakeholders and sponsors understand how well a project is meeting its goals. For sponsors, a project behind schedule may call for some type of intervention. Answer A is incorrect because, although it is important to create a project archive, it is not the purpose of distributing the information. Answer C is incorrect because project sponsorship should be resolved prior to project initiation. Occasionally, a project is cancelled because it no longer meets the needs of the sponsors or company, but distributing the project information is not intended to keep sponsorship of the project. Answer D is incorrect because conflicts need to be managed by the project manager and resolved apart from reporting on the project.

Question 8

What is solicitation used for?

○ A. Gathering requirements for a product purchase

○ B. Determining what vendors to buy from

○ C. Letting vendors know you have a need

○ D. Negotiating pricing

Answer C is correct. The solicitation process is the means by which you let vendors know what your requirements are. They then respond with a proposal on how they can meet your requirements. Answer A is incorrect because requirement gathering is done in the procurement planning stage. Answer B is incorrect because the actual determination of a vendor happens in the source selection phase. Answer D is incorrect because price negotiation happens in the source selection phase as well.

Question 9

A contract between buyer and seller is created at what point in the procurement process?

○ A. In procurement planning, based on the policies and procedures of the company

○ B. During solicitation, when a proposal from a vendor is received

○ C. During contract administration, when the vendor is actually producing the work requested

○ D. During source selection, based on evaluation criteria, procurement policies, and supplier history

Answer D is correct. Once the source selection is made, the end result is a contract to perform the requested activities. Answer A is partially correct because the corporate procurement policies do affect a contract, but that is not when it is created. Answer B is incorrect because the receipt of a proposal does not make a legal contract. Answer C is incorrect because a contract must be signed before work can be done. However, in certain circumstances, the actual act of work being produced can be considered a default contract. Project managers need to avoid this.

Question 10

What is the purpose of contract administration?

○ A. To manage the interfaces among various providers

○ B. To ensure the seller's performance meets the contractual requirements

○ C. To avoid change requests

○ D. To provide payment to the vendor

Answer B is correct. Contract administration involves all the execution phase tasks, including monitoring of the project plan, performance reporting, and quality assurance. Answer A is incorrect because, although managing the interaction between various providers is a key element, it is not the purpose of contract administration. Answer C is incorrect because, although change requests are a normal part of most projects, avoiding them because of contractual concerns would be inappropriate. Change requests should be managed according to the change-control process. Answer D is incorrect because payment to the provider is part of contract administration, not the purpose of it.

Need to Know More?

 Adams, John. *Principles of Project Management.* Project Management Institute Press, 1997. ISBN 1880410303.

 Kerzner, Harold. *Project Management.* Wiley, 2003. ISBN 0471225770.

 Verma, Vijay. *Organizing Projects for Success.* Project Management Institute Press, 1995. ISBN 1880410400.

Project Control

Terms you'll need to understand:

- ✓ Change control
- ✓ Integrated change control
- ✓ Control system
- ✓ Scope verification
- ✓ Gold plating
- ✓ Baselining
- ✓ Corrective action
- ✓ Lessons learned
- ✓ Feedback loop
- ✓ Variance
- ✓ Earned Value Management
- ✓ Risk trigger
- ✓ Budget at completion
- ✓ Estimate at completion
- ✓ Earned value
- ✓ Planned value
- ✓ Actual costs
- ✓ Change control board
- ✓ Configuration management
- ✓ Quality audit
- ✓ Pareto chart
- ✓ Risk response
- ✓ Workaround

Techniques and concepts you'll need to master:

- ✓ What factors cause change
- ✓ What the purpose of performance reporting is
- ✓ How change is approved
- ✓ What scope control and the WBS are
- ✓ What the difference between scope verification and quality control is
- ✓ What the quality control tools are
- ✓ How risk response control fits within the overall risk management process
- ✓ What "workarounds" are and when they should be used

Project Control Planning is the fourth project management process to execute in the project lifecycle. Project Control Planning comprises eight of the 39 PMBOK processes. Although the exam questions regarding the Controlling processes tend to be straightforward, and many project managers have considerable experience performing these activities, this is a subject area not to be taken lightly. The techniques and terms utilized in real-life project controls—risk management and scope change—are not always consistent with PMI's methodology and are used to varying degrees within projects. To streamline your exam preparations, we will focus on the "gotta-know" concepts and terms that are important to PMI and the "common" gaps between exam questions related to the core Project Management processes.

Project Control Defined

Controlling processes are found in all the project management areas to some varying degree. Project control is concerned with preventative measures, such as identifying and understanding variance, plus responding to trends, patterns, and changes in order to minimize the impact on the project.

PMI divides controlling processes into two categories—core and facilitating—as it does with all the other process areas. The Controlling processes are listed here:

➤ **Core Controlling processes**—These include performance reporting and integrated change control.

➤ **Facilitating Controlling processes**—These include scope verification, scope change control, schedule control, quality control, and risk monitoring and control.

Core Controlling Processes

The core Controlling processes include reporting the project work results and performance to the appropriate stakeholders and decision makers. This is a vital communicative act so that all involved can keep abreast of where the project stands and are able to make decisions on future needs and tasks the project will require.

Also, the core processes include integrated change controls. These controls are concerned with influencing the factors that cause change, determining that a change has occurred, and managing the change across the different areas, such as scope, time, and quality according to their respective change management plans.

The quantitative analysis of the control systems within each knowledge area is concerned with measuring and accessing the magnitude of variation to determine whether corrective action needs to take place.

Project changes should be expected, planned, and well managed.

Facilitating Processes

Facilitating processes are the activities within project control that monitor and measure the progress of project tasks. The purpose for this measurement is to detect variances, determine whether corrective action needs to take place, and act accordingly.

Variance is something that is contrary to the usual guidelines or rules. It's the irregularity sometimes associated with project duration. For example, let's say the amount of time it usually takes to build a new house is 8 days, but a recent home took 10 days to build. In this case, the variance would be 2 days. Variance is a comparison of the estimated (or scheduled) amount of time it normally takes to complete a certain activity and the *actual* amount of time it took to complete the activity.

Controlling activities help to ensure a project is on-time, on budget, of the appropriate quality, and meets the project objectives.

Therefore, project control consists of monitoring, measuring work results, and detecting change in a variety of project areas, including cost, schedule, quality, and risk.

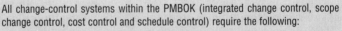

All change-control systems within the PMBOK (integrated change control, scope change control, cost control and schedule control) require the following:

➤ Influencing the factors that cause change

➤ Detecting that a change has occurred

➤ Obtaining agreement on a change activity

➤ Managing the change

Factors That Cause Change

Change within a project can occur from a variety of sources. PMI specifically lists the following:

➤ External events

➤ Errors and omissions

External Events That Cause Change

These events could include any event external to the project that causes a change in the direction or scope of the project. Examples include changes in corporate strategy, changes in project scope, and any new law that requires a product to conform to a specification not targeted in the project. It could also include something as dramatic as the World Trade Center tragedy.

Errors and Omissions That Cause Change

Errors committed and omissions of critical items are the most likely reasons for change in the real world, although PMI strongly encourages excellent planning to prevent errors and omissions. However, they do occur and some-times are only known when a project plan is being further elaborated in a technical design. Occasionally, a business requirement is missed and needs to be added in.

Value-Adding Change Versus Gold Plating

A *value-added change* is a change that adds to the return on investment (ROI) of a project. This can be a simple additional feature or a scope change. This involves payback analysis and the determination of costs in order to make informed decisions. For example, a customer might decide to choose high-speed Internet service over conventional dial-up service in order to enhance productivity and profitability. Ultimately this information could be quanti-fied to determine the effectiveness of the change.

Gold plating, on the other hand, is the addition of features that are not with-in the scope of the project and are not requested. They do not add value. Although they might be technically good ideas, they often add unexpected costs and risk to a project. PMI discourages gold plating because it involves activities outside the scope of the project.

An example of gold plating would be providing additional reports or infor-mation not originally part of the scope of the project. These types of changes should be monitored and controlled so they do not add to the cost of the project.

The Purpose of Performance Reporting

Performance reporting is the key, official method for communicating to your stakeholders about how project resources are being used and how project objectives are being met. Reporting methods, such as email, formal reports, and face-to-face meetings, and their frequency are outlined in the communications plan and communications matrix.

Performance reporting is performed against the project baseline, which is the original set of schedule dates, budget amounts, expected work, scope, and quality targets developed in the project planning phase. Project baselines are evaluated against actual performance of the project as the project is executed.

 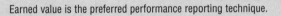
Earned value is the preferred performance reporting technique.

According to PMI, there are three types of reporting:

➤ **Status reporting**—Where is the project now? Is the budget over or under? Is the schedule over or under?

➤ **Progress reporting**—What has the team accomplished? What percentage of the project is completed and what percentage is still in progress?

➤ **Forecasting**—Involves predicting future progress, generally in terms of budget and schedule, an estimate at completion, and end date, respectively.

Most often, all three are combined in the real world as a weekly status report. Performance reporting will highlight the basic measurements of a project and will provide an analysis of cause, as well as a recommendation for action if necessary.

The purpose of performance reporting is to detect and raise issues early or to allow preventative measures to be taken by upper management. If a project is late or over budget, the project manager is responsible for analyzing and recommending action.

These recommendations can lead to change requests, corrective actions, or both.

Approving Change in Projects

The change-control system guides how changes may be approved. Generally there are guidelines based on the size and impact of the changes.

For all major changes that could alter the scope, timing, cost, or quality of the product or project, the change-control board needs to be contacted. The *change-control board* is composed of individuals from various areas of the company who join together to review and make decisions concerning scope changes to the project. This allows for objectivity concerning resources, scheduling, and financial decisions. The members of this board will make a recommendation and determine the tradeoffs involved in the triple constraints—*cost*, *scope*, and *time*—for approving the change. In a project, all these areas have an impact on one other. For example, if scope is enlarged, time and cost generally increase as well.

Any emergency changes made without approval of the change-control board need to go through the change-control processes to document the incidents and to provide approval after the occurrence.

Who can authorize change is often a question on the exam.

Once the change is approved or the corrective action is taken, more project reporting is necessary to determine whether the action was successful in bringing the project back on track.

Feedback Loop

The results of the monitoring and change detection are reported to stakeholders and other management figures. These results give critical insight into the progress of the project through status reports or informal communications. As change or variance occurs, the feedback cycle needs to take place. This includes determining whether the variance or change is significant and whether corrective action needs to take place. PMI also includes in this feedback loop the necessity to create *lessons learned*, which involves documenting any knowledge developed due to participation in and experience with the actual project.

Lessons learned are a key part of the Project Management Information System (PMIS) and are considered important resources for planning and future projects. Maintaining lessons learned during project control is important.

Providing Corrective Action

The purpose of corrective action is to bring a schedule or project back on track. This can involve root-cause analysis and schedule or budget adjustments as well as expediting.

Once a change or need for corrective action is determined, the project manager must revisit and perform the following planning tasks again:

➤ **Planning**—Project plans need to be revisited to determine how the corrective action or change will fit into the project.

➤ **Budgeting**—Many changes or corrective actions involve tradeoffs between cost, scope, and time.

➤ **Integrated change control**—Scope, quality, time, and cost all need to be reviewed in light of the change or corrective action. Each area's plans and change-control systems need to be updated with the changes and progress to determine the impact.

Re-baselining may be appropriate if a change is significant enough. It involves adjusting your performance measurement to the new tasks defined in the project plan. Without re-baselining, a project would appear to be significantly out of control, even though a change had been approved. Re-baselining allows management to see the progress of the project accurately after the change decision. However, re-baselining is considered a "last resort" because project historical data may be lost.

Scope Control and the WBS

Scope control involves managing any changes to the agreed-upon scope of the project as defined by the Work Breakdown Structure (WBS). Scope changes are "fed back" through the planning processes, documents are updated, and performance measurements are adjusted accordingly. Scope control involves the acknowledgement of a scope change and advising stakeholders of the impact on the timeline and costs for the project. If a customer wants a barn built, but later adds windows and doors to the project after everyone has agreed to the previous requirements, the new windows and doors will likely impact the cost and timeline.

PMI separates the control areas of scope, schedule, cost, quality, and Risk control because their techniques tend to differ. Scope change, however, most closely follows the work to be accomplished as defined by the WBS. Therefore, any change to the work is a change to the scope.

The Difference Between Scope Verification and Quality Control

Scope verification differs from quality control in that scope verification ensures that the work product is formally accepted, whereas quality assurance ensures the correctness of the work product. These two concepts are very close to one another and are easily confused.

Scope verification is when the customer verifies that the product fulfills the requirements of the project. Quality assurance verifies that the product does what it's supposed to do and that it's fit for use.

An example of a product might be a baby stroller. A couple looks at several strollers and decides that one does, in fact, have the advertised features they are looking for. This qualifies as scope verification. The quality control angle for the same product would be the company performing measurements and tests to ensure the performance is correct. Although the couple buying the stroller might perform tests to see whether it is what they want, they will not be determining whether the wheels will fall off, except in a very cursory way.

Scope verification measurements may be taken at the end of project phases. Stakeholders may review the work results and deliverables to accept continuation of the project into the next phase. This is sometimes known as *gate keeping*.

> **TIP** Out-of-scope extras add no value to the project and should be avoided.

Schedule Control

Schedule control focuses on monitoring and evaluating the schedule baseline. Any monitoring and evaluation that occurs with schedule control heavily involves detecting schedule variances, both positive and negative, on the project schedule. Determining the cause of the variance is important in the early correction of a schedule variance. Performance reporting on a project schedule involves reporting on which planned dates have been met and which have not.

Planned start and end dates are key to understanding the rudiments of schedule variance. However, just because a task does not start on time does not mean your project is at risk. Understanding slack, critical path, and subcritical tasks is important in order to see whether variances in specific tasks make a difference to the overall schedule.

Variance analysis, through the use of earned value methods, described later, is the key technique for project time management. Yet, when schedule updates occur, a change to the timing of the project needs to take place. Not all schedule updates require adjustments to other parts of the project plan. Also, be aware that a schedule revision will require approval because it could change the start or finish date of the project.

Cost Control

Cost control focuses on monitoring actual project costs against the planned costs for the project. It involves understanding the variances, ensuring changes are approved and accurately reflected in the cost baseline, and informing stakeholders of the results. Earned value, discussed in the next section, is also a key tool for cost control.

Using Earned Value Management

Earned Value Management is a good method for identifying schedule and cost variances. Table 7.1 summarizes the key elements of Earned Value Management.

Table 7.1 Elements of Earned Value Management	
Element	**Definition**
Planned value	Previously known as *budgeted cost of work scheduled* (BCWS). This involves an estimation of how much a project will cost before it occurs.
Earned value	Previously known as *budgeted cost of work performed* (BCWP). This is the actual physical work that is accomplished and includes an estimate of how much the work is valued at.

Table 7.1 Elements of Earned Value Management *(continued)*	
Element	**Definition**
Actual costs	Previously known as *actual cost of work performed* (ACWP). This calculation includes the total expenditures for the project.
Cost variance (CV)	The comparison between actual costs and budgeted costs. A negative number means you are over budget. BCWP − ACWP = CV
Schedule variance (SV)	The comparison between the actual project duration and the estimated duration. A negative number means you are behind schedule. BCWP − BCWS = SV
Cost Performance Index (CPI)	Used to calculate performance efficiency. Less than 1 means your project is costing you more than you planned. Greater than 1 means you are taking less money to do the project. BCWP / ACWP = CPI
Schedule Performance Index (SPI)	Used to calculate the efficiency level of the budgeted versus actual schedules. Less than 1 means you are behind schedule. Greater than 1 means you are ahead of schedule. BCWP / BCWS = SPI
Budget at completion (BAC)	This is the difference between the remaining budget and the work that has been completed. EAC = (AC + BAC) − EV VAC = BAC − EAC
Estimate at completion (EAC)	This calculation includes the actual project cost to date plus the expense of the remaining work. BAC / CPI = EAC
Estimate to complete (ETC)	This estimate includes the actual cost to date plus the estimated cost of work still left. EAC − ACWP = ETC

Earned value takes the planned value, or what you planned to do and how much that planned activity costs, and matches it against the actual costs, or what actually got done. These two metrics (measurements of value) provide a wealth of information about whether the project tasks are taking longer than they should (schedule variance, or SV), or whether they are actually requiring more work effort to complete (cost variance, or CV). The combination of the two provides you with the earned value. Budget at completion (BAC) and estimate at completion (EAC) are both metrics that help you determine whether your project will be on budget or whether you will need more money and time to complete the project. These metrics are used in performance reporting to help identify whether corrective action needs to take place.

Many of the project management software tools, such as Microsoft Project, include these calculations for you as features.

The formulas are key to actual performance reporting, and some questions on the exam require you to know the differences between them.

Be familiar with the schedule variance (SV) and cost variance (CV) formulas. Also, know what a negative value means (that you're behind schedule or over budget, respectively).

PMI changed the definitions of the earned value terms in the 2000 PMBOK. The following list contains the new terms you need to be aware of:

➤ BCWS is now *planned value*.

➤ BCWP is now *earned value*.

➤ ACWP is now *actual costs*.

Quality Control

Quality control involves a variety of quality measurements defined in the quality plan. These measurements should be items meaningful to determining whether the product of the project is of the quality required. Quality measurements can be statistical measurements that determine process control (whether the manufacturing process is within the acceptable tolerance of variation), or they can be more simple measurements for nonmanufactured goods, such as software, including walkthroughs, code inspections, and audits.

Quality control outputs help provide the feedback for improvements, acceptance, and, sometimes, rework.

Know the difference between quality control, which focuses on measurement, and quality assurance, which focuses on all the planned and systematic quality activities within a project.

Quality control tools are often associated with manufacturing and process control. Some key quality control tools are listed here:

➤ **Control charts**—These are plotted graphs of "tolerance in a process" measurements. Upper and lower boundaries are established, and when a product or process exceeds either boundary, it is considered "out of control," and improvements to the process are warranted. The boundaries are called *tolerances*.

➤ **Pareto analysis**—This is an 80/20 rule and generally involves mapping errors in a histogram to determine which 20% of the errors cause 80% of the problems.

➤ **Cause-and-effect diagrams**—Also called *fishbone* or *Ishikawa*, these diagrams are useful tools for uncovering root causes of quality problems.

➤ **Trend analysis**—This is used to determine whether corrective action needs to take place, or if a variance is simply an aberration. The "rule of sevens" is often cited. This means that if seven results in a row are out of bounds, then the process is likely to be out of control.

➤ **Statistical sampling**—This tool is used in manufacturing as well as other disciplines. It can take the form of random code reviews in IT or actual batch sampling of products produced in manufacturing. You are expected to understand statistical methods for the PMI exam.

Tracking Risks: Risk Monitoring and Risk Control

According to the PMBOK, "Good risk monitoring and control processes provide information that assists with making effective decisions *in advance of the event occurring*."

It is important to know that a project is the most at risk, and most likely to change, at the beginning of the project.

In our description of risk monitoring, pay special attention to the words *in advance of the event occurring* because preventative measures help create the least project variance. If a project runs smoothly and has been estimated correctly, schedule and cost variances will be minimal.

Risks are where the unexpected changes will most likely come in a project. PMI heavily recommends actively identifying and tracking risks so that when a risk occurs, the mitigation strategy identified can be implemented.

Do understand that risks happen. Understanding risk control according to PMBOK is relatively simple:

> "Identify risks early, monitor them often, and manage them when they occur. Risk management may require replanning, developing alternate strategies, and re-baselining the project, depending on the severity of the risk."

In practice, however, risks are sometimes tricky to identify. Management is often reluctant to consider risks outside the company environment.

 A *risk trigger* is an event that causes a risk to occur. For example, an employee leaving the company is a trigger for a staffing risk.

Exam Prep Questions

Question 1

> Getting the most productivity for the money can be a challenge for a project manager. The PMBOK talks about earned value and how to use it as a measurement. What is it?
>
> - ○ A. The difference between what should have been done and what was actually done
> - ○ B. The cost of the work accomplished
> - ○ C. The value of the project to the company defined in the business case
> - ○ D. How much is invested in a project

Answer A is correct. The cost of the work accomplished does not tell you how much you should have accomplished. Therefore, answer B is incorrect. The value to a company based on the business case is generally considered payback or return on investment. Therefore, answer C is incorrect (because the value is not yet earned). Answer D is incorrect because this is the definition of an investment.

Question 2

> Conflicts on a project can have an impact on control of the project scope. A control system is concerned with which of the following?
>
> - ○ A. Preventing change from affecting project execution and budgets
> - ○ B. Influencing factors that cause change, determining a change has occurred, and managing the implementation of the change
> - ○ C. Ensuring the change-control board is informed
> - ○ D. Managing conflict

Answer B is correct. Preventing change from affecting execution is impossible. Therefore, answer A is incorrect. Change control allows for the effective execution and incorporation of a change into the project plan. The change-control board is the body that accepts or rejects a change request. As such, it must be informed and is part of the change-control system. Therefore, answer C is incorrect. Answer D is incorrect because a project manager does not manage conflict for the change-control board.

Question 3

Monitoring progress on a project helps guide the project and provides a roadmap to milestone completion. One tool that allows the project manager to break down and describe tasks is the Work Breakdown Structure. The Work Breakdown Structure is a central input to which of the following?

○ A. Project schedule management.

○ B. Scope change control, because it defines the baseline tasks of the project.

○ C. Project payments to vendors.

○ D. Microsoft Project software

Answer B is correct. Although the WBS is key to creating the schedule, it is not used for schedule management. Therefore, answer A is incorrect. Payments to vendors may indeed be based on tasks in the WBS, but they are not the primary method for discerning payment. The contract is the method by which the payment obligations are defined. Therefore, answer C is incorrect. Answer D is incorrect because the information should go through change control before being put into a system.

Question 4

Scope verification consists of which of the following?

○ A. Ensuring the correctness of the work results

○ B. Ensuring formal acceptance of the work results

○ C. Verbal acceptance from a project sponsor

○ D. Preparing documents to capture the agreement

Answer B is correct. Scope verification is formal, and it cannot be verbal. Therefore, answer C is incorrect. It involves acceptance by the customer of the work results. Quality assurance is the process by which the correctness of the work results is verified. Therefore, answer A is incorrect. Answer D is incorrect because this is a communication deliverable.

Question 5

Which of the following is not an example of an item that causes a change request?

- ○ A. The programmer decides there is a neat feature he can add to the product.
- ○ B. An error in the project or product design is discovered.
- ○ C. The government has changed a regulation that impacts the project.
- ○ D. An identified risk has occurred and a contingency plan must be implemented.

Answer A is correct. Adding a "neat" feature is generally considered gold plating by the PMBOK. Extra features not requested by the customer should be avoided. The remaining items are all examples of when a change request should be initiated. Therefore, answers B, C, and D are all incorrect.

Question 6

A change-control system does not have _____.

- ○ A. paperwork
- ○ B. tracking mechanisms
- ○ C. approval requirements
- ○ D. referential authority

Answer D is correct. Referential authority is related to managing through another, more highly placed individual in an organization. Per the PMBOK definition, a change-control system must have paperwork, tracking mechanisms, and approval requirements. Therefore, answers A, B, and C, are all incorrect.

Question 7

Float time is the amount of time you can delay the beginning of a task without delaying the end date of the project. Float time is an important consideration in

_____.

- ○ A. detecting whether schedule variance needs to be remedied
- ○ B. scheduling tasks that are dependent on one another
- ○ C. final project reporting

Answer A is correct. Float is important in detecting whether schedule variance needs to be corrected. It is somewhat important with dependent tasks, but not until the float is actually used up. Therefore, answer B is incorrect. Float is not used in final project reporting. Therefore, answer C is incorrect.

Question 8

Project managers frequently monitor variances to determine where they should focus their attention on a project. What is schedule variance?

- O A. The difference between how much the project was expected to cost and how much it is actually costing.
- O B. It's not an issue for project managers because schedules do typically vary.
- O C. The difference between the amount of time a task was to take and the actual amount of time it took.
- O D. It's considered a major problem by PMI.

Answer C is correct. Answer A is incorrect because this is the definition of cost variance. Although answer B is true, a project manager must continually assess the variance to see whether corrective action must be taken. Therefore, answer B is incorrect. Answer D is incorrect because schedule variances can be positive and may not necessarily require corrective action.

Question 9

Project managers are decision makers in response to issues. What is corrective action?

- O A. The act of disciplining a project team member
- O B. An action taken to bring a schedule or project performance into line
- O C. Monitoring to detect and understand schedule variance
- O D. Taking notes, summarizing reports, and providing feedback

Answer B is correct. Although disciplining a project team member may well be a type of corrective action, this is not the *best* answer because the purpose of a corrective action is to bring a project back on schedule. Therefore, answer A is incorrect. Monitoring to detect and understand schedule variance is the definition of schedule control. Therefore, answer C is incorrect. Answer D is incorrect because these are tasks associated with communication and reporting.

Question 10

Earned Value Management consists of which of the following?

○ A. Monitoring project work results for conformance to requirements

○ B. Monitoring planned schedule and costs against actual schedule and costs to determine whether a project is ahead of or behind schedule or cost

○ C. Determining the amount of payment due to a contractor

○ D. Developing a lessons learned summary report

Answer B is correct. Answer A is incorrect because monitoring work results is quality control. Although earned value is sometimes used in contract payments, answer C is not the *best* definition. Therefore, answer C is incorrect. Answer D is incorrect because this is not related to earned value.

Need to Know More?

Project Management Institute, *PMBOK Guide 2000*.

PMI bookstore (www.pmibookstore.org)

Provides general project management references materials and other self-study texts.

PMI eLearning Connection (www.pmi.org)

Offers virtual, online seminars and study programs.

Commercial PMP prep courses

Search PMI (www.pmi.org) for a listing of PMI Registered Education Providers that offer PMP exam prep courses. Many of the courses are now offered online.

8

Project Closing

Terms you'll need to understand:

✓ Contract closeout
✓ Administrative closure
✓ Performance measurement documentation
✓ Product documentation
✓ Product verification
✓ Lessons learned

Techniques and concepts you'll need to master:

✓ The closing process steps: inputs, outputs, techniques, relationships, and differences
✓ Contract closeout: product verification, administrative closeout, procurement audit, formal acceptance
✓ Similarities between contract closeout and administrative closure
✓ Contract documentation that should be reviewed during contract closeout
✓ The criteria for project closure
✓ Benefits of lessons learned and why they are valued by PMI
✓ When administrative closure should be performed
✓ Methods for ending a contract or project

The fifth and final project management process in the project lifecycle is *Project Closing*. Project Closing encompasses only two of the 39 PMBOK processes, and only an estimated 7% of the exam questions will focus on this process.

The Project Closing exam questions are straightforward; however, it is very important that you have a thorough understanding of the terms and techniques within this process group. In real life, many projects are closed without following PMI standards. Unfortunately, project managers do not always view closing their projects as an important step, so many of the terms or techniques found on the exam may be foreign to some test-takers. It is imperative that you have a good understanding of PMI's definitions and concepts in this project management process. By focusing on the items in this section, you will be prepared for the exam questions covering the Project Closing process.

Closing Process Steps

PMI defines the Project Closing process as "formalizing acceptance of the project or phase and bringing it to an orderly end." For you to better understand what this means, we will provide an overview of the two subprocesses that comprise the Project Closing process in this section and then "drill down" into more detail on each process in subsequent sections.

Because there are only two processes in the Closing process group, it is not difficult to study and comprehend the material necessary to pass the exam questions pertaining to Project Closing. Table 8.1 gives a short description of the two closing steps, along with the PMBOK reference for additional information.

 You must know the definitions, relationships, and key inputs and outputs for each of the two closing processes.

Table 8.1   The Two Steps of the Closing Process

Step	Description	PMBOK Process Reference
1	Verify that the work was completed suitably. Resolve any open issues and settle the contract adhering to any specific guidelines in the contract.	12.6: Contract Closeout
2	Document the formal acceptance of the completion of the phase or project. Collect and archive project records.	10.4: Administrative Closure

Contract Closeout

The first Closing process is contract closeout. Contract closeout is a process that consists of the following activities:

➤ Product verification

➤ Administrative closeout

➤ A procurement audit

➤ Formal acceptance

It is helpful to have a solid understanding of these four items; however, at a minimum, make certain for the exam that you know they are a part of contract closeout, which is a step in the Project Closing process.

Product verification must be completed to ensure that all work was done according to the specifications in the contract.

Administrative closeout includes the updating and finalization of records. For exam purposes, it is also important to remember that contract payment and lessons learned are a part of administrative closure.

A *procurement audit* is a review of all steps in the procurement process to determine its successes and failures.

 The objective of a procurement audit is to gain insight into procurements and to transfer this knowledge to other procurements on the same project or other projects.

Formal acceptance should be provided to the seller, in writing, by the person responsible for contract administration.

 The requirements for formal contract closeout are defined in the contract terms and conditions.

Similarities Between Contract Closeout and Administrative Closure

It's important to remember that contract closeout and administrative closure are two separate process steps in the Project Closing process. This can be confusing, because as was described in the previous section, the *activity* of administrative closeout is part of contract closeout. However, the *process* of administrative closure involves the entire project, not just the contract. Plus, it should be executed at the end of each project phase.

 Contract closeout and administrative closure both involve verification of results and the updating and archiving of relevant documents.

Contract Documentation That Should be Reviewed During Contract Closeout

Contract documentation is listed in the PMBOK in Section 12.6.1.1, and it should be reviewed during contract closeout. It is important that you review the items on this list; the exam may try to trick you with a document that sounds similar to these but is not truly considered a part of contract documentation. Items deemed to be contract documentation by PMI include the following:

➤ The contract

➤ Supporting schedules

➤ Requested and approved contract changes

➤ Seller-developed technical documentation

➤ Seller performance records

➤ Financial documents such as invoices and payment records

➤ Contract-related inspection results

 Remember that the procurement audit is a key tool in the contract closeout process and is *not* contract documentation.

The Criteria for Project Closure

It's important to remember that project closure is a key output of administrative closure.

Here's a list of the criteria necessary to ensure project closure:

➤ Formal customer acceptance of the project results and deliverables

➤ Meeting the requirements of the delivering organization, such as the following:

  ➤ Staff evaluations

  ➤ Budget reports

  ➤ Lessons learned

 Keep in mind that although lessons learned are considered part of the criteria for project closure, lessons learned are also a separate key deliverable (or output) of administrative closure.

Benefits of Lessons Learned and Why They Are Valued by PMI

You should know that lessons learned are an output of administrative closure. The PMBOK defines *lessons learned* as any learning gained from the process of performing the project. Lessons learned are considered to be a project record.

 Lessons learned include both positive and negative aspects of the project.

It is important that you include both positive and negative information about the project. This will allow future projects to duplicate the constructive aspects of the project and to avoid similar downfalls or mistakes.

Documenting the lessons learned should not be delayed until the end of the project. This type of information should be logged throughout the project lifecycle in the project's PMIS, so that useful information is not lost and future projects can benefit from the historical data.

When Administrative Closure Should be Performed

It is important to perform administrative closure at the end of each phase in a project. As was mentioned regarding lessons learned, if administrative closure is delayed until project completion, valuable information will be lost.

Methods for Ending a Contract or a Project

A contract can end in one of three ways:

➤ Successful performance

➤ Mutual agreement

➤ Breach

Successful performance is what we think of as "getting the work done." All the work specified in the contract was performed by the seller and formally accepted by the buyer. The term *contract termination* refers to the other two ways a contract can end: mutual agreement and breach.

If there is *mutual agreement*, the contract is terminated because both the buyer and seller involved in the project agree that the project work should not continue. However, if a project contract is terminated due to breach, a party involved in the project work has failed to obey its side of the contract.

Although this describes how a contract can be completed or terminated, a contract closeout will not always signify the end of a project. However, the end of a project will almost always force a related contract to end. Reference Table 8.2 as a reminder of the various ways a project can be terminated.

Table 8.2	Methods of Project Termination
Method	**Description**
Completion	Successful performance; getting the work done.
Displacement	The project becomes obsolete due to another project.
Collapse	The project ends due to external factors, such as natural disasters, corporate mergers, and so on.
Absorption	The project becomes a permanent part of the sponsoring organization (a new department or division).
Deterioration	A "slow death." The sponsoring organization gradually reduces its support and budget for the project.

Contract termination refers to the end of a project contract through mutual agreement or breach.

Exam Prep Questions

Question 1

> A competing firm has acquired your organization. The CIO decides to terminate the network storage implementation project that you outsourced to Steve's Network Storage because he plans to migrate all existing applications and databases to his Storage Area Network (SAN) environment. As the project manager, what is the *best* thing for you to do next?
>
> ○ A. Initiate administrative closure on the project.
>
> ○ B. Set up a meeting with the new CIO and the account manager from Steve's Network Storage in an attempt to save the current project.
>
> ○ C. Initiate contract closeout with Steve's Network Storage.
>
> ○ D. Perform a procurement audit.

Answer C is correct. In this scenario, initiating contract closeout with Steve's Network Storage is the *best* thing to do first. Contract closeout should be initiated anytime a project is terminated. Answer A is incorrect because administrative closure on the project is performed after contract closeout. Answer B is reasonable, but setting up such a meeting is not the *best* thing to do first. By following the steps outlined for contract closeout, you ensure that proper communication takes place. Upon initiating this process, a meeting between the vendor and the CIO may indeed occur as a result. Answer D is incorrect because a procurement audit is part of the contract closeout process.

Question 2

> A project cannot officially close until what happens?
>
> ○ A. The lessons learned from the project have been captured.
>
> ○ B. All project products have been verified for correctness.
>
> ○ C. All chart of accounts associated with the project have been reconciled.
>
> ○ D. The customer has formally accepted the product of the project.

Answer D is correct. Project closure does not occur until the customer has officially and formally accepted the product of the project. In contractual arrangements, the specific nature of the formal acceptance is documented. Answers A, B and C are all part of the Project Closing process, but they can all occur while the project is still "active." Formal acceptance is the critical step.

Question 3

Contract closeout is similar to administrative closure in that they both involve
_____.

○ A. the use of the scope verification plan

○ B. product verification

○ C. project plan verification

○ D. quality assurance activities

Answer B is correct. In each closing process, it should be verified that the actual work product of the project meets the requirements. Answer A is incorrect because scope verification is performed as part of the Project Controlling process. Answer C is incorrect because project plans are verified and approved during project plan development. Answer D is incorrect because quality assurance is performed as part of the project management Executing processes.

Question 4

All of the following are part of administrative closure except which one?

○ A. ROI reports

○ B. Lessons learned

○ C. Formal acceptance

○ D. Updating resource pool information

Answer A is correct. Budget reports are a part of the administrative closure process, but not financial analysis reports such as ROI. Answers B, C, and D are all incorrect because each one of these is a part of the administrative closure process.

Question 5

> Contract closeout is different from administrative closure in that
> _____.
>
> - O A. administrative closure is performed only during the last project lifecycle phase
> - O B. administrative closure involves a procurement audit
> - O C. only contract closeout deals with formal acceptance of the final work product
> - O D. contract closeout is performed only once per contract

Answer D is correct. A contract is only closed once when the project has completed or has been terminated. Answer A is incorrect because administrative closure is performed at the end of each project lifecycle phase. Answer B is incorrect because it is *contract closeout* that involves a procurement audit. Answer C is incorrect because both closing processes involve formal acceptance.

Question 6

> All of the following documents should be reviewed during the contract closeout step except which one?
> - O A. Issues log
> - O B. Invoice and payment records
> - O C. Approved change requests
> - O D. Inspection reports

Answer A is correct. The key here is to understand what is considered contract documentation to PMI. Answer B, C, and D are all incorrect because they are all considered part of the project contract documentation.

Question 7

What is the main purpose of the procurement audit?

- ○ A. To gather evidence of vendor mistakes to use during final payment negotiations
- ○ B. To ensure the vendor is performing to quality standards
- ○ C. To improve the procurement management process within the performing organization
- ○ D. To ensure each participant in the procurement process is abiding by the organization's vendor management policies

Answer C is correct. The procurement audit is a structured review of each process step within the procurement management activity with the key objective of improving this process for future procurement initiatives. Answers A and B are incorrect because these options describe quality-related processes. Answer D is reasonable, but it describes only a part of the overall audit scope and is therefore incorrect.

Question 8

All of the following statements about lessons learned are false except which one?

- ○ A. Historical lessons learned are rarely used by projects.
- ○ B. Lessons learned should be kept in a secure, controlled file cabinet.
- ○ C. Lessons learned should be gathered during each phase of the project lifecycle.
- ○ D. Because lessons learned are documented, savvy participants will only note the positive aspects of the project.

Answer C is correct. Lessons learned should be accumulated during the entire project lifecycle rather than being put off until the end. By waiting until project closure, you risk losing valuable information and access to project team members. Answer A is incorrect because this is not consistent with PMI's vision. Answer B is incorrect because lessons learned are considered part of the project records (archives), which should be easily accessible in an indexed database repository for use by future projects. Answer D is incorrect because lessons learned should included both positive and negative experiences.

Question 9

The requirements for formal contract closeout can typically be found in the
_____.

- ○ A. charter
- ○ B. project schedule
- ○ C. Statement of Work
- ○ D. contract terms and conditions

Answer D is correct. If specific procedures for formal contract closeout are desired, they will be found in the contract terms and conditions. The project charter formally authorizes the project and defines the business need that the project addresses and the product description. Therefore, answer A is incorrect. Answer B is incorrect because the schedule includes dates for activities and milestones. Answer C is incorrect because the Statement of Work defines the product or service to be supplied.

Question 10

Which of the following processes are included in project closing?
- ○ A. Activity definition and activity sequencing
- ○ B. Contract closeout and administrative closure
- ○ C. Information distribution and contract administration
- ○ D. Schedule control and quality control

Answer B is correct. Contract closeout and administrative closure are the only two processes in Project Closing. Answer A is incorrect because activity definition and activity sequencing are processes within Project Planning. Information distribution and contract administration are Executing processes. Therefore, answer C is incorrect. Answer D is incorrect because schedule control and quality control are Controlling processes.

Need to Know More?

 PMBOK Guide 2000, Project Management Institute

 PMI Bookstore (www.pmibookstore.org). Offers general project management reference materials and other self-study texts.

 PMI eLearning Connection (www.pmi.org). Offers virtual, online seminars and study programs.

 Commercial PMP Prep Courses. Search PMI (www.pmi.org) for a listing of PMI Registered Education Providers that offer PMP exam prep courses. Many of the courses are now offered "online" to better support your lifestyle.

9

Professional
Responsibility

Terms you'll need to understand:

✓ Personal gain
✓ Conflict of interest
✓ Vendor gifts
✓ Stakeholder influence
✓ Truthful reporting
✓ Intellectual property
✓ Confidential information
✓ Association power
✓ PMI Code of Professional Conduct
✓ Ethical standards
✓ Integrity

Techniques and concepts you'll need to master:

✓ What a conflict of interest is
✓ What constitutes inappropriate payments
✓ What acceptable gifts are
✓ What affiliations and family connections are
✓ What defines professional ethics

Professional Responsibility and the Code of Professional Conduct

The PMP certification is a major goal for many people. After all the hours of studying and taking practice tests, you breathe a sigh of relief when you finally pass it. It reminds you of the days when you completed your college exams for the summer and were relieved about getting done.

While you celebrate your success, bear in mind that with your new certification comes a tremendous amount of responsibility. This involves looking at business agreements and monetary issues in a totally honest manner with an emphasis on integrity.

The Code of Professional Conduct is just a one-page document, but it accounts for more than 14% of the questions on the exam. *Make sure you read it thoroughly.*

This chapter explains professional responsibility and the ethics that provide the basis for the credibility of the project management profession.

Qualifications, experience, and honest performance of professional services are just some of the attributes you must consider when you evaluate your business practices. Much of this material is common sense, but it is emphasized so that everyone has a full understanding of expectations.

 Make certain you understand the concept of *conflict of interest* because it is one of the fundamentals tied to the other topics.

Where Do I Find the Information Concerning Professional Responsibility?

The Code of Professional Conduct is not part of the PMBOK. It can be found on the PMI Web site. Here's the current URL:

```
http://www.pmi.org/prod/groups/public/documents/info/pdc_
pmpcodeofconductfile.asp
```

If this URL does not work for you, the information can be found under the "Certifications" heading on the PMI Web site.

Although the Code of Professional Conduct is a small document, it contains a tremendous amount of information and constitutes a large percentage of questions.

The professional responsibility issues you will learn about in this chapter are summarized in Table 9.1.

Table 9.1 Professional Responsibility Summary	
Issue	**Recommendation and Summary**
Conflict of interest	Not recommended. This occurs when someone considers his or her personal interests above the project. Conflict of interest occurs when an individual can gain personally and therefore influences a decision.
Integrity	High integrity is recommended. Someone's integrity is linked to his or her morals and ethics.
Stakeholder influence	Not recommended. Powerful stakeholders can change the entire project instantaneously.
Personal enrichment	Not recommended. This occurs when someone inappropriately receives compensation or benefit for his or her actions. Often tied to conflict of interest.
Gifts from vendors	Not recommended. Ask what your company's policy on gifts is. This restriction may apply to free meals from sales reps or vendors. Most companies have a monetary limit that is considered acceptable. Use this as a guideline. Also, do not offer gifts that are inappropriate.
Affiliations and family connections	Business dealings for which an unknown linkage between the participants of the transactions exists. Someone receiving inappropriate personal enrichment is not recommended.
Ethics	The code stipulates that high professional ethics must be utilized at all times and in all circumstances.
Impact of team members	Not recommended. You should not allow team members' personal gain to diminish the importance of the project.
Professional behavior	Highly recommended. Your actions exemplify your professional standards. Always maintain control of your behavior and exercise emotional restraint in business situations.

Let's begin your journey through the topic of professional responsibility with *conflict of interest*. As you can imagine, PMI strongly discourages you from taking positions, money, gifts, and so on from people or organizations you have personal stakes with or interests in. Read on to find out just what PMI has to say about this issue.

Conflict of Interest

The Code of Professional Conduct has an underlying emphasis on viewing and performing project management as a truthful and ethical profession. The final section of the code discusses the importance of not compromising legitimate interests by receiving inappropriate compensation or benefits for personal or professional gain.

It also stresses the importance of not allowing personal gain to influence your decision making or performance of your duties as a project manager. Remember that we provide services to customers. The ethics of the profession places a lot of importance in maintaining the project management profession's integrity by conducting yourself in an upstanding and legitimate manner with high moral standing.

Both accepting and giving gifts, unjustified compensation, kickbacks, and any form of unjust enrichment are frowned upon. As with any other profession, the perception of accepting or offering inappropriate gifts will get you in trouble. The code makes this very clear by stating that it is not acceptable.

In order to show flexibility in its interpretation, the Code of Professional Conduct states that personal gain for project management services is negotiable in countries where it is acceptable according to applicable laws or customs of the country. Note, however, that for businesses based in the United States, bribery or "gifts" are illegal, even when you're doing business in a country where that practice is considered customary. If you have any doubt about a given situation, consult your corporate legal department or an attorney.

Truthfulness in the PMI professions is further extended to include the certification process and all activities associated with the collection of data and the preparation of applications. The assurance of honest and accurate information includes certifications or credentials from any academic organizations concerning your involvement with educational opportunities.

With all the corporate corruption in today's news, unjustified personal gain is one of the hottest topics on the exam. The practice of inflating hourly rates to complete a project or to make the outcome look better is not suggested. Providing untrue information to an organization is not ethical or appropriate for a project manager. We have standards to maintain, and the credibility of the profession is in the hands of the people who actually do the work.

Again, you *must* understand the concept of conflict of interest for the PMP exam. To help you with this concept, here are some questions that exemplify a potential conflict of interest:

➤ Did you receive money or benefits for work that was not performed?

➤ Did you have an unfair advantage in a business transaction?

➤ Did you receive benefits or compensation in order to influence your business decisions?

➤ Was your decision influenced by any personal gain you might receive as a result of the decision?

If you answer "yes" to any of these questions, you likely have a conflict of interest.

The compliance with all organizational rules and policies by utilizing accurate and truthful information is a key element to this requirement.

Affiliations

Using your relationships with friends and family in order to enrich yourself inappropriately in business arrangements is not recommended because it will likely be perceived as a conflict of interest. The key concept is *inappropriate compensation*, which includes gifts such as travel tickets, vacations, money, and entertainment.

Some of these affiliations may be with stakeholders within the organization as well. Stakeholder influence can have a significant impact on your career and credibility within the profession. Just make sure you are not placing your personal interests above those of the project when dealing with family affiliations, stakeholders, vendors, and employees.

Responsibilities to the Profession

The responsibilities to the profession include positive attributes that you would likely include on a list of "role model" characteristics, such as honesty and an emphasis on customer satisfaction. This area of the Code of Professional Conduct is composed of three areas:

➤ Compliance with all organizational rules and policies

➤ Candidate/certificant professional practice

➤ Advancement of the profession

What Are the Organizational Rules and Policies?

This section discusses the requirement that PMI members provide support and assistance to any PMI investigation, discuss conflicts of interests, and elaborate concerning truthful representation. The willingness to support the Code of Professional Conduct is paramount to membership in the organization. Although this text may seem to center on the certification process, the code also extends to truthful reporting of information to stakeholders and management involved with a project.

Table 9.2 provides a quick summary of the four subsections that discuss understanding organizational rules and policies.

Table 9.2 Organizational Rules and Policies	
Rule/Policy	**Action**
Truthful representations of information	Give all information accurately and honestly.
Responsibility to report violations	This is the process for reporting code violations.
Responsibility to cooperate with PMI concerning violations investigations	Provide support to encourage maintaining credibility for the profession.
Responsibility to disclose conflicts of interest to stakeholders and other individuals if they occur	Be up front and honest. Don't surprise anyone with perceived conflicts of interest.

Truthful Representations of Information

For the exam, you will need to know that members and certified PMPs are required to provide "accurate and truthful representations concerning all information." According to PMI, this includes the following:

➤ The entire PMI certification program

➤ Applications and all administrative paperwork

➤ Test banks

➤ Examinations and answer sheets

➤ Candidate information

➤ Continuing Certification Requirements Program reporting forms

➤ Truthful reporting of information to stakeholders and management involved with a project

For the exam, you must know that falsification of information can lead to disciplinary action up to and including membership and certification revocation. Consequently, the emphasis on accurate reporting is important to maintaining the credibility of the organization.

Reporting of Violations

This requirement offers a watchdog mechanism and process for anyone who wants to escalate code of conduct violations. You will likely see questions concerning this issue on the exam. As professionals in the project management arena, we maintain integrity in the organization by self-policing our operations and our membership.

Cooperating with PMI Concerning Code Violations

This sets the expectation that members should be willing to cooperate and provide assistance concerning code violations. The emphasis is on honesty and truthfulness. These issues will likely surface on the test at some point. There are no typical actions one might take if he or she is brought in on an investigation of code violations. It is generally handled on a case-by-case basis. For the test, you might have to discern scenarios and choose what actions you might have to take based on your ethical code.

Disclosing Situations That Could Be Seen as Conflicts of Interest or Improprieties

This requirement sets the expectation that you must provide full disclosure of a perceived conflict-of-interest situation to anyone associated with a project you are involved in, such as customers, contractors, owners, and clients. This allows them the opportunity to decide how to resolve the issue. This is a good standard for any business transaction so that there are no hidden agendas.

Candidate/Certificant Professional Practice

This section of the code maintains the same general theme as the other sections by advocating honesty as the best policy in regard to advertising, qualifications, experience, and performance of service. The code advocates maintaining these high standards regardless of the business setting or circumstances.

In addition to these guidelines, the document elaborates further by stating that PMI members and PMPs who offer a service, such as a project management service, must comply with state, province, and country laws, regulations, and ethical standards regarding his or her professional practices.

Ethical references are heavily emphasized in the document, so be prepared for situational questions involving morals and integrity on the exam. A typical scenario question will be several sentences long and could contain unnecessary information in order to confuse you. When you approach the question, begin to eliminate choices that you know are incorrect. This system will help to decrease your number of options and increase your chances of choosing the correct answer.

Advancement of the Profession

This section of the Conduct of Professional Code emphasizes the need to maintain privacy and security whenever you have access to intellectual property. As the world becomes more security oriented, regulations associated with national security and information privacy place an emphasis on maintaining good security processes whenever dealing with this type of information. As project managers, we must safeguard information and our reputations by being discreet and professional.

The support of the PMI Code of Professional Conduct and the willingness to distribute the information to other PMI members and PMPs is briefly discussed in this section. For the exam, you should know that the Code of Professional Conduct places an emphasis on communicating the honest philosophy and the principles of the Project Management Institute.

Responsibilities to Customers and the Public

As project managers, we must know that customer satisfaction is an important ingredient for a successful project. The test questions place an emphasis on this requirement. Handling ourselves as professional and trustworthy individuals is the general theme of this section.

The next section of the code is composed of two areas:

➤ Conflict-of-interest situations

➤ Performance, qualifications, and experience of professional services

Many of the exam questions will focus on the test-taker's interpretation of "conflict of interest" and what constitutes inappropriate behavior. When in doubt about one of these types of questions, always take a conservative approach and be overly cautious when interpreting a conflict of interest. The rule of thumb is to overcommunicate and provide 100% disclosure of all related issues so that no one can perceive any type of cover-up.

Dealing with Conflicts of Interest for Your Customer

In preceding sections we discussed the importance of communicating situations that are or may be perceived as conflicts of interest. Again, this is vital because you do not want a breach in the trust relationship of a project right out of the gates. If communicating conflict-of-interest possibilities is still unclear to you, be sure to review the preceding information before moving forward.

Performance, Qualifications, and Experience of Professional Services

The professional services requirement mandates that individuals and organizations utilize truthful advertising, estimating, marketing, and public statements when soliciting projects. Although most people would see this as common sense, keep in mind that it will likely be mentioned somewhere in the test.

Also, to successfully complete the professional services requirement you need to ensure that you are fulfilling the requirements associated with the scope and objectives of a project. The obligation to fulfill the scope and objectives is paramount to the success of a project, unless it is discontinued at the customer's request. This topic lends itself well to story-problem scenario-based questions, so expect one of these types of questions. Remember to use the process-of-elimination method for increasing your chances of choosing the correct answer.

Finally, to provide solid professional services you must ensure that the confidentiality and security of critical and sensitive business and project information are held in high regard. Respect of confidential materials is becoming more of an issue everyday, and the Code of Professional Conduct sets its standards by stating a responsibility to safeguard confidential and sensitive materials.

NOTE By now you should notice some duplicate guidelines in the "responsibilities to the profession" and "responsibilities to the customers and public" sections of the code of conduct.

Acting in a Professional Manner

Whenever you are involved in business affairs, you should always maintain composure and a willingness to control your responses to situations. Although this may be very difficult in some high-conflict situations, you must see it as a requirement for success. The ability to lead and set an example is an admirable trait for a project management professional.

Your interactions with your team will determine your effectiveness and ability to get things done. The Code of Professional Conduct has an underlying theme of being a role model for the members of your team as they develop. This includes providing them with guidance and encouragement as they go through the development process of PMP certification. Willingness on the part of the certified member to provide assistance to a student is encouraged.

Knowledge of the Project and Processes

As you go through a project, you develop skills and knowledge in order to keep current in the industry. Many careers utilize job-specific knowledge and development as part of the learning process. The commitment to stay current with the project management profession is a good goal as the discipline continues to mature and grow.

Cultural Differences in a Global Economy

The demographics of the world are changing. As project managers, it is our responsibility to understand the cultural differences individuals bring to a project. We must have respect for all types of nationalities and customs in order for us to be effective in our jobs. As process engineers, we are expected to utilize resources, regardless of their cultural background or ethic upbringing. As our economy becomes more global, we must acknowledge that we may need to use resources located on the other side of the planet.

Although this has pros and cons, it's a reality as society evolves. For the PMP exam, you will need to be aware of this concept and the requirement of a project manager to have proper diversity training in order to effectively perform his or her job. Because PMI is a global community, it is understandable that the organization and the PMBOK have an underlying emphasis of cooperation across all types of individuals with different religions, customs, and cultural standards. The Code of Professional Conduct does not explicitly discuss the topic of diversity or cultural differences.

Exam Prep Questions

Question 1

> You go to dinner at an expensive restaurant with a group of vendors from China. The bill is more than $500. After dinner, they offer to buy you dinner. How should you handle the situation?
>
> ○ A. Gracefully decline and pay for your own meal.
>
> ○ B. Accept the gift and thank them for their generosity.
>
> ○ C. Ask for a copy of the new vendor contract.
>
> ○ D. Offer to put it on your expense account.

Answer A is correct. Answer B is incorrect because you should not accept expensive gifts that may influence your decision making. Answer C is incorrect because you are potentially tying a business decision with a free meal. Answer D is incorrect because you should not provide or receive substantial gifts from vendors that could impact your decisions.

Question 2

> Good communication is vital in a project atmosphere, but this becomes more difficult when you're working with people who speak a different language than you do. As the member of a project team, the best way you can effectively communicate with other individuals who speak a different language is to
> _____.
>
> ○ A. use an interpreter
>
> ○ B. rely only on written communications so that a translator can be used
>
> ○ C. defer to another team member who knows their language
>
> ○ D. learn and communicate in their language

Answer D is correct. Although this isn't the easiest answer, the *best* way to effectively communicate with others is to use their language. When an outside individual is put into the situation, such as an interpreter or translator, important information can be lost.

Question 3

> Falsification of information on the PMP application could result in _____.
>
> ○ A. revocation of your PMP certification
>
> ○ B. legal prosecution
>
> ○ C. personal conflict
>
> ○ D. a fine

Answer A is correct. Revocation of your PMP certification is the *best* answer in this case. Falsification of information does not lead to a fine or prosecution. Therefore, answers B and D are incorrect. Although falsification of information could lead to a personal conflict, this is not the best answer, thus making answer C incorrect as well.

Question 4

> If your employment requires you to be dishonest or act in an inappropriate manner, what should you do?
>
> ○ A. Do as you're told.
>
> ○ B. Talk with your supervisor concerning the matter.
>
> ○ C. Report the activities to law officials.
>
> ○ D. Transfer out of the department.

Answer B is correct. Answer A is incorrect because it goes against the Code of Professional Conduct. Answer C is incorrect as well, unless the activities are illegal. Before you transfer out of your department, you should contact your supervisor, thus making answer D incorrect.

Question 5

> You are managing a project that incorporates some work in a foreign country. You need to interact with the country's government in order to gain its approval for the future import/export of supplies. What should you do?
>
> ○ A. Bribe the government to gain its approval.
>
> ○ B. Not knowingly engage in professional misconduct.
>
> ○ C. Follow the laws of your own country, even if they differ from the country whose government you are dealing with.
>
> ○ D. Not worry about the approval of the government.

Answer B is correct. Although you should be concerned about the approval of the foreign country's government, you should *never* stoop to bribery or knowingly break any laws or regulations to gain such approval.

Question 6

> When formulating a project team, is it fair to represent an individual as PMP certified if he or she has not passed the certification exam yet?
>
> ○ A. No.
> ○ B. Yes, as long as the individual will be taking the certification exam within the next 30 days.
> ○ C. Yes. As long as one other person on the team is PMP certified, it is fair to represent another individual as PMP certified even if he or she has not passed the exam yet.
> ○ D. Yes, as long as one other person on the team is PMP certified, and as long as the person who has not passed the exam is *not* acting as the project manager on the project.

Answer A is correct. It is never alright to misrepresent a person's qualifications, including his or her PMP status.

Question 7

> You have just been assigned to a project in a foreign country. You have never visited the country and know nothing about its culture. What should you do to prepare yourself for potential conflicts of interest for this project?
>
> ○ A. Go to the library and learn the native language.
> ○ B. Nothing. If you try to learn about the country before you get there, you will most likely do yourself a disservice by learning misconceptions about its culture.
> ○ C. Try to meet people who have visited or lived in the country to attempt to get valuable information about the culture.
> ○ D. Perform background research to determine the guidelines concerning vendor gifts in other countries.

Answer D is correct. Answer A is incorrect because it does not have an impact on project ethics. Answer B is incorrect because it is better to be overly cautious concerning conflicts of interest. Answer C could be partially correct, but answer D is the *best* answer.

Question 8

As a project manager on Wall Street, you have access to stock information through friends and colleagues. One day you hear that one of your stocks is going to plunge within 24 hours. What do you do?

- ○ A. Call your stockbroker and sell the stock.
- ○ B. Call your broker for advise.
- ○ C. Keep the stock until the information becomes public knowledge before you sell.
- ○ D. Tell your friends.

Answer C is correct. You should maintain confidentiality with the information until it becomes public knowledge. Then you can decide whether to hold or sell the stock.

Question 9

Due to circumstances outside of your project team's control, you have been unable to collect all the data needed to complete an analysis important to the project's completion. Because the deadline for this analysis is next week, your project manager has asked you to complete the analysis using incomplete data. What should you do?

- ○ A. Complete the analysis as the project manager requested.
- ○ B. Complete the analysis as the project manager requested, but send the project manager a separate memo documenting why the data was incomplete.
- ○ C. Complete the analysis as the project manager requested, but send the customer a separate memo documenting why the data was incomplete.
- ○ D. Do not complete the analysis. Instead, explain in writing that you cannot complete the analysis for project completion because of the incomplete data.

Answer D is correct. It is better to not complete the analysis and be truthful than to damage your integrity or the integrity of the project results.

Question 10

The sales team for a vendor has provided $100 bills to their customers for the company's 100th anniversary. You receive a check in the mail. What should you do?

- ○ A. Contact the vendor and explain that your company does not accept vendor gifts.
- ○ B. Send a thank-you card.
- ○ C. Cash it.
- ○ D. Donate the check to charity.

Answer A is correct. It is important to set expectations with vendors concerning gifts.

Need to Know More?

Heldman, Kim. *PMP Project Management Professional Study Guide.* Sybex. San Francisco, CA, 2002. ISBN 0782141064.

Practice Exam 1

Question 1

During what phase of the lifecycle is the project scope statement created?

- ○ A. Concept
- ○ B. Planning
- ○ C. Requirements definition
- ○ D. Feasibility study

Question 2

All the following statements about a WBS are true except which one?

- ○ A. It provides a framework for organizing and ordering a project's activities.
- ○ B. It breaks down a project into successively greater detail by level and can be similar in appearance to an organizational chart.
- ○ C. It's one of the methods available to build a project schedule.
- ○ D. It's a key project planning tool.

Question 3

During which phase of the project lifecycle is there the greatest degree of uncertainty?

- ○ A. Initiating
- ○ B. Planning
- ○ C. Executing
- ○ D. Controlling

Question 4

Which project-selection technique does not utilize a benefit measurement approach?

- ○ A. Linear programming
- ○ B. Murder boards
- ○ C. Cost-benefit analysis
- ○ D. Scoring models

Question 5

A consulting company first forms a pursuit team to develop a competitive bid and response to an RFP it received. After learning its response had been selected by the buyer, the company formed a negotiation team to settle on a final price. After the negotiation was complete and the contract was signed, the project manager was assigned to the engagement. The project manager was not part of either team or the process to date, so what should he, as a good project manager, do first?

- ○ A. Compare the proposal statement of work with the statement of work in the contract.
- ○ B. Develop a project charter and communications plan.
- ○ C. Develop an initial WBS.
- ○ D. Review the constraint and assumptions used in estimating process.

Question 6

In the early days of project management, project managers were typically selected from which organizational area?

- ○ A. Information Systems
- ○ B. Mid-level management
- ○ C. Engineering
- ○ D. Accounting

Question 7

SMART objectives are _____.

- ○ A. objectives that are easily achievable
- ○ B. objectives used with the MBO management approach
- ○ C. objectives aligned with the organization's strategic goals
- ○ D. objectives that are specific, measurable, assignable, realistic, and time based

Question 8

Of the following conflict management approaches, which is believed to lead to the *least*-sustaining positive results?

○ A. Avoidance

○ B. Problem solving

○ C. Compromise

○ D. Forcing

Question 9

Complex projects, involving multidisciplinary, multidepartment efforts, are *most* effectively managed by which of the following?

○ A. A strong matrix organization

○ B. A strong traditional manager

○ C. A functional organization

○ D. Multiple lead project managers

Question 10

Which document describes the business need, the quantifiable criteria that must be met by the project, the key deliverables, and the final product of a project?

○ A. Project charter

○ B. Signed contract

○ C. WBS

○ D. Scope statement

Question 11

All the following statements are false about the scope statement except which one?

○ A. It provides a documented basis for preparing the network diagram.

○ B. It is not the basis for the contract between the buyer and seller.

○ C. It does not include a description of project objectives, such as cost, schedule, and quality measures.

○ D. It is not developed by functional managers during the concept phase of a project.

Question 12

Effective stakeholder management includes all the following project elements except which one?

- ○ A. Taking key stakeholders to dinner
- ○ B. Clear requirements definition
- ○ C. Frequently soliciting stakeholder input and feedback
- ○ D. Scope change control

Question 13

Two types of network diagrams are precedence diagrams and arrow diagrams. Which statement best describes the primary difference between them?

- ○ A. The arrow diagram does not indicate the critical path.
- ○ B. The precedence diagram uses float as part of the activity duration.
- ○ C. The precedence diagram represents activities on nodes.
- ○ D. The arrow diagram incorporates PERT in the activity duration.

Question 14

Although several factors should be considered when developing estimates, the primary basis for estimating time and cost for an activity is _____.

- ○ A. resource usage and productivity rates
- ○ B. resource usage and resource availability
- ○ C. productivity rates and resource availability
- ○ D. activity risk rating and resource rates

Question 15

Using the following earned value metrics, calculate the SV, CV, and EAC for this project:

PV=$5,000, EV=$5,250, AC=$5,500, BAC=$25,000

- ○ A. SV=−$250, CV=$250, EAC=$26,315
- ○ B. SV=$250, CV=−$500, EAC=$24,038
- ○ C. SV=−$250, CV=−$500, EAC=$24,038
- ○ D. SV=$250, CV=−$250, EAC=$26,315

Question 16

When estimating activity durations, what inputs should you consider?

○ A. Management expectations, resource requirements, resource capabilities, and past project files

○ B. Management expectations, budget constraints, resource capabilities, and lessons learned from past projects

○ C. Stakeholder expectations, resource capabilities, project team knowledge, and past project files

○ D. Resource requirements, resource capabilities, project team knowledge, and past project files

Question 17

Due to an ethical violation by the original project manager, you have been hand-picked by the Director of Operations to take over the project. In addition to this major project change, you also discover the following on your first day on the project:

➤ Your team is distributed across three time zones.

➤ No risk response plan exists.

➤ The CPI is 0.9.

➤ A difficult critical path task is scheduled to start tomorrow.

➤ The SPI is 1.05.

Based on this information, what should be your two highest priorities?

○ A. Project team and stakeholders, cost

○ B. Schedule, cost

○ C. Cost, Director of Operations

○ D. Risk management, schedule

Question 18

The following activities are in the network diagram shown here:

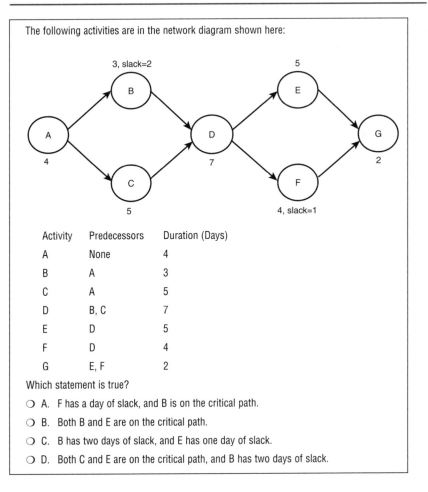

Activity	Predecessors	Duration (Days)
A	None	4
B	A	3
C	A	5
D	B, C	7
E	D	5
F	D	4
G	E, F	2

Which statement is true?

○ A. F has a day of slack, and B is on the critical path.

○ B. Both B and E are on the critical path.

○ C. B has two days of slack, and E has one day of slack.

○ D. Both C and E are on the critical path, and B has two days of slack.

Question 19

Lifecycle cost estimates consider which factors?

○ A. Cost of ownership, including the costs of operation and disposal

○ B. Acquisition costs only

○ C. Costs associated with the concept, planning, implementation, and closeout phases

○ D. Expected profits, measured by subtracting total costs from estimated gross revenues

Question 20

Accelerated depreciation allows a company to write off capital expenses from taxes more quickly. Which of the following is a recognized method of accelerated depreciation?

- ○ A. Double-declining balance
- ○ B. Straight-line
- ○ C. Rapid capital deduction
- ○ D. Benefit cost ratio

Question 21

On a top-secret biotechnology R&D project, the project performance reports indicate a Cost Performance Index (CPI) of 0.81 and a Schedule Performance Index (SPI) of 1.19. What is the most likely explanation for this situation?

- ○ A. Poor project management and estimating.
- ○ B. More experienced specialists have been used.
- ○ C. The project team is working overtime.
- ○ D. The special resources (equipment, materials) procured cost more than originally projected.

Question 22

All the following statements about analogous estimating are true except which one?

- ○ A. It has an accuracy rate of ±10% of actual costs.
- ○ B. It supports top-down estimating and is a form of expert judgment.
- ○ C. It is used to estimate total project costs when a limited amount of detailed project information is available.
- ○ D. It involves the use of the cost of previous, similar project(s) as the basis for estimating the cost of the current project.

Question 23

Which of the following estimates would most likely predict the actual cost of a project?

○ A. Definitive

○ B. Budget

○ C. Detailed

○ D. Order of magnitude

Question 24

Considering the project schedule during the cost budgeting process _____.

○ A. allows costs to be assigned to the time period when they will be incurred

○ B. identifies the project elements so that costs can be allocated

○ C. provides another way to help measure and monitor cost performance

○ D. allows the contingency allowance to be calculated correctly

Question 25

You are taking over a project during the planning phase and discover that four individuals have signed the project charter, including two company officers. Which of the following should *most* concern you?

○ A. That the charter was created during planning

○ B. Determining the reporting structure for the communications plan

○ C. Getting a single project sponsor

○ D. Determining the reason for the four charter signatures

Question 26

A former-CPA-turned-project-manager is selected to lead a groundbreaking information technology project. Because the project manager has very limited knowledge of this new technology, she decides to manage the project by delegating key planning activities, such as WBS development, schedule development, cost estimating, determination of specific tasks, and task assignments, to individual project team members. She decides it will be best to serve as a coordinator and coach for this initiative. What is the likely outcome of this approach?

- ○ A. Due to the work environment created by the project manager, a team characterized by moderate productivity levels and high commitment levels.
- ○ B. A team characterized by poor performance, low morale, high conflict, and high turnover.
- ○ C. Due to the work environment created by the project manager, a team characterized by high levels of productivity, creativity, and commitment.
- ○ D. A team destined to experience the normal "storming, norming, forming" phases. In time, however, the team will become highly productive.

Question 27

Which of the following is a chief characteristic of the Delphi technique?

- ○ A. Bottom-up approach
- ○ B. Extrapolation from historical records
- ○ C. Isolated opinion
- ○ D. Expert opinion

Question 28

To manage a project, a project plan should be realistic and achievable. Which of the following is the *best* method to achieve a realistic project plan?

- ○ A. The project manager creates the project plan based on input from the team.
- ○ B. The project manager creates the project plan based on input from senior management.
- ○ C. The functional manager creates the project plan based on input from the project manager.
- ○ D. The project manager creates the project plan based on the scope statement and organizational procedures.

Question 29

The WBS can be used to _____.

- ○ A. show calendar dates for each task
- ○ B. show the business need for the project
- ○ C. communicate with the customer
- ○ D. show the dependencies between work packages

Question 30

A new project manager asks you why he should use a WBS on his project. He does not see the value and feels it will take too much time to develop. What would be an effective response to his question?

- ○ A. A WBS will ensure that all the work to be done is accounted for.
- ○ B. A WBS is required if the project involves contracts.
- ○ C. A WBS is the only way to identify risks.
- ○ D. He can build a project schedule without a WBS.

Question 31

A new product-development project has five levels in the WBS and has been sequenced using the precedence diagramming method. The activity duration estimates have been received. Which activity would you do next?

- ○ A. Compress the schedule.
- ○ B. Finalize the schedule.
- ○ C. Create an activity list.
- ○ D. Create a code of accounts.

Question 32

You are now a project manager for a new nanotechnology carbon tube product development project. Most schedule development steps have been completed, including schedule compression. Which activity would you likely perform next?

- ○ A. Set up schedule change control.
- ○ B. Finish schedule development and gain approval of the schedule.
- ○ C. Develop a communications plan.
- ○ D. Update the project schedule with risk response strategies.

Question 33

A project manager is using weighted average duration estimates to calculate activity duration. What type of mathematical analysis is being used?

- ○ A. PERT
- ○ B. GERT
- ○ C. Monte Carlo
- ○ D. CPM

Question 34

A team member from the Web Creative Design department tells you that her work is too creative to provide you with a fixed, single estimate for the task. You both decide to use the average time the task has taken for past projects. This is an example of which of the following?

- ○ A. Parametric estimating
- ○ B. PERT
- ○ C. Monte Carlo
- ○ D. CPM

Question 35

A task has an early start date of day 3, a late start date of day 13, an early finish date of day 9, and a late finish date of day 19. What can be said about this task?

- ○ A. It's not on the critical path.
- ○ B. It's on the critical path.
- ○ C. It has a lag.
- ○ D. It's progressing well.

Question 36

Rearranging resources so that a constant number of resources are used each month is called what?

- ○ A. Balancing
- ○ B. Crashing
- ○ C. Fast tracking
- ○ D. Leveling

Question 37

The cost of choosing one project over another is called what?

- ○ A. Opportunity cost
- ○ B. Sunk cost
- ○ C. NPV
- ○ D. Indirect cost

Question 38

Which of the following is not needed in order to develop a project estimate?

- ○ A. WBS
- ○ B. Risks
- ○ C. Change-control procedure
- ○ D. Assumptions

Question 39

You have four projects from which to choose. Project 1 is a 5-year project with an NPV of U.S. $750K. Project 2 is a 3-year project with an NPV of U.S. $600K. Project 3 is a 1-year project with an NPV of U.S. $500K. Project 4 is another 3-year project with an NPV of U.S. $650K. Which project is preferred?

- ○ A. Project 1
- ○ B. Project 2
- ○ C. Project 3
- ○ D. Project 4

Question 40

During project planning, you are discussing estimating techniques with the project sponsor. The sponsor strongly recommends analogous estimating, but you want a form of expert judgment. What is the *best* thing you can do to resolve this situation?

- ○ A. Agree to analogous estimating. It's not worth the confrontation at this point in the project.
- ○ B. Determine why the sponsor wants such an accurate estimate.
- ○ C. Try to convince the sponsor to allow expert judgment because it is typically more accurate.
- ○ D. Agree to analogous estimating because it is a form of expert judgment.

Question 41

You've just completed initiating a small project and are preparing to start the planning phase when a project stakeholder asks for the project's budget and cost baseline. What should you tell the project stakeholder?

- ○ A. The project budget and cost baseline will not be finalized and accepted until the planning phase is completed.
- ○ B. The project will not have a budget and cost baseline due to its small size.
- ○ C. The project budget can be found in the project charter because it has just been completed.
- ○ D. It is impossible to create an estimate before the project plan is created.

Question 42

You are asked to prepare a budget for completing a project that was started last year and then shelved for 7 months after receiving a no-go decision after the design phase tollgate. All the following would be included in your budget except which one?

- ○ A. Sunk cost
- ○ B. Variable cost
- ○ C. Fixed cost
- ○ D. Direct cost

Question 43

Four projects are presented to the Project Portfolio Management Team. Project A has an IRR of 12%, Project B has a BCR of 2:3, Project C has an opportunity cost of U.S. $75K, and Project D has a payback of 6 months. Which project would you recommend?

- ○ A. Project A
- ○ B. Project B
- ○ C. Project C
- ○ D. Project D

Question 44

Project XYZ has a scope change probability of 75% and a cost increase change probability of 40%. What is the probability that Project XYZ will have a scope change and not see a cost increase?

- ○ A. 30%.
- ○ B. 45%.
- ○ C. 110%.
- ○ D. Not enough information is provided.

Question 45

Your project involves specialized equipment with a value of $500,000, and there is a 6% probability that the equipment could be lost. You decide to investigate the possibility of transferring this risk to an insurance company. The cost of the insurance premium is $19,000. Based on this information, what action would you recommend?

- ○ A. Buy the insurance premium, because the premium cost is less than the probable equipment losses.
- ○ B. Do not buy the insurance premium, because the premium cost is more than the probable equipment losses.
- ○ C. You cannot make a determination based on the information provided.
- ○ D. Develop a contingency plan.

Question 46

What are workarounds in project management?

- ○ A. Workarounds are alternative strategies.
- ○ B. Workarounds are the same as contingency plans.
- ○ C. Workarounds are responses to new risks that were previously not identified or accepted.
- ○ D. Workarounds are activities performed as part of fallback plans.

Question 47

Which of the following is a valid reason for re-baselining your project plan?

- ○ A. Cost variances
- ○ B. Missed target dates
- ○ C. Scope changes
- ○ D. Adding additional resources

Question 48

All the following are part of a risk management plan except which one?

- ○ A. Roles and responsibilities for managing risk
- ○ B. Individual risks
- ○ C. Budget for risk management activities
- ○ D. A description of the general risk management approach to be taken

Question 49

As the project manager for a new automated manufacturing system implementation project, you have contracted with a national robotics firm to develop a custom robotic arm for a critical step in your future design manufacturing process. The contract is fixed price with incentives for meeting targeted milestone dates. The payment schedule and accompanying incentives are as follows:

Payment	Milestone	Percentage	Amount	Incentive
1	Signed contract	5%	$50,000	—
2	Prototype	10%	$100,000	+10% if 5 days early
3	Robot design	15%	$150,000	+5% if 5 days early
4	Robot delivery	40%	$400,000	+ 5% if 1 week early, +10% if 2 weeks early
5	User acceptance	30%	$300,000	—

At this point, the robotic arm prototype has not been delivered, and it is now 1.5 weeks past due. The contractor's project manager has just called to request a change in the payment schedule. He wants to see the third payment changed to 30% and the final payment reduced to 15%. During the conversation, you sense the contractor has miscalculated the effort to do this work and may be in some financial trouble.

From the following options, what would be the best thing to do next?

- ○ A. Request that resolution of this request be delayed until after receipt of the prototype.
- ○ B. Schedule a risk management meeting with the contractor to better understand all the project risks before making any decision.
- ○ C. Ask him to provide justification for his demand.
- ○ D. Counteroffer his proposal of 30% and 15% with 22.5% and 22.5%, respectively.

Question 50

The project team has created a plan describing how it will gather and distribute project information. The plan describes the types of communication mechanisms that will be used and which stakeholders will receive which communications. If anything about this plan changes during the project, which other plan will also be affected?

- ○ A. Responsibility matrix
- ○ B. Project plan
- ○ C. Resource plan
- ○ D. Staffing management

Answers to Practice Exam 1

1. B	**18.** D	**35.** A
2. C	**19.** A	**36.** D
3. A	**20.** A	**37.** A
4. A	**21.** B	**38.** C
5. D	**22.** A	**39.** A
6. C	**23.** A	**40.** D
7. D	**24.** A	**41.** A
8. A	**25.** C	**42.** A
9. A	**26.** B	**43.** A
10. D	**27.** D	**44.** B
11. D	**28.** A	**45.** A
12. A	**29.** C	**46.** C
13. C	**30.** A	**47.** C
14. A	**31.** A	**48.** B
15. D	**32.** B	**49.** B
16. D	**33.** A	**50.** B
17. A	**34.** A	

Question 1

Answer B is correct. The scope statement is an output of scope planning (5.2 PMBOK), which is part of the overall Planning phase. Answer A is incorrect because *concept* is another term for *initiation*. Answers C and D are incorrect because they are not official names of project phases.

Question 2

Answer C is correct. A WBS is not a project scheduling method.

Question 3

Answer A is correct. As a project progresses through the lifecycle, the degree of uncertainty decreases. Also, Initiating is the first phase.

Question 4

Answer A is correct. Linear programming is an example of a constrained optimization project selection method. The other three answers are benefit-measurement methods of project selection and are therefore incorrect.

Question 5

Answer D is correct. For planning, a project manager must understand the constraints and assumptions that underlined the effort estimates developed to date. Answers B and C provide the steps that would follow next. Answer A may not be relevant because negotiations often alter the statement of work originally.

Question 6

Answer C is correct. This is a fine example of an "out-of-the-blue" type question that PMI occasionally includes on the exam.

Question 7

Answer D is correct. Although this topic is not covered in the PMBOK, it will serve you well in the real world.

Question 8

Answer A is correct. The avoidance approach does not resolve the main source of the original conflict. Answers B and C are incorrect because both address the central conflict and should result in longer-lasting solutions. Although answer D is generally not desirable either, due to the incentives/penalties involved, it should impact the conflict issue for a longer period of time compared to just avoiding it. Therefore, answer D is incorrect.

Question 9

Answer A is correct. A strong matrix organization provides the appropriate support and accountability structures to successfully accomplish projects of this type. A strong traditional manager and a functional organization are not regarded as effective in environments where strong cooperation, negotiation, communication, and compromise are needed. Therefore, answers B and C are incorrect. Although answer D may have been somewhat tempting, you generally want one lead project manager (or program manager) to oversee a team of project leads who represent the many disciplines and departments involved in the project. Therefore, answer D is incorrect.

Question 10

Answer D is correct. The tempting response is answer A. However, there is no mention of *authorization*, and a project charter does not have to list the quantifiable project objectives. Therefore, answer A is incorrect. Answer B is incorrect because a contract may not address the entire scope of the project and usually does not describe the business need of the project. Answer C is incorrect because a WBS does not describe the business need or the quantifiable criteria of the project.

Question 11

Answer D is correct. Functional managers do often develop the scope statement during a project's conceptual phase. Answer A is incorrect because it is the WBS and activity list that serve as the basis for the network diagram. Answers B and C are incorrect because the opposite of each statement is true about a scope statement.

Question 12

Answer A is correct. Answers B, C, and D are all "musts" for effective stakeholder management. Answer A "may" be an effective technique, but it depends on the code of conduct parameters that each party must abide by and the purpose of the dinner meeting.

Question 13

Answer C is correct. An arrow diagram represents activities on the arrow (and not the node). Answer A is incorrect because both types can represent the critical path. Answer B is incorrect because both types can use float. Answer D is incorrect because PERT is a scheduling technique that could use either network diagram type as input.

Question 14

Answer A is correct. The duration and cost estimate of an activity is chiefly a result of the number of resources needed, the quality/productivity of those anticipated resources, and the cost rates of those resources. Because answer A provides two of these factors, it is the *best* response, making answers B, C, and D all incorrect.

Question 15

Answer D is correct. Here's the breakdown:

➤ SV (schedule variance) = EV (earned value) – planned value (PV) = $5,250 – $5,000 = $250

➤ CV (cost variance) = EV (earned value) – actual costs (AC) = $5,250 – $5,500 = –$250

➤ EAC (estimate at completion) = BAC (budgeted at completion) / CPI (cost performance index)

➤ CPI = EV / AC = $5,250 / $5,500 = .95

➤ EAC = BAC / CPI = $25,000/.95 = $26,315

Question 16

Answer D is correct. Estimating activity durations should be focused on getting the best information on what the actual work effort is. Answers A, B, and C all included an external "expectation" influence that should *not* be a part of this schedule development process step.

Question 17

Answer A is correct. This question has several reasonable options listed; however, the best response is answer A. Due to the sudden change in project leadership, it will be most important that you establish yourself as the leader with your project team and the project stakeholders. In addition, the CPI of 0.9 (less than 1) indicates the project's current course will result in an over-budget condition. Answer B is incorrect because the SPI (Schedule Performance Index) is favorable (greater than 1). Answer C is incorrect because the cost performance issue is not the most critical item, and the Director of Operations is only one of the stakeholders you need to concentrate on. Answer D is incorrect because the lack of risk management is not as critical as the other items mentioned, and schedule performance is favorable.

Question 18

Answer D is correct. The critical path is A-C-D-E-G and is noted in red (bold) in the figure.

Question 19

Answer A is correct. Answers B and C are incorrect because they do not account for costs of operation and disposal. Answer D is incorrect because lifecycle cost estimates are not concerned with profitability measures.

Question 20

Answer A is correct. Double-declining balance is the only accelerated depreciation method listed. Therefore, answers B, C, and D are all incorrect.

Question 21

Answer B is correct. This is the best response because the use of more experienced specialists could translate into "higher resource costs" than originally estimated, but "more productive" than originally planned. Answer A is incorrect because all the performance indicators are not negative. Answer C is incorrect because earned value analysis accounts for each effort hour, so the SPI would not increase due to overtime. Answer D is very tempting, but it's not the *best* response. The higher equipment and materials costs explain the CPI rating, but not the SPI rating. If answer D stated that the special equipment resulted in faster work processes, then this could have explained the situation. Therefore, answer D is incorrect.

Question 22

Answer A is correct. The accuracy rate of analogous estimating is regarded to be in the –25% to +75% range. The other responses are all accurate descriptions of analogous estimating, thus making answers B, C, D incorrect.

Question 23

Answer A is correct. Definitive estimates are completed before project implementation and based on the project's design solution; they have an accuracy rate of −5% to +10%. Answers B and D are incorrect because these estimate types are not as accurate as definitive estimates. Answer C is not an official estimating accuracy type and is therefore incorrect.

Question 24

Answer A is correct. The cost budget is defined as the allocation of project costs to the proper time periods. Answer B is incorrect because the WBS and the resource plan identify the project elements for costing. Answer C is incorrect because the cost baseline is used to measure and monitor cost performance. Answer D is incorrect because the contingency allowance is figured as a result of risk management.

Question 25

Answer C is correct. It is imperative that the project have a single project sponsor. Answer A is not a concern at all, and answer B is a secondary concern compared to the alternatives listed. Therefore, answers A and B are incorrect. Answer D is tempting, and you should understand the background and reason for this situation, but it is not your *most* important concern. Therefore, answer D is incorrect.

Question 26

Answer B is correct. Without a defined and recognized "leader," it is unlikely that high productivity rates and team cohesion will occur. In addition, because the project manager has delegated all the individual planning parts, it is unlikely that any one person has all the information needed to complete his or her task properly. If the question would have mentioned a "team approach" to these planning tasks, the situation may be different. Answers A, C, and D are all incorrect in this case.

Question 27

Answer D is correct. The main characteristic of the Delphi technique is the use of "expert opinion." Although answer C may have been tempting, because the technique encourages isolating the identified experts from each other, this is not the *chief* characteristic. Therefore, answer C is incorrect. Answers A and B are incorrect because these are not characteristics of the Delphi technique.

Question 28

Answer A is correct. A strong point of emphasis from PMI is that the project team should be involved in the development of the project schedule and project plan. Answers B, C, and D are all incorrect in this case.

Question 29

Answer C is correct. The WBS is an effective stakeholder communication tool. Answer A is incorrect because there are no calendar dates on the WBS. Calendar dates are on the project schedule. Answer B is incorrect because the business justification is not part of the WBS. Answer D is incorrect because dependencies are shown on the network diagram and project schedule, not the WBS.

Question 30

Answer A is correct. A WBS is critical in making sure all the project work has been identified and that nothing slips through the cracks. Answer B is incorrect because all projects need a WBS, not just ones that involve contracts. Answer C is incorrect because analysis of the WBS is not the only way to identify risks. Answer D is tempting, but it's not the *best* response. It would be a secondary reason, because the project manager first needs to have all the project work identified to build a realistic project schedule. Therefore, answer D is incorrect.

Question 31

Answer A is correct. The next step would be to build the schedule, but because that is not listed, you should go to the next step in the schedule development process—compressing the schedule. Answer B is incorrect because you would not finalize the schedule until the compression activity has occurred. Answer C is incorrect because this is already done. The activity list would have served as input of the activity duration estimating step. Answer D is incorrect because this would have been done when the WBS was developed.

Question 32

Answer B is correct. The final schedule development step is schedule approval. Answer A is not correct because this occurs after schedule development and is not complete yet. Answer C is not correct because you need to complete schedule development first, and the communications planning should have occurred already because this work needs to be in the WBS. Likewise, answer D is incorrect. The initial pass at risk analysis should be complete before the schedule is compressed.

Question 33

Answer A is correct. PERT is the only mathematical analysis technique listed that uses a weighted average approach. Therefore, answers B, C, and D are all incorrect.

Question 34

Answer A is correct. Parametric estimating involves using past history to develop the task estimate. Answers B and D are incorrect because they are not the best descriptions of what is occurring. Answer C is not correct because Monte Carlo is a project schedule simulation technique and not an activity duration estimating technique.

Question 35

Answer A is correct. The task has slack because the early and late start dates are not the same, and slack tasks are not usually on the critical path. Therefore, answer B is incorrect. Answers C and D are incorrect because there is not enough information in the question to determine either of these.

Question 36

Answer D is correct. This is the definition of *resource leveling*. Answer A is incorrect because it is not the *best* response. Answers B and C are incorrect because they are schedule-compression techniques.

Question 37

Answer A is correct. This is the definition of *opportunity cost*, which is the only option that deals directly with comparing one project to another. Answer C is tempting, because NPV is often used to compare potential projects, but NPV is focused on the "value" of the project.

Question 38

Answer C is correct. A change-control procedure is part of project controlling and is, therefore, not involved with the project time and estimating process. Answers A, B, and D are incorrect because these items are all needed for an overall project estimate.

Question 39

Answer A is correct. Net present value (NPV) already incorporates the number of years, so you just select the project with the highest NPV, which in this case is Project 1, with an NPV of U.S. $750K. Therefore, answers B, C, and D are all incorrect.

Question 40

Answer D is correct. This is a bit of a tricky question if you are not clear on the definition of analogous estimating. Because analogous estimating is a form of expert judgment, answer D is the *best* response. Therefore, answers A, B, and C are all incorrect.

Question 41

Answer A is correct. The project budget and cost baseline are finalized and accepted during the planning phase. Answer B is incorrect because the project size would not dictate the development of a project budget and cost baseline. Answer C is incorrect because the project charter does not contain the project budget. Answer D is incorrect because it is possible to offer a preliminary cost estimate before the project plan is created. This is often a part of the project initiation process.

Question 42

Answer A is correct. Your budget would account for all cost elements to complete the project (variable, fixed, direct, indirect), but it would not account for money already invested into the project (sunk costs).

Question 43

Answer A is correct. Project A is the only one with a clear positive investment outlook. Answer B is incorrect because Project B is unfavorable, with a benefit cost ratio (BCR) of less than 1. The information presented for Projects C and D is not adequate to determine whether they would be good investments. Therefore, answers C and D are incorrect.

Question 44

Answer B is correct. A scope change of 75% times a 60% no cost increase equals .45 (or 45%), which makes answers A, C, and D all incorrect.

Question 45

Answer A is correct. The cost of probable loss is $500,000 times 6%, which equals $30,000. The cost of the insurance premium is $19,000. Therefore, answers A, C, and D are all incorrect.

Question 46

Answer C is correct. Workarounds involve unplanned work that is a response to a new, emerging risk not previously identified or accepted. Therefore, answers A, B, and C are all incorrect.

Question 47

Answer C is correct. Scope changes, properly tracked with a change-control system, are a valid reason to re-baseline the project plan. The other three options describe variances, which need to be tracked, but they are not reasons to re-baseline. Therefore, answers A, B, and D are incorrect.

Question 48

Answer B is correct. Individual risks and their planned responses would be documented in the risk response plan. Answers A, C, and D are all valid elements of a risk management plan and are therefore incorrect.

Question 49

Answer B is correct. This proactive approach will help identify any risks and issues that the contractor is experiencing. With better identification of risks and better information, the best response strategy can be developed. Answer A is incorrect because it further delays an understanding of what problems the contractor is having. Answer C is incorrect because it would be a part of the risk management meeting. Answer D is incorrect because it does not get to the root cause of the payment schedule change request.

Question 50

Answer B is correct. The question partially describes the communications management plan, and this plan is part of the project plan.

Practice Exam 2

Question 1

When working on a project in a country outside of your own, it is important that you not be viewed as ethnocentric by other team members and individuals around you. What is meant by ethnocentric?

- ○ A. Being homesick
- ○ B. Stereotyping others based on what you've heard about their culture
- ○ C. Having the opinion that one's own culture is inherently natural and superior
- ○ D. Believing that individuals from your country know how to better manage a project

Question 2

As the project manager for a marketing and sales extranet application tool project, you have contracted with a Web development firm to reengineer the existing extranet application in order to be compliant with the standards of the new corporate Web hosting center. The contract is fixed price with incentives for meeting targeted milestone dates. The payment schedule and accompanying incentives are as follows:

Payment	Milestone	Percentage	Amount	Incentive
1	Signed contract	10%	$50,000	—
2	Proof-of-concept	10%	$50,000	+5% if 5 days early
3	First iteration	15%	$75,000	+5% if 5 days early
4	Second iteration	15%	$75,000	+ 5% if 1 week early; +10% if 2 weeks early
5	Third iteration	15%	$75,000	+ 5% if 1 week early; +10% if 2 weeks early
6	User acceptance	35%	$175,000	—

At this point, the contractor has just delivered the second iteration 8 days early and requests the incentive bonus of 5%. You decide to not authorize the incentive bonus because the contractor had been 3 days late on the delivery of the first iteration and there were numerous performance issues with that iteration. The contractor's project manager threatens to halt application development until the milestone and incentive bonus payments are authorized. Which project document would be the most beneficial in the resolution of this dispute?

- ○ A. Procurement management plan
- ○ B. Solicitation plan
- ○ C. Signed contract (statement of work)
- ○ D. Scope statement

Question 3

You've completed a deliverable for a project and have gained acceptance and signoff by the customer. The project has now been closed for more than 30 days. When reviewing the deliverable with another project manager who is preparing for a similar project, you discover a flaw in the results communicated in the deliverable that may not depict possible safety issues in the future. The risk involved with these safety issues is very small. What should you do?

○ A. Because the project has been closed for more than 30 days, there is no need to bring these safety issues to the attention of the customer.

○ B. Because the risk involved with these safety issues is very small, there is no need to bring them to the attention of the customer.

○ C. Communicate your findings to your management, both verbally and in writing.

○ D. Immediately call the customer and let them know your concerns.

Question 4

Which of the following does not describe characteristics of a project plan ?

○ A. Formal and approved

○ B. A document or collection of documents that change over time

○ C. Only used by the project manager to execute the project

○ D. Includes methods for identifying milestones

Question 5

Which of the following statements is not true during project execution?

○ A. The majority of the budget is spent.

○ B. The product of the project is actually produced.

○ C. Project performance against the plan is monitored.

○ D. Decisions on when and with whom to communicate are made.

Question 6

As part of your project you implement a control system. What is a control system concerned with?

○ A. Preventing change from affecting project execution

○ B. Influencing factors that cause change, determining a change has occurred, and managing the implementation of the change

○ C. Ensuring the change-control board is informed

○ D. Ensuring the quality of the work products meet targeted standards

Question 7

Which of the following best describes *progressive elaboration*?

○ A. The process for better defining project scope

○ B. The step-by-step process by which project tasks are identified

○ C. A process for better defining project scope and product scope

○ D. A process that should not affect the project scope but that better defines the project's product characteristics over time

Question 8

What is the main difference between a program manager and a project manager?

○ A. A program manager is part of a PMO.

○ B. A project manager may direct one or more program managers.

○ C. A program manager coordinates and manages a group of projects to obtain benefits not available by managing them individually.

○ D. There are no major differences. The terms are interchangeable.

Question 9

You want to make certain you are not at a disadvantage in an upcoming negotiation session. What should you do?

- ○ A. Actively listen to all parties involved.
- ○ B. Speak louder than everyone else.
- ○ C. Make sure there are more people in the negotiation with your opinion than there are with an opposing opinion.
- ○ D. Sit at the head of the table.

Question 10

How often should a project plan be monitored?

- ○ A. Weekly.
- ○ B. Monthly.
- ○ C. Never. Once the plan is done, the team knows what to do and can do it.
- ○ D. Continuously.

Question 11

As part of your planning for a new chemical-processing plant construction project you have won, you identify the stakeholders involved with your project. Which of the following statements best describes who stakeholders are?

- ○ A. The company paying for the product or service.
- ○ B. Stakeholders exert influence over the project and its results.
- ○ C. Stakeholders include anyone whose interests are affected by the project.
- ○ D. Stakeholders are always external to the project team.

Question 12

A culture's approach to doing business is to initially spend a great deal of time getting to know the personal background of individuals through small talk. Questions are asked about such topics as family, education, and personal interests. This type of approach can be referred to as which of the following?

○ A. Lacking scope

○ B. High context

○ C. Low context

○ D. Overly friendly

Question 13

Project managers need solid communication and negotiation skills primarily because _____.

○ A. they often lead teams with no direct control over the individual team members

○ B. they must give briefings to senior management

○ C. procuring resources from vendors requires these skills

○ D. they must be able to effectively share their technical expertise

Question 14

What is the key difference between quality planning and quality assurance?

○ A. None. Prior to ISO 9000, they were considered the same thing.

○ B. Only quality planning involves the use of cost benefit analysis, benchmarking, flowcharting, and design of experiments.

○ C. Only quality assurance must be performed by the organization's QA department.

○ D. Quality planning focuses on identifying which quality standards to use, whereas quality assurance focuses on planned and systematic activities to ensure those standards.

Question 15

The ability of stakeholders to influence the final characteristics of a project's product is _____.

- ○ A. a major contributor to budget overruns
- ○ B. highest at the end of a project when stakeholders are engaged during product approvals
- ○ C. highest at the start of a project when the project and product requirements are defined
- ○ D. a constant issue for project managers

Question 16

If Project X has a Net Present Value (NPV) of $176K and Project Y has a NPV of $216K, what is the opportunity cost if Project X is selected?

- ○ A. $176K
- ○ B. $40K
- ○ C. $216K
- ○ D. −$40K

Question 17

When interacting with individuals from foreign countries in both personal and professional situations, people unfortunately sometimes judge others based on traits they assume everyone from that country has. While working on a project team in a foreign country, what should you do if you feel the team has categorized you based on your culture?

- ○ A. Use this to your advantage if possible.
- ○ B. Behave in a manner that contradicts their assumption about you.
- ○ C. Communicate verbally and in writing that you do not hold the cultural traits they are assuming you to have.
- ○ D. Ignore the situation.

Question 18

Which of the following is not needed in order to develop a project estimate?

- ○ A. WBS
- ○ B. Risks
- ○ C. Change-control procedure
- ○ D. Resource levels

Question 19

If you have a colleague ask you to describe the concept of Kaizen as related to project management, which of the following answers would be the best one to give?

- ○ A. It's a quality control technique.
- ○ B. It's a solicitation philosophy.
- ○ C. It's a quality assurance technique.
- ○ D. It's a quality planning organization.

Question 20

Which of the following statements regarding power types is true?

- ○ A. Legitimate power is based on an individual's organizational authority or position.
- ○ B. Referential power is based on the number of references on your resume.
- ○ C. With referential power, a project manager can enforce the execution of certain project tasks.
- ○ D. Legitimate power is based on fear.

Question 21

Which of the following statements is *not* true about a project phase?

- ○ A. A project phase is marked by the completion of one or more deliverables.
- ○ B. A project phase is marked by phase-end reviews designed to determine whether a project should continue.
- ○ C. Collectively, the sequential set of project phases are known as the *project lifecycle.*
- ○ D. A project phase is synonymous with a project management process group.

Question 22

Fast tracking can be best described as which of the following?

- ❏ A. The quickest way to achieve project manager status
- ❏ B. The practice of overlapping project activities on the critical path to speed a project's completion
- ❏ C. An accelerated method of monitoring project performance
- ❏ D. The practice of adding additional resources to critical path activities to compress the duration of the project

Question 23

Double-declining balance is a form of _____.

- ○ A. investment analysis
- ○ B. straight-line depreciation
- ○ C. constrained optimization
- ○ D. acceleration depreciation

Question 24

A status review meeting _____.

- ○ A. is ad hoc and only needed when problems arise
- ○ B. is regularly scheduled and used to exchange information about the project
- ○ C. should be avoided so that team resources can be spent on the project
- ○ D. is part of executing the project plan

Question 25

Which statement best describes a PMIS?

- ○ A. A PMI certification that is specifically designed for project management focusing solely on the Information Systems profession.
- ○ B. A repository used for project information so that future projects can learn from this information. It's used in the execution phase of a project for reference purposes.
- ○ C. A required log for timekeeping.
- ○ D. The tools and techniques used to gather, integrate, and disseminate the process outputs of project management.

Question 26

Business operations differ from projects because operations are not _____.

- ○ A. performed by people
- ○ B. constrained by limited resources
- ○ C. planned, executed, and controlled
- ○ D. temporary and unique

Question 27

Using the following earned value metrics, calculate the SV, CV, CPI and EAC for this project:

PV=$125,000, EV=$75,000, AC=$100,000, BAC=$225,000

- ○ A. SV=$50,000, CV=$25,000, CPI=.75, EAC=$300,000
- ○ B. SV=–$50,000, CV=–$25,000, CPI=.75, EAC=$300,000
- ○ C. SV=–$50,000, CV=$25,000, CPI=1.25, EAC=$180,000
- ○ D. SV=$25,000, CV=$50,000, CPI=.75, EAC=$168,750

Question 28

Which of the following is not an example of an item that causes a change request?

- ○ A. The programmer decides there is a neat feature he can add to the product.
- ○ B. An error in the project or product design is discovered.
- ○ C. The government has changed a regulation that impacts the project.
- ○ D. An identified risk has occurred and a contingency plan must be implemented.

Question 29

All the following statements about a WBS are true except which one?

- ○ A. It provides a framework for organizing and ordering a project's activities.
- ○ B. It breaks down a project into successively greater detail by level and can be similar in appearance to an organizational chart.
- ○ C. It's one of the methods available to build a project schedule.
- ○ D. It's a key project-planning tool.

Question 30

Which project-selection technique utilizes a constrained optimization approach?

- ○ A. Murder boards
- ○ B. Cost-benefit analysis
- ○ C. Linear programming
- ○ D. Scoring models

Question 31

Which of the following statements best describes a weighting system?

- ○ A. It's a tool used to evaluate vendors based on a value assigned to each criteria.
- ○ B. It establishes minimum performance requirements.
- ○ C. It judges the size and volume of the work to be accomplished.
- ○ D. It's not a recommended technique because it's subjective.

Question 32

Where is the best place to go to find out when individual people resources will be needed for the project?

- ○ A. The roles and responsibilities matrix
- ○ B. The project schedule
- ○ C. The staffing management plan
- ○ D. The communications plan

Question 33

A change-control system does not have which of the following?

- ○ A. Paperwork
- ○ B. Tracking mechanisms
- ○ C. Approval requirements
- ○ D. Referential authority

Question 34

Schedule control requires which of the following?

- ○ A. Continual meetings to update tasks and monitor personnel hours to ensure that all workers are sufficiently busy
- ○ B. Measuring and assessment of the magnitude of variation to a schedule to determine whether corrective action is needed
- ○ C. Re-baselining
- ○ D. A project scheduling system with a tightly integrated time-reporting capability

Question 35

Rework is the result of _____.

- ○ A. poor planning
- ○ B. a quality control finding
- ○ C. untrained project resources
- ○ D. a quality improvement process

Question 36

Risk monitoring and control _____.

- ○ A. only need to take place during the initial phases of a project
- ○ B. detect new risks as the project matures
- ○ C. keep track of identified risks, monitor residual risks, identify new risks, and ensure the effectiveness of risk plans at reducing risk to the project
- ○ D. D. are part of the PMIS and are the most neglected risk management processes

Question 37

The characteristics of a project lifecycle include all the following except which one?

○ A. A defined beginning and ending

○ B. A phase to transition the project to ongoing operations

○ C. Deliverable approvals

○ D. High risk

Question 38

What does Earned Value Management consist of?

○ A. Monitoring project work results for conformance to requirements

○ B. Measuring project performance by relating planned value, earned value, and actual costs

○ C. Determining the amount of payment to a contractor

○ D. Monitoring planned schedule and costs against actual schedule and costs

Question 39

Schedule variance is _____.

○ A. the difference between how much the project was expected to cost and how much it is actually costing

○ B. not an issue for project managers because schedules do typically vary

○ C. the difference between the amount of time a task is scheduled to take and the actual amount of time it takes

○ D. considered a major problem by PMI

Question 40

You are meeting with a business that has never had a professional project manager work with it before. The president asks you what's the best environment for your team to work in. She is concerned about giving you the optimal environment to succeed with the project. What do you tell her in response to her question?

- O A. A team in the same room that reports directly and only to the project manager
- O B. A team that meets frequently face to face but has other functional duties
- O C. A loosely connected group of functional experts who help direct the project
- O D. A team that resides offsite

Question 41

Which of the following is a good team-building technique?

- O A. Involving the team in the planning process
- O B. Having a barbeque
- O C. Doing a "lessons learned" session
- O D. Letting individual team members operate independently

Question 42

The key purpose of distributing project information is _____.

- O A. to create an archive of project information that can be used by other projects
- O B. to inform stakeholders in a timely manner of work results
- O C. to make sure the project continues to have sponsorship
- O D. to resolve conflicts between project members

Question 43

A scope change is _____.

○ A. a request by a stakeholder to change the project schedule

○ B. any modification to the agreed-upon scope, as defined by the WBS

○ C. necessary for any change request

○ D. a change in the level of involvement of the project manager

Question 44

The Work Breakdown Structure is a central input to which of the following?

○ A. Project schedule management

○ B. Scope change control, because it defines the baseline tasks of the project

○ C. Project payments to vendors

○ D. Project initiation

Question 45

The WBS can be used to _____.

○ A. show calendar dates for each task

○ B. show the business need for the project

○ C. communicate with the customer

○ D. show the dependencies between work packages

Question 46

Your project is about to get underway. You perform a solicitation at the start. Which of the following best describes what you are doing in the solicitation?

○ A. Gathering requirements for a product purchase

○ B. Determining what vendors to buy from

○ C. Letting vendors know you have a need

○ D. Negotiating the pricing

Question 47

A contract between buyer and seller is created at what point in the procurement process?

- ○ A. In procurement planning, based on the policies and procedures of the company
- ○ B. During solicitation, when a proposal from a vendor is received
- ○ C. During contract administration, when the vendor is actually producing the work requested
- ○ D. During source selection, based on evaluation criteria, procurement policies, and supplier history

Question 48

Scope verification consists of _____.

- ○ A. ensuring the correctness of the work results
- ○ B. ensuring formal acceptance of the work results
- ○ C. a verbal acceptance from a project sponsor
- ○ D. verification that all the project's teams have signed off on their respective duties

Question 49

A good work authorization system is _____.

- ○ A. mandatory and includes all tasks
- ○ B. informal
- ○ C. intended to prevent projects from spending money unnecessarily
- ○ D. designed to balance the value of the control provided against the cost of that control

Question 50

All of the following statements about project plan execution are true except which of the following?

○ A. Tasks are completed

○ B. Change requests are generated based on new information

○ C. Information for project reporting regarding costs and quality is gathered

○ D. Team members are trained

Answers to Practice Exam 2

1. C	**18.** C	**35.** B
2. C	**19.** C	**36.** C
3. C	**20.** A	**37.** D
4. C	**21.** D	**38.** B
5. D	**22.** B	**39.** C
6. B	**23.** D	**40.** A
7. D	**24.** B	**41.** A
8. C	**25.** D	**42.** B
9. A	**26.** D	**43.** B
10. D	**27.** B	**44.** B
11. C	**28.** A	**45.** C
12. B	**29.** C	**46.** C
13. A	**30.** C	**47.** D
14. D	**31.** A	**48.** B
15. C	**32.** C	**49.** D
16. B	**33.** D	**50.** B
17. B	**34.** B	

Question 1

Answer C is correct. When a person is ethnocentric, he or she judges others based on his or her own culture. This results in an individual being less open to other people and their viewpoints.

Question 2

Answer C is correct. The signed contract (or statement of work) should indicate the acceptance criteria for each milestone deliverable, and it should indicate the authorization criteria for milestone and bonus payments. Answer A is incorrect because the procurement management plan describes how the overall project procurement process will be managed and would not include the type of details needed to resolve this conflict. Answer B is incorrect because the solicitation plan deals with the selection of the contractor, not with the administration of the contract. Answer D is incorrect because the scope statement does not deal with payment schedules and terms.

Question 3

Answer C is correct. Even though the project has been closed, it is important to bring this information to the attention of your management. They will need to verify your concerns and then address the findings with the customer.

Question 4

Answer C is correct. A project plan is used by the entire project team and helps to communicate the tasks needed during a specified timeframe. The project plan is distributed to the project staff according to the communications plan.

Question 5

Answer D is correct. Although certain ad hoc communications and information requests are handled during project execution, decisions on how, when, and with whom to communicate are defined in the planning stage in a communications plan.

Question 6

Answer B is correct. Preventing change from affecting execution is impossible. Change control allows for the effective execution and incorporation of a change into the project plan. The change-control board is the body that accepts or rejects a change request. As such, it must be informed and is part of the change-control system.

Question 7

Answer D is correct. Progressive elaboration is focused on the definition of the product of the project (pages 5–6, PMBOK) and should not affect the project scope if done properly. Answer A is incorrect because it is focused on the product. Answer B is incorrect because this better describes *decomposition*. Answer C is incorrect because progressive elaboration is not focused on project scope.

Question 8

Answer C is correct. This incorporates the definition of *program* straight out of the PMBOK. Answer A is incorrect because a program manager does not have to be part of a PMO. A PMO may have both program and project managers in its organization, but this depends on the nature of the PMO and the sponsoring organization. Answer B is incorrect because a program manager deals with multiple projects, so a program manager would normally direct one or more project managers. Answer D is incorrect because the terms do mean different things and are not interchangeable.

Question 9

Answer A is correct. The best way to make sure you are not at a disadvantage is to listen to the opinions of all parties. Through listening you not only build the trust of everyone involved, but you also become more knowledgeable about the subject at hand.

Question 10

Answer D is correct. Although some projects may have tasks that can be monitored monthly or weekly (and will depend on the project itself), the PMBOK's best answer is continuously. This way, a project manager can ensure budget adherence and timeliness of the project.

Question 11

Answer C is correct. A stakeholder is anyone whose interests are affected by the project. Answer A is incorrect because the company paying for a project is the customer (although the company is a stakeholder, this is not a full definition). Answer B can be true, but not all stakeholders can exert influence over the outcome of a project. Answer D is incorrect because the project manager, customer, project team, and sponsors are always stakeholders.

Question 12

Answer B is correct. Such a culture is referred to as *high context*. The business environment is very relationship centered; therefore, a great deal of time can be spent getting to know the individual(s) and the performing organization.

Question 13

Answer A is correct. It focuses on the key challenge facing project managers—getting things done without direct control. Answers B, C, and D are all incorrect because none is the *best* response. Each of them describes a valid function of a project manager, but these are not tasks a project manager does on a daily basis.

Question 14

Answer D is correct. Although part of answer A is correct, the part indicating no differences is not correct. Answer B is incorrect because both quality planning and quality assurance use the same tools and techniques. Answer C is incorrect because it is not a requirement that a QA department perform the quality assurance function on a project.

Question 15

Answer C is correct. Although answer A may be true in some circumstances, a good project manager will manage budget overruns so that projects are brought in on time and on budget. Answer B is incorrect because approval time would be the costliest time to influence product characteristics because rework would be necessary.

Question 16

Answer B is correct. Opportunity cost is defined as the difference in the returns from a selected investment and another that is passed up.

Question 17

Answer B is correct. The best way to handle such a situation is to not draw attention to their possible categorization of you but rather reveal through your actions that you do not hold such traits.

Question 18

Answer C is correct. A change-control procedure is not needed to provide a project time or cost estimate. However, the WBS, the identified risks, and committed resource levels are needed to provide the estimate. Therefore, answers A, B, and D are incorrect.

Question 19

Answer C is correct. *Kaizen* is the Japanese term for continuous improvement. The purpose of quality assurance is improvement in the project. Answer A is incorrect because quality control measures against quality standards. Answer B is incorrect because Kaizen has to do with quality, not solicitation. Answer D is incorrect because there is no quality planning organization named Kaizen.

Question 20

Answer A is correct. Legitimate power is based on an individual's organizational authority or position. Answers B and C are incorrect because referential power is based on the ability to use authority, other than your own, to get a project done. Answer D is incorrect because *coercive* power is based on fear.

Question 21

Answer D is correct. A project phase and a project management process group are not the same thing. Each of the project management process groups occur within a project phase.

Question 22

Answer B is correct. Answers A and C are incorrect and are both plays on the words *fast tracking*. Answer D is incorrect because this describes another popular schedule compression technique, called *crashing*.

Question 23

Answer D is correct. This is an example of the fundamental accounting concepts that need to be understood for the PMP exam. Double-declining balance is an accelerated depreciation accounting technique.

Question 24

Answer B is correct. Status review meetings should be regularly scheduled, although the frequency of the meetings may depend on the project (that is, weekly versus monthly). Although ad hoc meetings are generally called when a problem arises, they are not status review meetings. Therefore, answer A is incorrect. Project team participants should be involved in status review meetings. Therefore, answer C is incorrect. Although status meetings are part of executing, they are not part of actually accomplishing project tasks. Therefore, answer D is incorrect.

Question 25

Answer D is correct. This definition of Project Management Information System is straight from the PMBOK (page 44). Answer B is tempting, but it describes lessons learned more than the PMIS and is therefore incorrect.

Question 26

Answer D is correct. These are the characteristics that distinguish operations from projects. Answers A and B are both true but are not complete answers because they also apply to projects. Answer C is a trick, because we generally consider planning, execution, and control to be project-oriented topics.

Question 27

Answer B is correct. Here's the breakdown:

➤ SV (schedule variance) = EV (earned value) – planned value (PV) = $75,000 – $125,000 = $-50,000

➤ CV (cost variance) = EV (earned value) – actual costs (AC) = $75,000 – $100,000 = –$-25,000

➤ EAC (estimate at completion) = BAC (budgeted at completion) / CPI (cost performance index)

➤ CPI = EV / AC = $75,000 / $100,000 = .75

➤ EAC = BAC / CPI = $225,000/.75 = $300,000

Question 28

Answer A is correct. This is generally considered *gold-plating* by PMBOK. Neat, extra features not requested by the customer should be avoided. Answers B, C, and D are all examples of when a change request should be initiated and are therefore incorrect answers.

Question 29

Answer C is correct. A WBS is *not* a project-scheduling method. Answers A, B, and D are all true statements concerning a WBS and are therefore incorrect answers.

Question 30

Answer C is correct. Answers A, B, and D are all benefit-measurement methods of project selection and are therefore incorrect answers.

Question 31

Answer A is correct. A weighting system is a method of applying quantitative methods to qualitative data to minimize subjectivity. Answer B is incorrect because minimum performance requirements define a screening system. Answer C is incorrect because it deals with scope definition and estimating. Answer D is incorrect because it is a recommended technique.

Question 32

Answer C is correct. The staffing management plan documents when and how each person starts on the project and plans to leave the project. Answer A is incorrect because the roles and responsibilities matrix does not describe the "timing" elements. Answer B is tempting, but it is not the best source for this information. Answer D is incorrect because the communications plan does not deal with the use of a project's human resources.

Question 33

Answer D is correct. Referential authority is related to managing through another, more highly placed individual in an organization. Per the PMBOK definition, a change-control system must have paperwork, tracking mechanisms, and approval requirements, thus making answers A, B, and C incorrect.

Question 34

Answer B is correct. Although meetings are often required to update a schedule, this can be done through other means, such as email. Therefore, answer A is incorrect. Re-baselining is only necessary if a major change to the scope or timeline of the project has occurred. Therefore, answer C is incorrect. Answer D is tempting, because a project scheduling system with a tightly integrated time-reporting capability would be a great asset for the schedule control process, but it is not a requirement for doing schedule control.

Question 35

Answer B is correct. Although answers A and C may be true, rework is detected and required only through the quality control process.

Question 36

Answer C is correct. Answer A is incorrect because risk control must take place throughout a project. Answer B is incorrect because it's only partially true. This leaves answer C to be the best answer.

Question 37

Answer D is correct. Although risk is higher earlier in a project lifecycle, it is not part of the definition. Answers A, B, and C are all characteristics of a lifecycle definition and are therefore incorrect answers.

Question 38

Answer B is correct. Answer A is incorrect because monitoring work results is quality control. Answer C is also incorrect, although earned value is sometimes used in contract payments. Answer D is tempting, but it is incorrect due to the focus on "monitoring" rather than "measuring" and the incomplete definition.

Question 39

Answer C is correct. Answer A is incorrect because this is the definition of cost variance. Although answer B is true, a project manager must continually assess the variance to determine whether corrective action must be taken. Answer D is incorrect because schedule variance can be positive and may not necessarily require corrective action.

Question 40

Answer A is correct. Collocation and a projectized environment are the best situations for a project team. Although the scenario in answer B can work effectively, team members with other functional duties will have conflicts of priorities. Therefore, answer B is incorrect. Answer C is incorrect because it's the definition of subject matter experts. Answer D is tricky because off-site team building is often encouraged in team literature. However, in this case, it's an incorrect answer.

Question 41

Answer A is correct. Involving the team in the planning of the project helps to develop buy-in by all members and provides them with a better understanding of the project. Although having a barbeque can be a team-building technique, it isn't the best one in this case. Therefore, answer B is incorrect. Lessons learned sessions are typically done at the end of phases or the end of a project. These can be team-building events by airing difficulties, but they are intended to correct project direction, not to build a team. Therefore, answer C is incorrect. Allowing individuals to operate independently is a good management technique in general. However, if they're allowed to do so without supervision or project control, it could actually cause team problems. Therefore, Answer D is incorrect.

Question 42

Answer B is correct. Project information is important so that stakeholders and sponsors understand how well a project is meeting its goals. For sponsors, a project behind schedule may call for some type of intervention. Answer A is incorrect because, although it is important to create a project archive, it is not the purpose of distributing the information. Answer C is incorrect because project sponsorship should be resolved prior to project initiation. Occasionally a project is cancelled because it no longer meets the needs of the sponsors or company, but distributing the project information is not intended to keep sponsorship of the project. Answer D is incorrect because conflicts need to be managed by the project manager and resolved apart from reporting on the project.

Question 43

Answer B is correct. Answer A is incorrect because a schedule change may not mean there is a scope change. Likewise, answer C is incorrect because a change request may not require a scope change. Answer D is incorrect because a change in resource allocation does not mean a scope change has occurred.

Question 44

Answer B is correct. Although the WBS is key to creating the schedule, it is not used for schedule management. Therefore, answer A is incorrect. Payments to vendors may indeed be based on tasks in the WBS, but they are not the primary method for discerning payment. The contract is the method by which the payment obligations are defined. Therefore, answer C is incorrect. Answer D is also incorrect because the WBS is created after project initiation.

Question 45

Answer C is correct. The WBS is an effective stakeholder communication tool. Answer A is incorrect because there are no calendar dates on the WBS. Calendar dates are on the project schedule. Answer B is incorrect because the business justification is not part of the WBS. Answer D is incorrect because dependencies are shown on the network diagram and project schedule, but not the WBS.

Question 46

Answer C is correct. The solicitation process is the means by which you let vendors know what your requirements are. They then respond with a proposal on how they can meet your requirements. Answer A is incorrect because requirement gathering is done in the procurement planning stage. Answer B is incorrect because the actual determination of vendor happens in the source selection phase. Answer D is incorrect because price negotiation happens in the source selection phase as well.

Question 47

Answer D is correct. Answer A is only partially correct because the corporate procurement policies do affect a contract, but that is not when it is created. Answer B is incorrect because the receipt of a proposal does not make a legal contract. Answer C is incorrect because a contract must be signed before work can be done. However, in certain circumstances, the actual act of work being produced can be considered a default contract. Project managers need to avoid this.

Question 48

Answer B is correct. Scope verification deals with formal acceptance of the project work results. Answer A is incorrect because this describes quality assurance. Answer C is incorrect because verbal acceptance is not adequate. Answer D is incorrect because it is focused on verification of assigned tasks rather than work results.

Question 49

Answer D is correct. Work authorization is intended to ensure the proper tasks are done at the proper time. It is usually a formal system with written authorizations. A work authorization system does prevent projects from spending money at the wrong times. However, it doesn't prevent them from spending unnecessarily. A good work authorization system is designed to work for the scale of the project.

Question 50

Answer B is correct. Execution will result in completed tasks, development of team members and information gathering regarding costs and quality. So, Answers A, C and would not be correct. It *can* also result in change requests, but it does not have to.

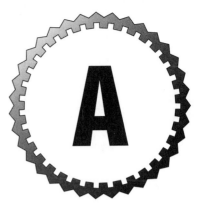

What's on the CD-ROM

This appendix is a brief rundown of what you'll find on the CD-ROM that comes with this book. For a more detailed description of the *PrepLogic Practice Tests, Preview Edition* exam-simulation software, see Appendix C, "Using the *PrepLogic Practice Tests, Preview Edition* Software."

PrepLogic Practice Tests, Preview Edition

PrepLogic is a leading provider of certification training tools. Trusted by certification students worldwide, PrepLogic is, we believe, the best practice exam software available. In addition to providing a means of evaluating your knowledge of the *Exam Cram 2* material, *PrepLogic Practice Tests, Preview Edition* features several innovations that help you improve your mastery of the subject matter.

For example, the practice tests allow you to check your score by exam area or domain to determine which topics you need to study more. Another feature allows you to obtain immediate feedback on your responses in the form of explanations for the correct and incorrect answers.

PrepLogic Practice Tests, Preview Edition exhibits most of the full functionality of the *Premium Edition* but offers only a fraction of the total questions. To get the complete set of practice questions and exam functionality, visit PrepLogic.com and order the Premium Edition for this and other challenging exam titles.

Again, for a more detailed description of the *PrepLogic Practice Tests, Preview Edition* features, see Appendix B.

Using the *PrepLogic Practice Tests, Preview Edition* Software

· ·

This *Exam Cram 2* includes a special version of *PrepLogic Practice Tests*— a revolutionary test engine designed to give you the best in certification exam preparation. PrepLogic offers sample and practice exams for many of today's most in-demand and challenging technical certifications. This special *Preview Edition* is included with this book as a tool to use in assessing your knowledge of the *Exam Cram 2* material, while also providing you with the experience of taking an electronic exam.

This appendix describes in detail what *PrepLogic Practice Tests, Preview Edition* is, how it works, and what it can do to help you prepare for the exam. Note that although the *Preview Edition* includes all the test-simulation functions of the complete, retail version, it contains only a single practice test. The Premium Edition, available at PrepLogic.com, contains the complete set of challenging practice exams designed to optimize your learning experience.

Exam Simulation

One of the main functions of *PrepLogic Practice Tests, Preview Edition* is exam simulation. To prepare you to take the actual vendor certification exam, PrepLogic is designed to offer the most effective exam simulation available.

Question Quality

The questions provided in the *PrepLogic Practice Tests, Preview Edition* are written to the highest standards of technical accuracy. The questions tap the content of the *Exam Cram 2* chapters and help you review and assess your knowledge before you take the actual exam.

Interface Design

The *PrepLogic Practice Tests, Preview Edition* exam-simulation interface provides you with the experience of taking an electronic exam. This enables you to effectively prepare for taking the actual exam by making the test experience a familiar one. Using this test simulation can help eliminate the sense of surprise or anxiety you might experience in the testing center because you will already be acquainted with computerized testing.

Effective Learning Environment

The *PrepLogic Practice Tests, Preview Edition* interface provides a learning environment that not only tests you through the computer, but also teaches you the material you need to know to pass the certification exam. Each question comes with a detailed explanation of the correct answer and often provides reasons the other options are incorrect. This information helps to reinforce the knowledge you already have and also provides practical information you can use on the job.

Software Requirements

PrepLogic Practice Tests, Preview Edition requires a computer with the following:

➤ Microsoft Windows 98, Windows Me, Windows NT 4.0, Windows 2000, or Windows XP.

➤ A 166MHz or faster processor (recommended).

➤ A minimum of 32MB of RAM. (As with any Windows application, the more memory, the better your performance.)

➤ 10MB of hard drive space.

Installing *PrepLogic Practice Tests, Preview Edition*

Install *PrepLogic Practice Tests, Preview Edition* by running the setup program on the *PrepLogic Practice Tests, Preview Edition* CD-ROM. Follow these instructions to install the software on your computer:

1. Insert the CD-ROM into your CD-ROM drive. The Autorun feature of Windows should launch the software. If you have Autorun disabled, click Start and select Run. Go to the root directory of the CD-ROM and select setup.exe. Click Open and then click OK.

2. The Installation Wizard copies the *PrepLogic Practice Tests, Preview Edition* files to your hard drive; adds *PrepLogic Practice Tests, Preview Edition* to your Desktop and Program menu; and installs test engine components to the appropriate system folders.

Removing *PrepLogic Practice Tests, Preview Edition* from Your Computer

If you elect to remove the *PrepLogic Practice Tests, Preview Edition* product from your computer, an uninstall process has been included to ensure that it is removed from your system safely and completely. Follow these instructions to remove *PrepLogic Practice Tests, Preview Edition* from your computer:

1. Select Start, Settings, Control Panel.

2. Double-click the Add/Remove Programs icon.

3. You are presented with a list of software installed on your computer. Select the appropriate *PrepLogic Practice Tests, Preview Edition* title you want to remove. Click the Add/Remove button. The software is then removed from your computer.

Using *PrepLogic Practice Tests, Preview Edition*

PrepLogic is designed to be user friendly and intuitive. Because the software has a smooth learning curve, your time is maximized because you start practicing almost immediately. *PrepLogic Practice Tests, Preview Edition* has two major modes of study: Practice Test and Flash Review.

Using Practice Test mode, you can develop your test-taking abilities, as well as your knowledge, through the use of the Show Answer option. While you are taking the test, you can expose the answers along with detailed explanations of why the given answers are right or wrong. This gives you the ability to better understand the material presented.

Flash Review is designed to reinforce exam topics rather than quiz you. In this mode, you will be shown a series of questions but no answer choices. Instead, you will be given a button that reveals the correct answer to the question and a full explanation for that answer.

Starting a Practice Test Mode Session

Practice Test mode enables you to control the exam experience in ways that actual certification exams do not allow:

➤ **Enable Show Answer Button**—This option activates the Show Answer button, allowing you to view the correct answer(s) and full explanation(s) for each question during the exam. When this option is not enabled, you must wait until after your exam has been graded to view the correct answer(s) and explanation(s).

➤ **Enable Item Review Button**—This option activates the Item Review button, allowing you to view your answer choices and marked questions, and to facilitate navigation between questions.

➤ **Randomize Choices**—This option randomizes answer choices from one exam session to the next. This makes memorizing question choices more difficult, thus keeping questions fresh and challenging longer.

To begin studying in Practice Test mode, click the Practice Test radio button from the main exam-customization screen. This enables the options detailed in the preceding list.

To your left, you are presented with the option of selecting the preconfigured practice test or creating your own custom test. The preconfigured test has a fixed time limit and number of questions. A custom test allows you to configure the time limit and the number of questions in your exam.

The *Preview Edition* included with this book has a single preconfigured practice test. You can get the compete set of challenging PrepLogic practice tests at PrepLogic.com to make certain you're ready for the big exam.

Click the Begin Exam button to begin your exam.

Starting a Flash Review Mode Session

Flash Review mode provides you with an easy way to reinforce topics covered in the practice questions. To begin studying in Flash Review mode, click the Flash Review radio button from the main exam-customization screen. Select either the preconfigured practice test or create your own custom test.

Click the Best Exam button to begin your Flash Review of the exam questions.

Standard *PrepLogic Practice Tests, Preview Edition* Options

The following list describes the function of each of the buttons you see. Depending on the options, some of the buttons will be grayed out and inaccessible or missing completely. Buttons that are appropriate are active. The buttons are as follows:

➤ **Exhibit**—This button is visible if an exhibit is provided to support the question. An exhibit is an image that provides supplemental information necessary to answer the question.

➤ **Item Review**—When you click this button, you leave the question window and go to the Item Review screen. From this screen you will see all questions, your answers, and your marked items. You will also see correct answers listed here when appropriate.

➤ **Show Answer**—This option displays the correct answer with an explanation of why it is correct. If you select this option, the current question is not scored.

➤ **Mark Item**—Check this box to tag a question you need to review further. You can view and navigate your marked items by clicking the Item Review button (if enabled). When grading your exam, you will be notified if you have marked items remaining.

➤ **Previous Item**—Use this button to view the previous question.

➤ **Next Item**—Use this button to view the next question.

➤ **Grade Exam**—When you have completed your exam, click this button to end your exam and view your detailed score report. If you have unanswered or marked items remaining, you will be asked whether you would like to continue taking your exam or view your exam report.

Time Remaining

If the test is timed, the time remaining is displayed in the upper-right corner of the application screen. It counts down minutes and seconds remaining to complete the test. If you run out of time, you will be asked if you want to continue taking the exam or if you want to end it.

Your Examination Score Report

The Examination Score Report screen appears when the Practice Test mode ends—as the result of time expiration, completion of all questions, or your decision to terminate early.

This screen provides you with a graphical display of your test score with a breakdown of scores by topic domain. The graphical display at the top of the screen compares your overall score with the PrepLogic Exam Competency Score.

The PrepLogic Exam Competency Score reflects the level of subject competency required to pass this vendor's exam. Although this score does not directly translate to a passing score, consistently matching or exceeding this score does suggest you possess the knowledge to pass the actual vendor exam.

Reviewing Your Exam

From your Examination Score Report screen, you can review the exam you just completed by clicking the View Items button. Navigate through the items, viewing the questions, your answers, the correct answers, and the explanations for the questions. You can return to your score report by clicking the View Items button.

Getting More Exams

The *PrepLogic Practice Tests, Preview Edition* that accompanies this *Exam Cram 2* book contains a single PrepLogic practice test. Certification students worldwide trust PrepLogic practice tests to help them pass their IT certification exams the first time. You can purchase the *Premium Edition* of *PrepLogic Practice Tests* and get the entire set of all the new challenging practice tests for this exam. PrepLogic Practice Tests—Because You Want to Pass the First Time.

Contacting PrepLogic

If you would like to contact PrepLogic for any reason, including information about our extensive line of certification practice tests, we invite you to do so. Please contact us online at www.preplogic.com.

Customer Service

If you have a damaged product and need a replacement or refund, please call the following phone number:

800-858-7674

Product Suggestions and Comments

We value your input! Please email your suggestions and comments to the following address:

feedback@preplogic.com

License Agreement

YOU MUST AGREE TO THE TERMS AND CONDITIONS OUT-LINED IN THE END USER LICENSE AGREEMENT ("EULA") PRESENTED TO YOU DURING THE INSTALLATION PROCESS. IF YOU DO NOT AGREE TO THESE TERMS, DO NOT INSTALL THE SOFTWARE.

Glossary

acceptance
The term *formal acceptance* is generally used in project management. This is the key output of scope verification and entails the project stakeholders formally agreeing that the project deliverables meet their satisfaction.

activity definition
Identifying the specific tasks that must be performed to produce the various project deliverables.

activity duration estimate
Estimating the number of work periods that will be needed to complete the individual activities.

activity list
After a work packet is decomposed, this is the list of tasks associated with the project that have to be completed.

activity sequencing
Identifying and documenting the logical relationships between project activities.

actual cost (AC)
Total costs incurred over the specified reporting period.

actual cost of work performed (ACWP)
A legacy earned value term that has been replaced with *actual cost (AC)*.

administrative closure
Generating, gathering, and disseminating information to formalize phase or project completion.

analogous estimating
Also known as *top-down estimating*. This type of estimating uses historical data from one project to determine the duration of another, similar project.

application area

A category or type of project that has elements not common for all projects. An application area is usually defined by the product of the project (such as software development or commercial building construction) or the type of customer (such as government versus commercial).

Arrow Diagramming Method (ADM)

A network diagramming technique in which activities are represented by arrows. The tail of the arrow represents the start of the activity, and the head represents the finish. Activities are connected at nodes (points) to illustrate the expected performance sequence. ADM uses dummy activities to show logical dependencies.

assumptions

Factors considered to be true that affect project planning. These factors should be identified, documented, and validated throughout the planning process and throughout the elaboration of the project.

bar chart

A graphic depiction of schedule-related information. Also called a *Gantt chart*. Normally, activities are listed down the left hand side of the chart, dates are list along the top, and activity durations are shown as date-placed horizontal bars.

baseline

The original approved plan. Types of project baselines include cost baseline, schedule baseline, and performance measurement baseline. Baselines are used to measure project performance.

bidder conference

A meeting of bidders that provides an opportunity to ask the customer questions and confirm expectations before the submission of a proposal for the project.

bottom-up estimating

A type of estimating where the project is broken into numerous smaller tasks and all the tasks are estimated. After all the estimates are completed, they are added together to calculate the estimate for the entire project.

budget at completion (BAC)

The sum of the total budgets for the project.

budgeted cost of work performed (BCWP)

A legacy earned value term that has been replaced with *earned value (EV)*.

budgeted cost of work scheduled (BCWS)

A legacy earned value term that has been replaced with *planned value (PV)*.

change-control board (CCB)

A formally constituted group of stakeholders responsible for approving or rejecting changes to the project baselines.

change requests

Documents that are prepared to describe the changes made to a project and the impact on the pricing and the timeline. The form usually requires approvals before it is incorporated into the project.

chart of accounts

Any numbering system used to monitor project costs by category (such as labor, supplies, materials, equipment, and so on). Usually based on the chart of accounts of the primary performing organization.

closing processes

Also known as *project closeout processes*. These are the activities associated with the closing out of a project.

code of accounts

Any numbering system used to uniquely identify each element of the Work Breakdown Structure (WBS).

collocation

The close physical proximity of team members, where they work together in a central location.

communication planning

Determining the information and communication needs of the project stakeholder—who needs what information, when they will need it, and how it will be given to them.

confidential information

Secret or private information that is associated with the project.

configuration management

A supporting process that manages control, versioning, and tracking of changes to work products used, created, and maintained in executing a project.

conflict of interest

Whenever someone's personal interests exceed the interests of the project.

constraints

Factors that limit a project team's options. Examples include predefined budget, contractual provisions, and specific external requirements.

contingency (reserve)

The amount of money or time needed above the estimate to reduce the risk of overruns of project objectives to an organizational acceptable level.

contingency plan

A management plan that identifies alternative strategies to be used to ensure project success if specified risk events occur.

contract

A mutually binding agreement that obligates the seller to provide the specified product or service and obligates the buyer to pay for it.

contract administration

Managing the relationship with the seller during project execution.

contract change-control system

The process by which a contract can be modified. It includes the forms, tracking procedures, dispute-resolution procedures, and approval levels for authorizing changes. This system should be integrated with the project's overall integrated change-control system.

contract closeout

Completion and settlement of the contract. This process involves product verification and administrative closeout steps. Contract closeout precedes project administrative closure.

contract negotiation

The discussions and meetings intended to set the framework for contract development. These discussions can lead to compromises and likely lead to a signed agreement.

control charts

Graphic displays of process results over time and against specified control limits. Used in quality control to determine whether a process is "in control" or needs adjustments.

control system

The system used to compare actual performance with planned performance, to analyze variances, to evaluate alternatives, and to take corrective actions.

controlling processes

The processes used to monitor and measure project performance to identify variances that may impact the accomplishment of project objectives.

core processes

Project management processes that must be performed in approximately the same order on all projects.

corrective action

Steps taken to bring future project performance in line with planned project performance.

cost baseline

The agreed-upon costs associated with the project. The cost baseline sets the guidelines for expenses and is the expected total cost for the project.

cost budgeting

Allocating the overall cost estimates to individual work activities. The result is a cost baseline.

cost control

Controlling changes to the project budget (cost baseline).

cost estimating

Developing a cost approximation of the resources needed to complete the project activities.

cost management plan

Describes how cost variances will be managed.

cost of quality

The costs incurred to ensure quality.

Cost Performance Index (CPI)

An Earned Value Management ratio used to measure the efficiency of earned value (EV) to actual costs (AC).

$$CPI = EV / AC$$

CPI is often used to predict the total project costs at completion (EAC) using the formula EAC = BAC / CPI.

cost variance (CV)

Any difference between budgeted cost and actual cost.

$$CV = EV - AC$$

cost-reimbursable contracts

This contract type involves payments to the seller for its actual costs. These contracts can also incorporate incentives for meeting or exceeding certain project objectives.

crashing

A schedule compression technique that relies on adding resources to critical path activities to reduce project duration.

critical path

The series of activities that determine the duration of a project. The critical path is the longest path in a project and is usually defined as those activities with zero float.

Critical Path Method (CPM)

A network analysis technique used to predict project duration by determining the critical path(s) of the project. This technique calculates four dates for each activity (early start, late start, early finish, and late finish).

decision tree

A diagram that describes a decision under consideration and the implications of selecting each alternative. The diagram will also show the probability (risk) and the cost (reward) of each option.

decomposition

The process of breaking down a work packet into smaller tasks. This process can be used when developing the Work Breakdown Structure (WBS).

deliverable

Any measurable, tangible, verifiable item produced to complete a project work package.

dummy activity

An activity of zero duration used to show a logical relationship (dependency) in the Arrow Diagramming Method. (Depicted as dashed arrow lines.)

duration compression

Shortening the project schedule without reducing the project scope.

earned value (EV)

The sum of the cost estimates for project activities completed during a given time period.

Earned Value Management (EVM)

A project controlling technique that integrates scope, schedule, and resources for measuring project performance. EVM compares the planned amount of work (and cost) with the actual work earned and actual costs incurred.

effort

The number of labor units required to complete an activity. (Not the same as *duration*.)

estimate at completion (EAC)

The predicted total costs at completion for one or more project activities.

EAC = budgeted at completion (BAC) / Cost Performance Index (CPI)

estimate to complete (ETC)

The expected additional cost needed to complete one or more project activities.

ethical standards

Professional standards and morals that are tied with integrity, honesty, and respect.

executing processes

The project management activities that coordinate the resources and people to implement the project plan.

external feedback

Receiving or requesting feedback from individuals who are outside of the project. This allows for objective opinions.

facilitating processes

Project management processes that vary depending on the nature of the project. Facilitating processes are performed intermittently throughout the project and are not optional.

fallback plan

A backup plan option.

fast tracking

A schedule compression technique that overlaps critical path activities that would normally be done in sequence.

feedback loop

The channels of communication developed to allow opinions to be distributed among the team members and stakeholders.

fixed-price contracts

Also known as *lump-sum contracts*. This contract type involves a fixed total price for a well-defined product. These contracts can also incorporate incentives for meeting or exceeding certain project objectives.

float

The time that an activity can be delayed from its early start date without impacting the project's finish date. Also called *slack* and *total float*.

free float

The time that an activity can be delayed without impacting the early start date of any immediate successor activities.

functional organization

An organizational structure that groups staff hierarchically by area of specialty.

Gantt chart

See *bar chart*.

gold plating

Performing extra work outside the approved project scope. Gold plating is not an approved practice of PMI.

Graphical Evaluation and Review Technique (GERT)

A network analysis technique that allows for conditional and probabilistic logical relationships (such as branching, repeat loops, and optional activities).

information distribution

Making needed information available to project stakeholders in a timely manner.

initiating processes

Project management processes that authorize a project or phase.

initiation

Formally authorizing a new project or an existing project to continue into the next phase.

integrated change control

Coordinating changes across the entire project.

integrity

Adherence to a code of values or morals.

intellectual property

The nontangible things developed by a company or organization that have commercial value.

lag

A mandatory delay in the logical relationship between two tasks. For example, in a finish-to-start dependency with a five-day lag, the successor activity cannot start until five days after the predecessor has finished.

lessons learned

The learning gained from the process of performing the project. These lessons can be identified and captured at any point in the project.

lifecycle costing

The costing method that accounts for the entire life of the product, including acquisition, development, operating, and disposal costs.

Management by Objectives (MBO)

A management technique that focuses on setting goals, checking progress on those goals, and taking necessary corrective actions.

matrix organization

An organizational structure that cuts across functional departmental boundaries. Project managers drive projects and share responsibility with functional managers for determining work priorities and work direction of project staff.

milestone

A significant event in the project. Usually the completion of a key project deliverable or phase.

Monte Carlo simulation

The technique used to estimate the likely range of outcomes by simulating the process a large number of times, thereby identifying key risks.

operational definitions

A quality management term for "metrics." Describes a quality standard in very specific terms and describes how it is to be measured by the quality control process.

organizational planning

The process of identifying, documenting, and assigning project roles, responsibilities, and reporting relationships.

organizational policies

Standards and rules of an organization that set guidelines for professionalism within the organization.

parametric estimating

An estimating technique that uses a statistical relationship between historical data and other variables to calculate an estimate.

performance measurement baseline

An approved plan against which deviations are compared for management control.

performance reporting

The process of collecting and disseminating project performance information. This includes status reporting, progress measurement, and forecasting.

personal gain

Receiving monetary gain or benefits through business dealings, arrangements, or negotiations.

planned value (PV)

The budgeted cost of the planned (scheduled) work for a given time period.

planning processes

Project management activities that clarify the project objectives and determine the best course of action to take to accomplish those objectives. These activities are ongoing throughout the project.

PMI Code of Professional Conduct

Ethical standards for project management professionals concerning business practices and interactions.

Precedence Diagramming Method (PDM)

A network diagramming technique in which activities are represented by boxes (or nodes). Arrow lines are used to show the sequence and relationship between the activities.

preventive action

The proactive steps taken to keep an event or activity from occurring or existing.

process

Gradual changes that lead toward a particular result. Includes results that are brought about by a series of actions.

procurement management plan

The document that describes how the processes from solicitation planning through contract closeout will be managed. This is the key output of procurement planning.

procurement planning

The process of determining what to procure and when.

product documentation

The set of reviewable project documents that describes the final product of the project.

product lifecycle

The timeline associated with the entire lifespan of a product, from inception to disposal.

product verification

The process of ensuring the key deliverables of the project are complete, accurate, and satisfactory to the project stakeholders.

program

A group of related projects managed in a coordinated way.

Program Evaluation and Review Technique (PERT)

A network analysis technique used to estimate project duration when there is uncertainty in activity duration estimates. Activity duration estimates are computed by a weighted average of optimistic, pessimistic, and most likely duration estimates.

Estimated duration = (O + 4ML + P) / 6

progressive elaboration

The evolutionary steps associated with the development and refinement of a product.

project

A temporary endeavor undertaken to create a unique product, service, or result.

project charter

The document issued by senior management that formally authorizes a project and gives the project manager authority to use organizational resources to complete project activities.

Project Communications Management

A subset of project management processes that ensures timely and appropriate generation, collection, dissemination, storage, and disposition of project information.

Project Cost Management

A subset of project management processes that ensures the project is completed with the approved budget.

Project Human Resources Management

A subset of project management processes that makes the most effective use of the people involved with the project.

Project Integration Management

A subset of project management processes that ensures that the various elements of the project are properly coordinated.

project lifecycle

The collection of sequential project phases.

Project Management Information System (PMIS)

The techniques and tools used to gather, integrate, and distribute the outputs of project management processes. It includes both manual and automated processes.

project management office (PMO)

Groups developed by organizations to maintain standards, processes, and procedures associated with project management in their organizations.

project management software

A type of software application designed to assist the planning and controlling of project costs and schedules.

project network diagram

Any schematic display of the logical relationships of project activities.

project plan

A formal, approved document used to guide both project execution and project control.

project plan development

The process of integrating and coordinating all project plans to create a single consistent, coherent document.

project plan execution

The process of performing the activities included in the project plan.

Project Portfolio Management

The choosing and support of program or project investments based on an organization's strategic plan and resources.

Project Procurement Management

A subset of project management processes that acquires goods and services from outside the performing organization to achieve the project objectives.

Project Quality Management

A subset of project management processes that ensures the project will satisfy the needs for which it was undertaken.

Project Risk Management

A subset of project management processes that identifies, analyzes, and responds to project risk.

project schedule

The planned dates for performing activities and the planned dates for meeting milestones.

Project Scope Management

A subset of project management processes that ensures the project includes all the work required, and only the work required, to complete the project successfully.

project sponsor

The person who provides the financial resources to the project.

Project Time Management

The subset of project management processes that ensures timely completion of the project.

projectized organization
An organizational structure in which the project manager has complete and total authority over the resources assigned to the project.

proposals
Written documents prepared by vendors that make an offer for consideration by the customer.

qualified seller lists
Listings of preferred vendors that have developed a reputation for being honest and fair. This list is used as a resource for organizations so they can choose reliable vendors.

qualitative risk analysis
The process of performing a qualitative analysis of risks and conditions for the purpose of prioritizing their effects on project objectives.

quality assurance
The process of evaluating overall project performance on a regular basis to ensure the project will satisfy the targeted quality standards.

quality audit
The process of reviewing and evaluating the performance of a project to determine whether it is fulfilling quality standards.

quality control
The process of monitoring specific project results to determine whether they comply with targeted quality standards and of identifying corrective actions for any unsatisfactory performance.

quality improvement
A positive increase in quality standards and the fulfillment of project requirements.

quality management plan
The monitoring and control of quality standards to maintain or increase quality performance.

quality planning
The process of identifying which quality standards are relevant to the project and determining how to satisfy them.

quantitative risk analysis
The process of measuring the probability and consequences of project risks.

reserve
A provision in the project plan to mitigate cost and/or schedule risk. Also known as *management reserve* or *contingency reserve*.

residual risk
A risk that remains after risk responses have been implemented.

resource leveling
Any form of network analysis in which scheduling decisions are driven by resource management concerns.

resource planning
The process of determining what people, equipment, and materials are needed in what quantities to perform project activities.

resource pool

Available employees, stakeholders, and people associated with the project that can be utilized in a project.

resource requirements

The list of the type and quantity of each person, role, skill, material, and equipment needed to complete the project.

responsibility matrix

Also known as *responsibility assignment matrix (RAM)*, this is a document that relates the project organization to the Work Breakdown Structure. This matrix ensures that each element of the WBS is assigned to a responsible individual and that each project team member understands his or her project responsibilities.

rewards and recognition systems

A plan developed to reward and provide positive reinforcement to team members for their participation on a project through monetary or nonmonetary means.

risk

An uncertain event or condition that can have a positive or negative effect on the project objectives if it occurs.

risk avoidance

A risk response strategy that changes the project plan to eliminate the risk or to protect the project from its impact.

risk event

A discrete occurrence of a project risk.

risk identification

The process of determining which risks might affect the project and documenting their characteristics.

risk management plan

This plan documents how the risk management processes will be executed during the project. This is the output of risk management planning.

risk management planning

The process of deciding how the risk management processes will be executed during the project.

risk mitigation

A risk response strategy that seeks to reduce the probability and/or impact of a risk to an acceptable threshold.

risk monitoring and control

The process of monitoring residual risks, identifying new risks, executing risk response plans, and evaluating their effectiveness throughout the project lifecycle.

risk rating matrix

A table that's developed to list the risks associated with a project and to determine a quantitative rating system for providing rankings based on several criteria.

risk response

The steps, procedures, or techniques to implement if the risk occurs. The four risk response strategies are avoidance, mitigation, transference, and acceptance.

risk response plan

A document detailing all identified risks, their probability of occurrence, possible impacts on objectives, and the proposed response to each risk.

risk transference

A risk response strategy that seeks to shift the impact of a risk and ownership of the response to a third party.

risk trigger

An indicator that a risk has occurred or is about to occur.

rolling wave planning

Progressive detailing of the project plan. At the end of each project phase, the next phase is planned in detail and reestimated.

schedule control

Controlling changes to the project schedule.

schedule development

The process of analyzing activity sequences, activity durations, and resource requirements to create the project schedule.

Schedule Performance Index (SPI)

An earned value management ratio used to measure the efficiency of earned value (EV) against planned value (PV). SPI describes what portion of the planned schedule has actually been accomplished.

$$SPI = EV / PV$$

schedule variance (SV)

Any difference between scheduled activity completion and actual activity completion.

$$SV = EV - PV$$

scope change control

Controlling changes to project scope.

scope definition

The process of subdividing the major deliverables into smaller, more manageable components to provide better control.

scope management plan

This plan provides an analysis of the stability and reliability of the scope for the project.

scope planning

The process of progressively elaborating the work of the project and developing the scope statement.

scope statement

A document used to develop and confirm a common understanding of project scope among the stakeholders. The scope statement is used as a basis for making future project decisions.

Key elements include project justification, major deliverables, and project objectives.

scope verification
The process of formalizing accept-ance of the project scope.

screening system
The process of interviewing ven-dors to determine whether they ful-fill the needs of the project.

secondary risk
A risk that arises as a direct result of implementing a risk response.

solicitation
The process of obtaining seller responses.

solicitation planning
The process of documenting prod-uct requirements and identifying potential sources.

source selection
The process of choosing a seller from the potential group of sellers.

staff acquisition
The process of getting needed human resources assigned to and working on the project.

staffing management plan
A plan used to determine staff lev-els and scheduling.

stakeholders
Any organization or person who has a vested interest in the outcome of the project.

status report
A summary report that is provided by the project team for the stake-holders to keep them informed about project-related issues, deliv-erables, and timelines.

status review meeting
Regularly scheduled meetings of project stakeholders to exchange information about the project.

team development
The process of developing individ-ual and group competencies to enhance project performance.

time and material contracts
A vendor calculation that incorpo-rates the costs of materials and labor into a proposal or customer billing.

truthful reporting
The ethical requirement that ensures project management pro-fessionals will provide honesty in composing reports, providing analysis, and communicating status on projects.

vendor gifts
Compensation or benefits that are provided by vendors to customers. These can be seen as potential con-flicts of interest based on some company's standards.

war room
The physical location where team members are co-located with other resources to focus exclusively on a project.

WBS Dictionary
The collection of work package descriptions.

weighting system
The quantification analysis used to judge vendors for selection.

work authorization system

A formal procedure to ensure project work is sanctioned, done at the right time and in the right sequence.

Work Breakdown Structure (WBS)

A deliverables-oriented grouping of project elements that organizes and defines the total scope of the project.

work package

A deliverable that is at the lowest level of the Work Breakdown Structure (WBS). A work package includes the bundling of several activities that will be decomposed into tasks to populate the WBS.

work results

The outcome of an activity associated with a project.

workaround

The development of alternatives in response to a problem. This process allows you to get beyond the issue by utilizing creative problem solving.

Index

quality management, 106-107
  compared to project management, 108
  costs of, 109
  leading personalities, 110
  PMI principles, 107
  responsibilities, 108
  relationships among quality planning, quality assurance, and quality control, 109-110
  relationships among quality, risk and procurement, and HR management, 98-99
  relationships among resource, organizational, and communications planning, 100-101
  risk management compared to risk response, 99-100
facilitating processes, project control and, 171
failure risk, 23
fast tracking, shortening project schedule, 84
feedback loop, project control and, 174
fishbone diagrams, 180
fixed costs, 50
Flash Review mode (PrepLogic Practice Tests), 286-287
forecasting reports, 173
formal acceptance (Project Closing), 191
functional organizations, 24-25

G

Gantt charts, 13
  project schedule presentation, 83
gate keeping, 176
general management, 21
GERT network diagram, 73
gifts from vendors (professionalism), 203
go/no-go decisions, 42
gold plating, project control and, 172
Grade Exam button (PrepLogic Practice Tests), 287
Guide to the Project Management Body of Knowledge, A (PMBOK Guide), 2000 Edition, 57

H

Herzberg's Hygiene Theory, 150
historical information, time estimates, 76
HR responsibilities, 106
human resource management, 20

I-J

indirect costs, 50
information distribution, 151-152
  communication skills, 153
  information retrieval systems, 153
  outputs, 154
  techniques, 153
information retrieval systems
  project execution, 153
Initiating processes, 29
initiation (projects), 42
  cost accounting, 49-51
    accelerated depreciation, 51
    BCR (benefit cost ratio), 49
    direct costs, 50
    fixed costs, 50
    indirect costs, 50
    IRR (internal rate of return), 49
    lifecycle costing, 51
    NPV (net present value), 49
    opportunity cost, 50
    payback period, 49
    PV (present value), 49
    straight-line depreciation, 50
    sunk cost, 50
    variable costs, 50
    working capital, 50
  exam prep questions, 52-54, 56
  expert judgment, 46-47
  go/no-go decisions, 42
  importance of, 42
  MBO (Management by Objectives), 47
  project charters
    elements of, 43
    importance of, 44
    issuing, 44
    purpose of, 43
  project manager assignment, 45

interface design, 284
learning environment, 284
license agreement, 289
Practice Test mode, 286
PrepLogic contact information, 289
product suggestions/comments, 289
question quality, 284
software requirements, 284
time remaining, 288
uninstallation, 285
time
    estimates
        project management guidelines, 76-77
        project schedule building, 75-77
    management, 20
Time Management component, project scheduling and, 69
time remaining (*PrepLogic Practice Tests, Preview Edition*), 288
tracking project performance, 12
training (team development), 146
trend analysis, 180
triple constraint, 28-29
truthful representations of information (Code of Professional Conduct), 206

U

unapproved project management practices, 11
uninstalling *PrepLogic Practice Tests, Preview Edition*, 285
'use the pencil' questions (PMP exam), 3

V

value-added change, project control and, 172
variable costs, 50
variance, project control and, 171
vendors, source selection, 156-157
verification (scope verification), quality control comparison, 176

W-X-Y-Z

war rooms (team development), 146
watches, 8
WBS (Work Breakdown Structure), 13, 33, 67
    benefits, 68
    breakdown structure types, 69
    development techniques, 67-68
    Project plan comparison, 64
    scope control, 175-177
weak matrix organizations, 25
Web sites
    Code of Professional Conduct, 202
    PMI (Project Management Institute), 4
    PMI Bookstore, 57
    PMI eLearning Connection, 57
weighting vendors, 157
working capital, 50

How can we make this index more useful? Email us at indexes@quepublishing.com

informIT